JOHN TRAVOLTA
KING OF COOL

WENSLEY CLARKSON

JOHN BLAKE

Published by John Blake Publishing Ltd,
3, Bramber Court, 2 Bramber Road,
London W14 9PB, England

www.blake.co.uk

First published in Hardback in 2005

ISBN 1 84358 125 8

British Library Cataloguing-in-Publication Data:

A catalogue record for this book is available from the British Library.

Design by www.envydesign.co.uk

Printed in Great Britain by Creative Print and Design

1 3 5 7 9 10 8 6 4 2

Papers used by John Blake Publishing are natural, recyclable products made
from wood grown in sustainable forests. The manufacturing processes conform
to the environmental regulations of the country of origin.

Every attempt has been made to contact the relevant copyright-holders,
but some were unobtainable. We would be grateful if the appropriate people
could contact us.

JOHN TRAVOLTA
KING OF COOL

'I'm the guy who keeps haunting everyone. I should
have been dead by forty. I was supposed to leave behind
wonderful memories of a young guy in his twenties.'

JOHN TRAVOLTA

'There is no business in this world so troublesome
as the pursuit of fame: life is over before you have
hardly begun your work.'

CHARACTERS (1688)

To Polly, who needs to read more books.

'What was that?'

VINCENT (John Travolta)

'Nothin'. Let's get into character.'

JULES (Samuel L. Jackson)
From *Pulp Fiction* by Quentin Tarantino

CONTENTS

ACKNOWLEDGEMENTS

I owe many individuals, who have helped make this book possible, my deepest thanks. All told, I interviewed more than 120 people, among them friends, acquaintances, writers, directors, producers, actors, editors, artists, lawyers, publishers, managers, agents, publicists, college professors, cops, private eyes, models, reporters and down-on-their-luck dropouts. Many of these sources have chosen to remain anonymous, even though most of them had nothing but positive things to say. I offer a note of great appreciation for the help they provided and subtly refer to some of them below.

Also, my heartfelt thanks to everyone in the charming town of Englewood, New Jersey, whose help and guidance while investigating John Travolta's early life was unswerving. John's two best friends during his early days in Hollywood were a source of many interesting anecdotes. They stayed close to John for many years and clearly remembered the problems and frustrations John faced in those early, somewhat tragic, days.

Jonathan Krane is John's personal manager and he kindly kept in contact with me and did not stand in the way of my enquiries.

Film Threat magazine were very helpful, particularly editor Paul Zimmerman, who provided some fascinating reference material. A number of John's friends from his school days came up with details of his difficult teens. And David Bourgeois' account of how he stalked the *Pulp Fiction* team at Cannes was highly amusing and incisive.

The section on the build-up to actually shooting *Pulp Fiction* owes a great deal to Cathryn Jaymes and Craig Hamann. They welcomed me into their lives and provided the inside information that lies at the heart of that section. Two crew members from *Pulp Fiction* also contributed some vivid recollections.

Others who deserve much appreciation include: Mark Sandelson, John Glatt, Alex Stone, Mark La Femina, Rupert Maconick, Jon Ryan, Martin Dune, Roger Hitts, Kate Edwards, Viola Johnson, Brendan Bourne, Graham Berry, Jo Solomon, Anthony Bowman, Jim Franklyn, Lisa Samuels, Sofia Crusero, Stuart White, Judy McGuire, Alex Widlock, Nick Howell and George Stewart.

The Academy of Motion Picture and Science Library (Los Angeles), the Englewood Office of Records, the Englewood Library, the Lincoln Center (New York), the *LA Times*, Associated Newspapers, News International, the *New York Times*, *Vanity Fair*, *Time* magazine, *Newsweek*, *Entertainment Weekly*, *Los Angeles Magazine*, the *Village Voice*, Fagi at the *New York Daily News* library, *Variety*, the *Hollywood Reporter*, *Interview* magazine, *LA Weekly*, *Premiere*, *Empire*, *TV Guide*, *Playboy*, *Playgirl* and the Mirror Group provided much of the background information.

Also invaluable were *The John Travolta Scrapbook* (Sunridge, 1976) by Suzanne Munshower; *Travolta -A Photo Bio* (Harcourt Brace Jovanovich, 1978) by Michael Reeves; *John and Diana* (Bantam, 1978) by Mary Ann Norbom; *True Romance* screenplay (Faber and Faber, 1993) by Quentin Tarantino; *Pulp Fiction* screenplay (Faber and Faber, 1994) by Quentin Tarantino; *The Misbegotten Son* (Headline, 1993) by Jack Olsen; *Nancy Reagan* (Pocket Star, 1991) by Kitty Kelley; *Great Movie Quotes* (Fawcett Columbine, 1995) by Dale Thomajan; *Valentino* (Leslie Frewin, 1967) by Irving Shulman; *Halliwell's Film Guide* (HarperCollins, 1995) edited by John Walker.

'Don't make me sound like a pretentious jerk.
I'm really not.'
JOHN TRAVOLTA

'Opportunity, like fortune, does not change a man –
it unmasks him.'
CLIFFORD IRVING, AUTHOR

AUTHOR'S NOTE

Some of the dialogue represented in this book was constructed from available documents, some was drawn from tape-recorded testimony, and some was reconstituted from the memory of participants.

INTRODUCTION
STRAIGHT TO THE HEART

Like many others, I first came across John Travolta when he was strutting his stuff across the big screen in *Saturday Night Fever* in 1978. I observed as the excitement and adoration built to fever pitch, catapulting him to more fame than anyone could imagine. I also watched with fascination as John hit the first of many Hollywood declines.

But now he is back where many say he has always belonged – riding on the crest of a wave. He is so used to the disappointments as well as the elation that this time most believe he is here to stay.

Check it out! Man walks down the street so fine. Strides easy. Long. Looking right. Then left. Then ahead, then left ...snap! ... again, follows that little sister in the tight pants a ways, then back on the beam. Arms arc. Could be some old trainman, swinging an imaginary lantern in the night. Smiling.

Stepping so smart. Roll, almost. Swings his butt like he's shifting gears in a swivel chair. Weight stays, sways, in his hips. Shoulders straight, shift with the strut. High and light.

The street's all his, no doubt. And there's more if he wants it. Could be he might step off that concrete. Just start flying away.

It was all there in the walk that John Travolta took through the opening credits of *Saturday Night Fever*.

John Travolta inspired a generation – for what seemed like two minutes. He was Mr Flares, he was Mr Musical, he was Mr Cool and he had tens of millions of teenage fans wanting a piece of him. He swaggered on to the big screen like Mussolini on his platform shoes, strutted like Schwarzenegger in his black bikini briefs, and danced like Greco in his white suit. And then the whole world turned against him. In *Saturday Night Fever* he was Tony Manero – he was a quiff, a groovy dude in tight pants; he was as camp as a man's man could get; he was the guy who pumped his pelvis to the Bee Gees; he was disco dancing; he was, in many ways, the seventies male personified. Everybody loved him then.

John was a brilliant actor who could hold your attention as he swept across a crowded screen, a great mover, a great deliverer of lines.

His early start left him without a true adolescence, and emotionally Travolta is an odd combination, half boy, half man – a middle-aged man at that. The man plans his career. The boy buys a DC-3 and collects model planes.

Something in John's childhood must have given him an irresistible affinity with the darker side of life. All the signature roles of his career, from *Fever* through to *Pulp Fiction*, have cast him as hard men: cocky, macho, amoral. John is nothing like that in real life. 'But it fascinated me in others,' he explains. '*The seduction of dangerous charm*. People that can lure you, and maybe burn you, and you know you ought to steer clear, but somehow you keep falling in.'

Now he's been rediscovered for the umpteenth time, but the key to his repeated success is the fact that he has never stopped being cool. The way he delivers lines in Quentin Tarantino's *Pulp Fiction* had many wondering why he ever went away. He's now as famous as he once was.

Back in 1977, John could have avoided a total career crash if he'd remained locked into playing Tony Manero-type characters, but he wanted more from Hollywood. He tried to pick and choose carefully but ended up making some disastrous mistakes. Before long, he was poised on the edge of oblivion.

It looked set to be a painful death. The entire ethos of the discotheque – everything John had represented – died a sudden, and painful death. He seemed to have been abandoned. Today, John considers that he was simply replaced by a new generation of actors – Hanks, Costner, Cruise. But it wasn't as simple as that. John became the part of everyone's past that we all feared and loathed. He was the victim of a sort of cultural revolution.

In the early eighties John entered a kind of death zone. He was accepting bad parts, and turning down good ones, with unerring consistency. By 1989, he was seriously considering a new career. His movies were sinking without trace at the box office. He was depressed and washed up, with no place to go. Then he got a part in a movie featuring a talking baby, put on two stones in weight and found himself starring in the surprise hit of the year.

But that wasn't enough for John because he still felt desperately unfulfilled. It took a phone call from young director Quentin Tarantino in 1993 to bring him back to the top of the tree. Tarantino told him to get smart and accept a role in his movie *Pulp Fiction*. It was the best career move John ever made.

The feeling inside Hollywood is that John is now on the ultimate roll. He's survived too much to go under again; people have been renting his old movies on video because there is a certain nostalgia about watching *Saturday Night Fever*, *Blow Out*, *Staying Alive* and, even, *Grease*.

Today, teenagers who were not even alive when *Fever* came round the first time are renting it and watching his every move avidly. The cultural revolution has gone full circle and John's clothes and persona are once again hip and groovy.

In *Pulp Fiction*, when John and Uma Thurman – the gangster's moll he is reluctantly minding for the evening – fetch up at a theme restaurant staffed by Monroe, Buddy Holly and James Dean-alikes, Thurman asks him if he wants to twist with her on the dance floor. As celluloid homages go, watching John Travolta shift his hips to the dance music is the ultimate evidence.

John Travolta always knew how to dance like an inspired, or possessed, amateur. Like someone fantasising. Once you take this on board, then you can read Travolta the actor. He's never been great with lines, but he sure knows how to move, stand and pose like no-one else the big screen has ever known. Just look at how he walked his stuff as he and hitman Samuel L. Jackson quit the Hawthorne Diner at the end of Pulp Fiction. He was strutting, floating along in a hilariously self-conscious type of way.

It was the role that marked his return and he hasn't looked back since.

CHAPTER ONE
AN INDEPENDENT WOMAN

BANK OF THE HUDSON RIVER, HACKENSACK, NEW JERSEY, SUMMER 1932

Pretty young college grad Helen Burke had a look of steely determination on her face as she ploughed through the murky waters of the Hudson, much to the astonishment of the crowds gathered on both sides of the river.

However, her attempt to be the first woman to cross this treacherous stretch of the Hudson was being endangered by painful cramps in her legs. Helen knew the currents were so strong that she risked being swept away. Here she was, a gutsy twenty-year-old Irish-American girl risking life and limb just to break an obscure record. All her friends had said she was crazy to attempt the crossing, all except her boyfriend Sam, a well-known local football star.

And then there was Helen's family. No one seemed particularly surprised when she announced her plans to cross the Hudson. The Burke family took everything in their stride.

Helen ploughed on through the choppy river, her chin held

1

high out of the cloudy brown water. She glanced across at the far bank, where she could just make out Sam's bulky figure waving her on.

'Come on, Hellie. You can do it!' he screamed in his broken Italian, New Jersey accent.

Others in the crowd cheered her on. Cameras snapped as the press recorded this historic event. There wasn't a person on the riverbank that day who did not want Helen Burke to succeed. The cheers went up the moment she touched land and struggled up the slippery, squelching river bank straight into Sam's arms. As her team of supporters gathered around and offered their congratulations, Helen made up her mind to marry Sam and have lots and lots of children.

When Helen got home a few hours later, her mother – a hot-blooded Irishwoman with a very down-to-earth attitude – accusingly asked her daughter, 'Why is your hair wet?'

Helen replied, 'Because I just swam across the Hudson.'

'Well,' said her mother. 'You'd better dry it before you catch cold.'

Salvatore 'Sam' Travolta – also known as 'Dusty' – was the son of an Italian immigrant. His rugged good looks undoubtedly contributed to the Travolta features that would later provoke so much adoration.

Helen reckoned that Sam was the handsomest man in the world – she never forgot the chiselled features and Cary Grant looks which had first attracted her to him when they met in 1932. Sam had been the all-American football hero at college and came complete with cleft chin, dimples and floppy black hair.

Strong-willed Helen Burke entranced Sam from the moment they first met at a high-school dance. Sam had never encountered anyone like Helen before. She was strong, independent, warm and so damn good at organising his life for him.

Helen always seemed to have the energy and determination to do anything she wanted; she made such a good impression during her theatrical debut in a school play at the age of nine that her teachers told her parents she definitely belonged on the stage. During the early 1930s in Helen's home town of Hackensack, New Jersey, she even had her own performing radio group called the Sunshine Sisters.

Helen and Sam soon became known as the most glamorous couple in Hackensack, although they only dated once a week, under the watchful eyes of both their strict Catholic families.

Helen later went to Columbia University to study drama while Sam headed for college on a football scholarship. Sam's continuing education was all the more remarkable because he came from such a poor background. His mother worked in a New York City sweatshop and made every single item of clothing for her four sons. His father eventually managed to scrape together enough money to start a tyre shop in Hillsdale, New Jersey. The family never forgot the day that Sam's father decided he finally had enough money to buy each of his sons a $25 suit, but instead gave the cash to a down-on-his-luck distant cousin who lived in a rat-infested New York City tenement.

Helen did not marry Sam until she was twenty-six years old. Both of them wanted to make sure they were financially secure before they had children. Meanwhile, she decided to devote all her spare time to working as a drama coach, actress and director of student productions in local New Jersey high schools. Sam had already found a place in the New Jersey Hall of Fame, thanks to his prowess on the football field. By small-town standards, they were certainly a go-ahead couple.

Helen directed one of her favourite plays, Thornton Wilder's *Our Town*, seven times at various schools. 'It was almost like being on Broadway' she later explained. (She was particularly flattered because both her family and Sam's used to compare her with Hollywood movie star Barbara Stanwyck.)

The couple's first and only house was purchased in the New Jersey city of Englewood after their marriage in the mid-1930s. Englewood, situated in the southern part of Bergen County's Northern Valley region, just north of the great Jersey meadowlands, was only three miles from the George Washington Bridge and ten miles from Times Square, New York.

Like all good Catholics, the newly wed Travoltas immediately decided to start raising a family, the bigger the better.

'This is the beginning of our real life,' Sam told his wife. He meant every word.

CHAPTER TWO
MOM'S THE WORD

ENGLEWOOD, NEW JERSEY, 18 FEBRUARY 1954

Marilyn Monroe, Betty Grable, Lauren Bacall and William Powell were starring in *How To Marry a Millionaire* in Cinemascope at the local movie theatre. The smaller place down the street was offering moviegoers Hal Wallis in *Ceasefire*, plus *Forbidden* with Tony Curtis, both in 'Thrilling Realism' thanks to the new three-dimensional screen system that became one of Hollywood's finest ever five-minute wonders.

But movies were the last thing on Helen Travolta's mind as she went into Englewood Hospital to give birth to yet another child. At forty-three, Helen was considered extremely old to have a child, even though it was going to be her sixth baby. There were already Ellen, fourteen; Sam, ten; Margaret, eight; Annie, five; and Joey, two.

Some of her friends had rather cruelly told her it was 'disgusting' to have a child at such a late age. She was very irritated by their narrow-minded attitude. How dare anyone tell a mother that she shouldn't have a child! Years later she reflected, 'I can't imagine what my world would have been like without that child.'

Yet six months earlier, when Helen had first gone to see her doctor complaining about feeling nauseous, she had presumed she was going through 'the changes in life'. Even the doctor was surprised to find that she was pregnant.

As all five of Helen's other children had been extremely difficult births, she was amazed and delighted when this baby arrived after only three contractions. It made her feel a special affection for this child because he was 'so darned easy'.

The birth of John Travolta was announced on page seven of the *Englewood Press-Journal* edition of 25 February 1954, in a column entitled 'Society and Personal Events':

BIRTH ANNOUNCEMENT

Mr and Mrs Samuel J. Travolta, 135, Morse Place, Englewood, have announced the birth of a son, John Travolta, at the Englewood Hospital on Thursday Feb. 18. Mr and Mrs Travolta are also the parents of Ellen, Margaret, Ann, Joseph and Sam Travolta.

Other important articles on that same page included a report on a Valentine's Day party given by a Mr and Mrs Carl Bruce for their daughter Clair and an announcement of the impending card party of the Catholic Daughters of America local branch. The same week that John Travolta was born, a local woman was given a suspended sentence of ten days in the Bergen County Jail for cursing at a police officer. Englewood was *that* sort of place.

Elsewhere in the *Press-Journal* there was plentiful evidence of the healthy financial state of the area with a big full-page advertisement for some impressive savings at the A and P supermarket chain, which included fresh top-grade chickens available at just 43 cents a pound. Two huge cans of freestone peaches were on sale for only 65 cents. The cost of living in Middle America in the mid-fifties was probably more reasonable than anywhere else in the world.

The front page of the *Press-Journal* was more colourful, but then this was a town less than half-an-hour's drive from New York City. The lead story was about how a local man had 'miraculously returned from the grave' when another man was mistakenly identified as him after being found dying on the steps of a hospital.

The other big story of the day was indicative of the problems the United States has always had with its war veterans – even before Vietnam. A crazed Iwo Jima vet. had murdered his landlord, a man who, it was revealed, had killed his own wife ten years earlier.

The only vaguely famous resident of Englewood at the time was sportsman Dick Button, who won more international and national figure-skating championships than any other male athlete in the United States. Englewood even held a 'Dick Button Day' following his triumphant return from the 1948 Olympic Games after winning the figure skating gold medal at the age of just eighteen.

Almost twenty years before that, local resident Dwight W. Morrow gained Englewood a place on the world map thanks to his efforts as a senator and ambassador. He also happened to be the father of Ann Lindbergh, whose husband was Charles Lindbergh. Morrow died in 1931.

But in the summer of 1954, the famous residents of Englewood meant little to Helen Travolta. Here she was, a mother with a young child at an age when most local women were preparing to become grandmothers. To make matters worse, there were no other young children on the block where the Travoltas lived, so Johnny tagged along with his mom most days, while his older brothers and sisters attended school.

Englewood started life as a small community of merchants, artisans and small businessmen. Many of them were immigrants from Europe during the mid- and late 1800s and a small number were black. The name of the town was registered on 15 August 1859 by a New York lawyer called J. Wyman Jones who was so impressed by the beauty of the surrounding countryside that he decided it would make an ideal place to develop into a town.

The Wisconsin Glacier, the last of three glaciers that had covered this part of New Jersey, was responsible for many of the features which made the area desirable to early European settlers. Tumbled rocks provided building material; many streams could be dammed to create water power for lumber and grist mills; the soil of the valley was rich enough for good crops and grazing land.

The predominant religion in the mid-1800s was Dutch Reformed and, when the town was founded, Englewood residents raised funds to build their own chapel.

By the time John Travolta was born, Englewood had become a bustling town with 25,000 inhabitants. It was a thriving and diverse place with something close to a city atmosphere. Small businesses and light industry were booming and the population was very varied in terms of wealth, occupation, age, race and religion. High- and low-income families co-existed in the town as well as a large percentage of elderly citizens. About one-third of the population was black and there were more and more Spanish and Oriental communities sprouting up. In religious terms, Englewood was roughly 50 per cent Protestant, 25 per cent Catholic and 25 per cent Jewish. In other parts of the United States, these elements might have represented a social tinder box, but in Englewood everyone seemed to get along together. For once, the American dream was working.

When John was born, Sam Travolta and his brother were co-owners of the tyre shop in nearby Hillsdale which their father had started before the First World War. Sam worked hard, so Helen took on most of the parental duties and, as a keen aficionado of the theatre, she naturally sparked an interest in the arts in her young son.

'Johnny', as his mother always called him, was so skinny and frail for the first year of his life that Helen became convinced he would die in infancy. Virtually every week, she'd call up her local doctor seeking reassurance on her son's health.

In between raising three boys and three girls, Helen directed, taught and acted in drama workshops. Her special interest in her youngest son was fuelled by a mother's natural protectiveness towards the baby in the family. John was taken everywhere by his mother while the other children were left to fend more for themselves.

Meanwhile, Sam Travolta continued earning the reasonable income that enabled Helen to encourage all her children to share her healthy infatuation with acting. It soon became an accepted element of life within the Travolta household. Helen was also different from most mothers in Englewood in other ways: she wore daring turtleneck sweaters and slacks, which was considered fairly revolutionary, beatnik-type stuff in the mid-fifties.

Even as a toddler, John became so infected by his mother's acting bug that she later insisted he was forever saying, 'I want to be a star when I grow up.' At least, that's how the family legend goes ...

At the age of three, John saw *Peter Pan* on television and decided that he could fly. His father explains, 'He'd stand on the third step up the stairs in the hallway of the family home and start flapping his arms like he'd seen Mary Martin do, jump off and fall flat on his stomach. He'd pick himself up and do it again and again and again. Johnny would never settle for anything less than what he wanted.'

By the time John was nine years old, his three older sisters, Ellen, Margaret and Annie, had all become actresses. One of John's earliest recollections was seeing Ellen off at the airport every time she left town on an acting job. He grew up believing that acting and flying were in some way inextricably linked.

At nights, John would lie awake in bed listening to the planes soaring overhead from nearby Teterboro Airport. 'That world of airplanes and theatre seemed like a route to freedom,' he recalled many years later.

John got into movies like any child growing up in Middle America. He saw *Mary Poppins* five times and The Beatles' *A Hard Day's Night* ten times.

John's two older brothers, Sam Jnr and Joey, also got involved in performing and set up their own rock and roll bands.

There is no doubt that Helen was the single most important influence on John's life. She later insisted that she nurtured, rather than pushed, her children's talents and she was especially adept at ensuring that they all had plenty of confidence. Helen always made a point of telling them they were the best, whether or not it was actually true. But she also noticed that Johnny was a very sensitive little boy and later recalled, 'I always had to think before I said anything even faintly critical to Johnny. His feelings were so easily hurt. If I raised my voice to him, he'd run up to his room and slam the door. Then, like the good little actor he was, he'd yell down, "I'm throwing myself out of the window!" I'd race up the stairs, my heart in my throat. Johnny would be hiding behind the dresser.'

John was forever seeking reassurance. He might begin a typical breakfast table conversation as follows: 'Am I good enough, Ma? Pa, what do you think? Am I doing good?'

Other interesting characteristics were also starting to emerge, like Johnny's habit of always asking his mother her opinion on what clothes to wear. 'Ma, which shirt should I wear to school today, the blue one?' he'd ask Helen Travolta.

'I think the green one would look best with those pants, Johnny,' came the reply.

'Thank you, Ma. I think I'll wear the pink one.'

Years later Helen explained, 'Johnny was always asking our opinion – and then doing exactly what he was going to do anyway. He's that way with lawyers and managers and agents now. He wants their advice and their approval, but he's too smart to let other people control his life. He trusts his instincts.'

At the age of three or four, John became so entranced by showbusiness that he would regularly interrupt his mother and ask, 'Momma, can we sit down and play-act?'

With five other children in school and a vast, chaotic home to keep clean, one might have expected Helen to have had little time for her youngest child, but she would immediately drop everything and devote hours to coaching John. He even got into the habit of waiting up until his mother got home from whatever show or play she was working on that evening. The moment she walked through the front door he would rush downstairs and beg her to tell him all about her evening. As a result, even at that early age, John found it difficult to sleep before midnight – a habit that would cause him problems in later life.

Helen's own father had forbidden her to audition for a Hollywood movie role after she had been spotted when performing with the Sunshine Sisters back in the mid-thirties. She felt she had been deprived of a superb opportunity and decided to encourage all her children if they wanted to enter showbusiness. They became a way of fulfilling the hopes and ambitions she had never managed to achieve.

Young Johnny Travolta was fortunate in many ways. He was growing up as part of a remarkably solid family in civilised surroundings, with all the classic American conveniences nearby, including a movie theatre, pizza shops, toy stores, excellent schools, a municipal pool, good public transport and a superb library.

Englewood had a remarkably peaceful, rural atmosphere considering its proximity to New York City. Set amongst dozens of small hills, it boasted three or four luscious green parks and clean, neat tree-lined streets of healthy-looking housing. Playing ball and cycling were encouraged by every parent in Englewood.

The Travoltas grew up on a charming street called Morse Place. Their three-storey Victorian frame house was reminiscent of the large clapboard one inhabited by *The Munsters* (one of John's favourite TV shows while he was growing up). Bootsie, his terrier, stood guard on the big front porch each and every night.

The house itself was painted a dark, musky blue, with an awning surrounding three sides of the front porch. The white window shutters, white trim and red tile roof perked up the appearance of the property. There was even a screen door with a large 'T' in the front entrance, and five steps leading up to it, covered with blue lawn carpet.

On the porch itself, there were nearly always bright-red geraniums in a window box and a cheerful assortment of garden furniture, including a wicker table, a wooden rocker painted white and a wrought-iron chair.

In later years, the Travoltas installed a large above-ground swimming pool in the garden for the younger kids.

Inside, Helen Travolta kept a neat, comfortable home that was extremely welcoming. The furniture was a combination of interesting antiques and functional American tables and chairs. In the corner of the sitting room was a worn red rocker which became known as 'Johnny's chair' because the youngster loved rocking back and forth as his mother regaled him with some theatrical tale or other. Plastic flowers and doilies, cut-glass bowls and a banjo clock on top of a hand-carved nineteenth-century Czechoslovakian chest sat in one corner. A framed reproduction of Andrew Wyeth's *Christina's World* painted by Helen's father hung over the mantelpiece and there was a liberal collection of photos of all the children everywhere. Old-fashioned white net curtains graced the windows at the front of the house in an effort to keep out the prying eyes of passers-by.

Back in those early years, John's best friend was a shabby black teddy bear called Audi to which he formed a strong and understandable attachment. John also tried to construct model planes from the age of four. Helen always went up to his bedroom to tuck him in before he fell asleep – a habit that continued well into adulthood.

Long after stardom struck, John candidly admitted he was a bit of a momma's boy, protected from the outside world by a large and loving family. 'I never knew too much threat. In all sincerity, street life kind of scared me. Inhibited me, I guess. But I always liked to observe.'

Sam Travolta's attitude following the birth of his six children is worth noting because it gives an insight into the sacrifices he and his wife made for their family. 'Once we had those kids,' said Sam, 'my life became unimportant: theirs were the important lives. Helen and I wore second-hand clothes. It didn't matter: we weren't out to make a show. The main thing was the kids saw Pop wasn't putting on a $100 suit while they went without. They knew nobody was loved more than anybody else. One of us was always at home. I could have belonged to a dozen organisations. I didn't. I don't think I spent more than ten nights out all the time the kids were growing up. My own mother and father were always home when we came home from school. I've never forgotten how important it was for me to hear my parents' voices and to know they were always there ... and Helen and I made up our minds that we'd be home for the kids. We believe that kids don't forget.'

There was ample evidence throughout the Travolta clan's childhood that this was indeed the case. The other children – especially the oldest child Ellen – protected John like a baby even after he reached his teens.

Ellen was the first of the Travolta offspring to perform publicly. When she was seven, she sang 'If I Knew You Were Comin', I'd 'Ave Baked a Cake' on a TV programme called *Star for a Day*. She eventually married a cattle rancher she met when she was performing in a Chicago nightclub, and moved to Wyoming.

Throughout his early childhood, John seemed to have an endless supply of questions for his parents beginning with 'Why?', 'What?', 'When?' and 'Who?' He rapidly learned to stay five steps ahead of most kids his age and his father even dubbed him the 'Why-Is-The-Sky-Blue Kid'.

Amongst his favourites were 'How far up is the sky, Pa?' and 'Why can't you make me an airplane that can fly?'

Sam Travolta would often say to his youngest, 'Son, you ask too many questions I can't always answer.'

But John's curious nature was undoubtedly intensified by his loneliness at home during the long hours when his brothers and sisters were away at school, college and work. To compensate, the Travoltas continued to spoil him outrageously.

John was allowed to eat as much candy as he liked and the sweet tooth he developed would give him continual weight problems in later life. Mars bars were his favourite and no one at the time pointed out that each one had the calorific content of a entire loaf of white bread. John also had a weakness for hot fudge sundaes and tuna-melt sandwiches.

During those early years about the only exercise John got was when his father picked him up and pretended to fly him around in circles. 'Fly me Daddy! Fly me!' he would demand at the top of his voice. His mother rewarded him in another way by taking him to watch rehearsals at her high school-drama classes and sometimes even the shows themselves. It was those outings that fuelled Johnny's most ambitious dreams.

CHAPTER THREE

DRESSING-UP TIME

MORSE PLACE, ENGLEWOOD, NEW JERSEY, SUMMER 1960

To this day, John continues to insist that his mother did not push him into acting. He considered it a real treat to watch Helen's drama students in action and would come home and mimic the actors and singers on musical comedy records. Another favourite pastime was dancing in front of the TV screen whenever the 1942 James Cagney film *Yankee Doodle Dandy* was rerun. He'd keep tap dancing for hours and the family would eventually reward him by each offering him a dime to stop.

John later reflected on his mother's interest in the theatre by explaining, 'It was like dominoes – the oldest of her children got interested in acting … and the next … and the next one … It was the accepted thing in our family to perform. It was looked up to.'

His father recalled that Johnny was also an excellent mimic. 'He would take one of my cigars, make believe he was smoking it and do a pretty good imitation of me.'

John soon began nagging his mother to let him do some dancing and singing, so eventually Helen let him enrol in a tap-dancing class taught by Fred Kelly, brother of the legendary Gene.

Older sister Ellen – who was earning her living as an actress – also continued to keep a close eye on her baby brother's progress. She had been impressed by John's enthusiasm and fully appreciated his strong attraction to all things theatrical.

When John was just six years old, Ellen landed a part in the touring version of the musical *Gypsy*, starring Ethel Merman, and she decided to put her brother's obvious talents to the test. After getting both Sam and Helen's consent, Ellen offered John the chance to join her on the show's tour so he could see what it was really like to be in a professional musical. The little boy was ecstatic about the opportunity, especially since it involved flying to Chicago, where the tour would begin. To be with real actors and fly in a real plane was like a dream come true for John.

His mother recalled, 'He was always such a proud little boy. When we let him go to see *Gypsy*, he went on his own on that plane and, as we watched him board, he knew we were watching so he never turned round. He wanted to show how grown up he was.'

Every night during the show, John hung about backstage and followed his sister around until the early hours of the morning. Sometimes he would wander off by himself and enter the theatre's prop room where he would lovingly touch all the props and imagine what they were used for. He would occasionally engage some of the other performers in conversation but was far more adept at chatting with the stagehands.

On his return to Englewood, John could talk about nothing but *Gypsy*. Sam Travolta even splashed out on a record of the show which John listened to endlessly in the basement of the family home. Sitting down there in the children's den all alone, the young boy would act out every single part in the show. He even borrowed his big sisters' dresses and frilly underwear and put them on for the female roles. He enjoyed dressing up because it made him feel closer to the characters he was trying to portray.

On one occasion, he invited Sam and Helen down to the basement to witness his carefully rehearsed one-man show, including his sister Ellen's striptease number 'Let Me Entertain

You'. Instead of being surprised by her youngest son's performance, Helen appreciated John's acting ability, as he stripped down to his sister's underwear in front of them.

John was particularly enthralled by the storyline of *Gypsy* and it undoubtedly gave further inspiration to the youngster to make it in showbusiness. The story is about two young sisters whose mother keeps pushing them on to the stage. The mother insists that the theatre is the only life that holds any glamour or excitement.

John swallowed *Gypsy*'s message hook, line and sinker. However, unlike the heroine of the play, he didn't need his mother to convince him. Besides playing the music from *Gypsy* virtually round the clock, John's basement performances got better and better as he learned that practice did, in fact, make perfect.

Helen Travolta explained, 'John sang and danced all the parts, male and female. He dragged all the dress-up clothes from my costume trunk – and he was tremendous even then: he had the timing and the talent.'

John did all his acting and dancing in the basement because he did not want his brothers and sisters to catch him and tease him. After all, he was dressing up in his sisters' clothes and he knew what sort of ribbing that would provoke.

'Even before he went to kindergarten, he could get into the skin of any character – man or woman,' explained Helen. 'I think I knew even before Johnny was born that he would become a performer. He danced in my womb.'

John's ability to play male and female parts at such a tender age may explain what critics later referred to as an almost androgynous quality, a combination of street-smart virility and vulnerable sensuality that leaves men unthreatened and appeals enormously to women. While there is absolutely no suggestion that John got any sexual pleasure from wearing his sisters' dresses and underwear, there is little doubt that he learned to sympathise with the feelings of women because he was so close to them.

According to Helen Travolta, even at the age of six or seven her son's good looks were beginning to blossom. John's eyes were a dazzling sky blue and his smile was a weapon of charm that easily won over everyone he met. Also, despite the endless supplies of candy, John was a very long, lean youngster.

He actually became so tall and gangly at this time that his brothers and sisters nicknamed him 'Bone'. John's older brother Joey recalls, 'We all had nicknames. I'd be sitting at home with 'Dut' – that was our father's nickname – who'd be reading the paper. Johnny would be sitting with us, too. I'd say to my father, "Dut, when you have a chicken and take all the meat off it, what do you have left?" And Dad would say, "Bones," and Johnny would go, "Aaaahhhh!" and start screaming. He'd go hysterical.'

While all the Travolta boys and girls remained close in many ways, John was considered a spoiled brat and the others couldn't resist an opportunity to tease him.

John has openly admitted that he was 'the kind of kid who liked to play on people's emotions'. And he continued to do things like threatening to jump out of windows if his mother wouldn't take him with her to see his sister in a play.

Yet John later insisted that he was only testing his mother's reactions because he actually wanted her to discipline him. Perhaps the most drastic example of this type of behaviour came when John was eight years old. His sweet tooth was already well developed and he was throwing a tantrum because his mother had refused to cook a chocolate cake that evening. John became increasingly hysterical about not getting his own way.

Eventually he yelled, 'I'll cut off my weenie if you don't make a cake, Mom!'

Helen Travolta was so appalled by this threat that she immediately got to work on the cake. Some would say she should have ignored Johnny's threat, but Helen couldn't do that to her baby.

Eventually Helen developed her own strategy for dealing with her conniving offspring. Knowing that young Johnny had been awestruck by James Cagney, she would pretend to telephone

Cagney saying to John, 'Jim here wants you to do as you're told!'

'OK!' John would reply in abject terror. 'Does he, does he like me?' Naturally, the young boy was too afraid to go to the phone and actually find out if Cagney was on the other end of the line. He never quite worked out whether he was afraid because it might not be true or whether he was afraid he'd be too nervous to talk to the Hollywood star. Meanwhile, John continued to barrage his mother with questions about acting. Then he would spend hours alone in his bedroom daydreaming about the fame he believed he could one day achieve.

CHAPTER FOUR

FLYING HIGH

MORSE PLACE, ENGLEWOOD, NEW JERSEY, SPRING 1964

John was so excited. He'd managed to persuade his father to build a 'real' plane in the backyard. The wings and fuselage were made of wooden planks, and car batteries powered the propellers. John watched in wonder as Sam carefully assembled the machine.

'But what if it don't fly, Pop?'

'Just wait and see, kid.'

John dreamed of soaring up into the sky and following his sisters to the theatre where they seemed to be having the time of their lives. 'Right, let's try her out,' said Sam as he put the finishing touches to the plane. He looked at the bright expression on his youngest son's face and realised that it was time to bring him down to earth with a bump. 'Don't ever try to take her up on your own, Johnny.'

'Why not, Pa?'

'Cos she only works when I'm around.'

'Right,' replied John, nodding his head enthusiastically.

Not long after this, John attended a church social at the

21

Catholic church where he had been baptised and confirmed, just down the street from the Travolta family home. When a local band started playing the 'Twist', Johnny got up and began dancing. However, the group did an incredibly long version of the classic dance tune.

Helen takes up the story. 'That poor kid looked so trapped and exhausted. I kept gesturing to him, "Johnny, it's ok, you can walk off the stage." But he didn't dare stop.'

John's love of travel was fed by his father's insistence that the family manage at least one vacation together each year. They would usually head for the Jersey shore and then on to the mountains where Uncle John and Aunt Mildred had a house.

With each passing year, the boy's urge to travel became stronger. Once, when Sam hinted that he might not be able to afford their annual vacation, John led a deputation of his brothers and sisters and begged his father to let them take some sort of holiday. In the end, he caved in and they went up to the mountains once again.

Another significant childhood love for John was music. Besides all the singing and dancing he did, the youngster was encouraged by his mother to take up the guitar. But it was a struggle for Sam to pay for the lessons.

As brother Joey explains, 'Dad couldn't afford to buy music lessons for us, so we cut piano keys out of a box and we'd "play" them. We'd play and hum and say, "How's that? Pretty Good?" And then say, "Yeah, that's *real* good." And then I remember Dad got Johnny a guitar.'

Books also became an important influence in John's life. His parents encouraged him to read from an early age and he became particularly interested in any books that were even vaguely related to aviation.

On the sporting front, John enjoyed basketball and tennis, but did not share his father's passion for football. This seemed to be yet more evidence of his closeness to his mother.

As John grew up, he continued the dancing lessons that

especially fuelled his dreams of stardom. All through grade school, he tagged along with Helen to her drama classes, carefully listening to how she trained her students.

Helen Travolta, meanwhile, was more than a little concerned about her youngest son's appetite for showbusiness, even though she had clearly encouraged it in the first place. She felt an obligation to point out the good, the bad and the ugly aspects of such an insecure career.

'It's not all about glamour and glitz,' she would tell John. 'It can be a real lonely life.'

Helen also had a very straight-down-the-line attitude when it came to the art of performing.

'You have to be quiet on stage when it is not your turn to speak. And you don't make an entrance by running into a room. You let people have a look at you as you walk in,' she told John.

It was simple enough advice but it would stand him in good stead. The ten-year-old boy never forgot those words of wisdom.

As an accomplished drama coach, John's mother also knew that good speech was essential. She believed that an actor had to be able to speak like any character, from Hamlet to Sgt Bilko. She would spend hours teaching correct speech and dialects to her children.

All the Travolta children should have had strong New Jersey accents like their friends, but Helen was always correcting John and his siblings. Whenever they said 'wata', she'd snap back 'water'. She was relentless.

When John was ten years old, Helen Travolta decided that her youngest child was ready to audition for one of her carefully planned school drama productions. The show was a musical revue called *Spats*. John had his heart set on a major role but, when his older brother Joey won the lead, John threw a tantrum and refused to appear in the show if he could not have the lead.

The rest of the family put John's spoiled behaviour down to the fact that he was the youngest and used to always getting his own way. As is typical in a big family, no one took much notice.

John immediately soothed his hurt feelings by organising an attention-grabbing carnival in the backyard of the family home and starting a bowling alley in the basement using croquet balls and milk bottles. Each game cost 20 cents and soda was a nickel extra. It was a big hit with the local children.

Sam Travolta Snr recalled, 'The backyard became the playground for the entire block. I used to buy hotdogs and sauerkraut and rolls for everybody.'

Eventually the carnival became a regular event and had the desired effect of drawing the family's attention back to youngest child John. He also persuaded brother Joey to help him, although a slight competitive edge was starting to develop between the two brothers.

Joey recalls, 'We used to do shows to records. We even ran regular spook houses and things like that. We were always putting something on, always doing something, performing somewhere or playing. It was very entertaining.'

The carnivals were only really created by John to avoid the issue of why his acting career had suddenly come to a standstill. He recalls, 'A couple of times one of my sisters took me along with her on auditions, but things just didn't seem to gel.'

He sometimes went to New York City with his mother to audition for TV commercials but he failed to get any. Years later, John put all this failure down to fate, but clearly the disappointment of losing the role in *Spats* to his older brother had dented his confidence.

At the age of twelve, John began delivering groceries for a local store and repairing furniture for the neighbours as a way of raising some extra cash for the family. All the Travolta children worked at an early age because they felt obliged to help ease the financial burden on their parents.

'The kids knew we didn't have much,' explained a proud Sam Travolta many years later. 'Our daughter Margaret made good money – $100 a week – as a waitress, and she gave $10 to Helen and $10 to me ... and she knew she had to share with the little ones, too.

'We have a saying in Italian: "Even the little ones want." Margaret would slap a couple of dollars in front of Johnny and say, "Here you are, brat." She loved the brat. None of them ever got into trouble.' But John's latest nickname, 'The Brat', was certainly indicative of the way he was treated within the family.

The basis of John's upbringing was a good, solid traditional combination of Irish good sense and Italian warmth. Even though the Travoltas were all expected to attend church every Sunday, there was never any question of their being forced to become nuns or priests like a few of their close relatives.

Sam and Helen never even went down the traditional route of telling their youngest son to become a doctor or a lawyer or anything so predictable.

Years later, Sam Travolta Snr came up with an interesting theory as to why their approach to parenting worked so well. 'You know why so many stars don't seem to have any past or any parents? It takes a long time to make it in showbusiness and, when a kid is out on the road making no money, his parents think he's a bum. Johnny wasn't a bum. He knew he could always count on us. We looked after him even after he left home.'

During this period, John's mother decided it was time to give her youngest son another chance to perform publicly. A friend of hers had just taken over the newly formed local branch of the Actors' Studio, at the New Dimension Theater, in Englewood. The original Actors' Studio in New York City was made famous by many notable performers including Marlon Brando, Al Pacino and Robert De Niro. The first play scheduled at the Englewood branch was a drama by Frank Gilroy called *Who'll Save the Ploughboy*.

Initially, John attended rehearsals as an observer. He explains, 'My mom didn't have to urge me. Man, nobody pushed me into showbusiness. I was aching for it! And seeing those rehearsals knocked me out!

'The first time I visited, I came in when some of the studio people, the advanced students from New York, were in the middle of doing a scene. After a couple of minutes they, like, broke character to ask the director a question, and I was *stunned*. I mean, I didn't know they'd been *acting* – that's how believable they were.'

John was invited to audition for a role in *Ploughboy* and won the small speaking part of a child. He only had two or three lines but, according to his family, he stole the show because he said them 'so meaningfully'. John knew this was an extremely important opportunity. He also enjoyed the way his role allowed him to escape into being somebody else. He had already become adept at imitating people; from an early age he stored things up about people he encountered and used their habits and mannerisms to build a character. He now realised that he could be anyone he wanted to be. He no longer had to be just the baby of the family, 'The Brat' or 'Bone'. Acting was going to provide him with a means to survive, perhaps even thrive.

CHAPTER FIVE
SCHOOL DAZE

DWIGHT MORROW HIGH SCHOOL, ENGLEWOOD, WINTER 1968

Located in twenty-seven acres of beautiful lush countryside on the edge of town, Dwight Morrow High School had a picturesque college-style campus. At its centre was a handsome brick building with a tower, surrounded by spacious soccer and baseball fields, a pool, dozens of vast trees and a tranquil lake. It looked more like a country club than a school. But that didn't make it any more enjoyable for John.

He had just finished yet another awful day. Over the previous eight hours he had put up with constant teasing, jibes about his lack of academic prowess and a series of playground threats from school bullies. As he rushed down the leafy street on his way to the safe refuge of his home, tears began streaming down his cheeks. He couldn't stand much more of this. He hated it so much in that place. He had to make sure his acting dreams came true otherwise he might never escape the classroom.

It's hard to imagine John Travolta ever being considered a wimp and a nerd. But he really did go through a lonely, tough time at high school. His shyness, his strong attachment to his

27

family and his preoccupation with showbusiness all combined to establish him firmly as an outsider. Many kids in his class called him the 'dumb hunk' – and, not surprisingly, it hurt.

John believed that few of his classmates understood him and he soon gave up trying to be friends with them. They called him names because of his obsessive interest in acting and he was convinced he had nothing whatsoever in common with them. When his family weren't around, John felt he had absolutely no one to turn to.

His isolation from other children was unintentionally reinforced by his brothers and sisters who happily play-acted along with him back home. They made him believe that being different was no big deal – and that turned his school days into an even more painful, anguished experience.

'I would come home from school and I'd play a Broadway musical record instead of running to do my homework,' explains John. 'That made me different from my peers. My reality was different from theirs. I was interested in showbusiness and they weren't.'

Feeling so alone inevitably caused him a great deal of anxiety, especially as John was at an age when most children start to break away from their families and develop outside friendships. John's family – and especially his mother Helen – must take a portion of the blame because they expected so much from him.

'When I acted like a baby, they told me to act like an adult,' explains John. 'When I acted like an adult, they didn't like that either.'

It was a classic situation: his strong-willed parents and domineering older brothers and sisters had cosseted John so much that he was unable to cope with anything or anyone in the outside world.

This also meant that John had a hard time forming relationships with girls when he was younger. 'I wasn't popular with girls. Most of the time I was a little too young for them.'

He tried to use his sense of humour to win favour but ended

up earning a reputation for being nothing more than a clown. But there was one incident when he was on the school bus with football team members, returning from a game, that did at least help to ease his classmates' attitude towards John.

It all started when black team members began to sing a chorus from the James Brown classic: 'Say it loud/I'm black and I'm proud.' John let out his own version: 'Say it light/I'm white and outasight!' It was a rare moment when he actually started to break down the barriers of suspicion amongst his peers.

One of John's few close schoolfriends at Dwight Morrow was a boy named Jerry Wurms. Jerry explains, 'We were both taught to dance by the blacks at the school. Somebody in the corridors or outside always had a radio, and somebody was always dancing.'

Eventually, whenever a new dance craze came to the school, Jerry and John learned it. They soon found that the black pupils were accepting them as if they were true soul brothers. Wurms later surmised that this was because both he and John actually cared about being accepted by the black pupils. 'They seemed to have a better sense of humour, a looser style. We wanted to be like that,' says Wurms.

John then got into watching the legendary Motown TV show *Soul Train*, and would pick up dance moves, which he'd then practise in his room just before going to bed. Dancing was an excellent way to communicate with people and it definitely helped John to be accepted by a few classmates.

But he wasn't the only talented dancer in the Travolta family in those days. Brother Joey, only two years older, was also at Dwight Morrow and he had a reputation that was almost on a par with the fictional character Tony Manero from *Saturday Night Fever*.

Joey was renowned for doing back flips and the splits in the school yard while his classmates applauded. It wasn't really disco in those days (the late sixties) but 'Cool Jerk' and other funky soul songs dominated the dance halls of Englewood.

Joey was a regular at local haunts like the Jewish Community

Center where he won a number of dance contests. Some nights he would go from there to the nearby St Mary's Club and also win. Joey tended to pick as his partner any pretty young girl who he reckoned was the best mover on the floor. He even won a contest, with his older sister Annie, at an expensive privately run Englewood girls' school called St Cecilia's.

Some summer nights, John would hang out in the nearby park, sitting by a sewer, underneath a street lamp, just watching. Studying the activity amongst the other kids nearby, John seemed to be biding his time in preparation for the real world.

When he was thirteen, he met Denise Wurms, the pretty fourteen-year-old sister of his good friend Jerry. For the next few years, she came home to the Travolta house every single day after school.

They would make snacks together, study together, listen to music on the radio. Helen and Sam watched John gradually becoming infatuated with Denise. Everyone presumed they were sweethearts, although both of them insisted they were just good friends. The Travolta clan decided to leave them alone and let the relationship take its own course. Denise, a friendly good-natured girl, became a familiar and welcome face at the big house on Morse Place.

Academically speaking, John was not one of the brightest prospects at Dwight Morrow. He was barely in the average-student category and was constantly distracted from earning anything more than marginal grades by all that dancing and singing.

Teachers found John difficult to handle. He was obstinate, cheeky and bad at accepting any form of discipline. When he got into trouble, he would just try and charm his way out of it. He later explained that he was 'trying to communicate with them on a more adult level'.

John was continually being suspended from Dwight Morrow for a whole range of offences, from bad language to not handing in his homework on time. He later claimed that he was bored at school and got a kick out of fooling around and acting the clown.

As an adult, John would be labelled by many as being a real-life 'dumb hunk' because of his limited education. He was even accused of being stupid by journalists during interviews when he was promoting movies. Yet, although he was undoubtedly very academically unsophisticated, his knowledge of the theatre, music, dancing and aviation was exceptional.

John Travolta was ready to become an adult by the time he hit his early teens. He felt bored and trapped by school and couldn't wait to make his way in the world.

Even today he says, 'Most schools are a one-way flow, guaranteed to put a kid to sleep. The teacher dishes it out and the students listen, then get bored.'

Throughout his troubled stay at Dwight Morrow, John was forever being described by teachers as 'having great potential', even though he preferred to spend his time daydreaming instead of memorising academic facts and figures. His mind was focused on his potential as an actor and performer. Sitting behind a desk staring at a blackboard certainly wasn't going to help him realise his ambitions.

During the late sixties, when John attended Dwight Morrow, Middle America was trying to cope with an onslaught of illicit drug-taking amongst teenagers. At his own school, John witnessed kids taking cannabis, amphetamines and cocaine but he never once felt tempted to experiment.

'I remember the most popular athletes being killed by overdoses,' he recalls, 'and they were guys with really incredible abilities. Drugs were like an outside force that sort of came in and contaminated the whole school.'

John insists to this day that he managed to avoid the trap of using drugs because 'I knew I didn't like it. I knew it wasn't going to help me, and I felt uncomfortable even thinking about it. But also I was not in a group of people who were into that kind of stuff.' In some ways, John's loner mentality helped him resist the lure of drugs.

Meanwhile, John kept up with his dancing and singing and continued to absorb everything his mother, brothers and sisters had to say about the world of entertainment. He also started going to auditions on his own.

The summer after tenth grade, John went to try out for a role at a New Jersey dinner theatre called the Club Bernay in Fort Lee. The play, *Bye Bye Birdie*, had been a smash hit on Broadway in 1960 and John landed the second lead. It was 1970 and he was just sixteen years old. John's salary was a princely $50 a week and he was staggered that he was actually getting paid for something he really wanted to do.

John's parents were delighted that their youngest child had found something to occupy himself with during the long summer holidays. They had no idea just how important this move would prove to be.

John Travolta's first professional acting role as Hugh Peabody in *Bye Bye Birdie* convinced him that he had to leave school as early as possible and try to make a living as an actor.

The part of Peabody in many ways mirrored the sixteen-year-old's life up until that point. For Hugh Peabody was a washed-out loser; a shy ordinary fellow who gets called 'stupid' by his friends and then hooks up with a girl called Kim. She and the rest of the townsfolk betray Hugh when an Elvis-like rock'n'roll star called Conrad Birdie invades their home town and sets teenage hearts aflutter. The John of those days was definitely more like Hugh than Conrad.

John found the role very satisfying; he was able to reach inside himself and use his own experiences as a shy loner. He also had a real-life girlfriend, Denise Wurms, who was struggling to develop her role in his life from that of school sweetheart.

John's relationship with Denise was crucial in helping to shape his complex attitude towards romance in later life. Until he met her, his experience of females had been confined to his strong mother and three noisy sisters.

John dated Denise for nearly five years and he actually believed at one point that they would eventually marry and settle down. Throughout that five years, he never once went out with anyone else.

Back on the stage of *Bye Bye Birdie*, John recognised that he had to take full advantage of the wonderful opportunity he had been given. Each night of the show he tried to improve on his previous performance and eventually he was spotted by an agent called Bob LeMond, who had originally visited the theatre to see the actor playing rocker Conrad Birdie.

LeMond recalled, 'John was the only presence on stage. He had something special going. When John came on stage, everyone else looked like they should go home.'

Backstage after the show that evening, LeMond was introduced to John and immediately asked if he could be his representative. John was flabbergasted by LeMond's directness and mumbled something non-committal in reply; in any case he was due to go back to school at the end of the summer break.

'Thanks for asking me. I'll call you about it sometime,' replied the shy, awkward teenager.

It took John more than a month before he could muster the courage to contact LeMond.

During that month, John did some serious thinking. He was actually considering quitting school altogether, but he feared his parents would never allow it, especially as all his older brothers and sisters had graduated from high school. John also had all the usual fears about not getting a decent job and being trapped in poverty through insufficient qualifications.

However, he had undoubtedly caught the acting bug and genuinely believed he had the talent to make it to the top. But then so did tens of thousands of young hopefuls throughout America.

Also, certain individuals besides his mother had encouraged John to believe that he had real talent. His dance teacher at high school, Derrick Wolshenak, even encouraged him to drop out and try performing full time. And then there were the words of agent Bob LeMond still ringing in his ears. 'I have no doubt you've got the talent, John. Now you just need the correct guidance to get it right.'

John knew the only solution was to ask his parents to let him try acting full time. He might not get another chance. He finally popped the all-important question when he was offered another show to do after *Birdie*. The youngster called his father on the phone. 'Pop, please don't make me go back to school.'

Sam Travolta was almost stunned into silence by what he was hearing. John then broke down in tears. 'Please, Pop. I need this chance. I'll regret it for the rest of my life if I don't do it.'

Sam Travolta appreciated his son's situation but was naturally worried. He had sat back and watched his wife encourage and nurture the young boy's appetite for acting over many years. He took a deep breath. 'Hold on while I tell your mother.'

There was a pause as Sam Travolta put his hand over the receiver. But John could still hear their conversation.

'No,' his mother almost screamed. 'He might not find enough work acting.'

Sam came back on the phone.

But John pleaded, 'Gimme a chance, Pop, please.'

'OK, I'll let you stay out, but it's got to be for only a year, and then you've got to go back.'

'It's a deal.'

Sam was very worried about his son's situation and Helen Travolta shared her husband's fears. In fact she felt doubly guilty because she had encouraged John in the first place.

However, the Travoltas' attitude was consistent with the way they had treated all their children. As Joey later explained, 'All of us kids, we were pretty well adjusted. I think it was because of our freedom. You never heard our parents say, "You have to be home at this time" or "You have to be home at that time." Our parents didn't put too many restrictions on us so we had our own restrictions. There was that kind of trust that made it real nice.'

John was relieved that his parents had been so reasonable

about his request to quit school. He considered his father's suggestion of a one-year trial to be sensible, as he fully appreciated just how difficult it was to make it as an actor. He also reckoned that if he did belly flop then he could go back to school, take his exams, go to college and qualify as a pilot.

John was incredibly excited about his prospects and determined to make it work. He didn't see himself as a typical star-struck kid. He had a chance and he was going to make an impact.

Interestingly, shortly after dropping out of school, John signed up for a mail-order high-school diploma course so that he could still get some qualifications. But he never actually finished the course.

In September 1970, when all his classmates from Dwight Morrow High School were starting eleventh grade, John found himself in the high-rise New York City offices of Bob LeMond.

The agent introduced the shy teenager to everyone in his office and they were impressed by his confident appearance. Shortly afterwards, LeMond signed John up as a client and immediately began sending him out for work.

The first few auditions were for TV commercials, a useful way for an actor to earn some good money (from residual payments) while pounding the pavement searching for work in the theatre. LeMond advised John to go after every available commercial as it would help him avoid more mundane jobs like delivering groceries or waiting at tables, which would eat into his potential auditioning time.

John received several thousand dollars for some of those early commercials, which seemed like a small fortune to a young actor just starting out.

It was a good beginning, but there was a long way to go yet.

CHAPTER SIX

THE TRIP BEGINS

MORSE PLACE, ENGLEWOOD, NEW JERSEY, FALL 1970

John sat in his bedroom too exhausted even to practise his dance moves before flopping into bed. He was extremely worried because his mother had just been taken very seriously ill. She was in hospital and, the way everyone else in the family was talking, he knew she might never come home.

Helen Travolta was the centre of John's existence. She provided an ever-present shoulder for him to cry on. She urged him on and encouraged him every step of the way. He couldn't bear to even think about what life might be like if she wasn't around.

Helen had been rushed to hospital for a serious operation on her legs following a recurrence of health problems that had been dogging her for years. Fortunately, the surgery was a success and she did recover.

On her return home, the family were instructed to look after Helen very carefully. But John insisted that he must be the only one to change his mother's bandages and apply salve to the gaping wound where the surgeon's knife had sliced through her flesh. He did it without embarrassment: his only concern at the time was that *she* might be embarrassed.

John was not in any way repulsed by his mother's illness: he actually embraced his responsibilities towards her and threw himself into the job in hand. This devotion was something that would characterise him in later years.

In 1971, John landed acting jobs in summer productions of two musicals, *The Boyfriend* and *She Loves Me*, at the Allenbury Playhouse in Boiling Springs, Pennsylvania.

When he returned from Pennsylvania, John lived at home with his parents. He was still dating Denise Wurms and there was something reassuring about getting home from his travels and slipping back into normal life with his close-knit family and sweetheart.

John and Denise vowed to continue their romance even though there would be lengthy separations while John pursued his acting career and Denise completed her studies back in Englewood. John felt so attached to his girlfriend, he was convinced their relationship could still lead to marriage and he wasn't about to turn his back on her.

Every day, he commuted from Englewood across the nearby George Washington Bridge into New York City. As he later explained, being so near the city was a big help: 'For a person growing up in New Jersey, it's very easy to get into showbusiness. You're just a bus ride away from New York. You get the theatrical papers, go to auditions. If you have any talent at all, you'll be spotted.'

But, as the number of auditions plus acting, singing and dancing classes increased, the daily commuting became more gruelling and John realised that it would be much better if he moved into the city. His sister Annie – who was also trying to build an acting career – lived in New York. He figured he could stay with her for a short time until he found a place of his own.

John approached his parents and Bob LeMond about his plans and they all agreed it was a good idea. He was just seventeen years old and the yellow brick road to stardom seemed to be opening up in front of him. At first, John felt completely lost in the bright lights of the big city. He was used to a cosy house with a yard and his terrier Bootsie to come home to each evening. There had always been someone to talk to, a brother to share a joke with. Now there was only his older sister Annie and she was out most of the time.

The self-discipline John had learned at home helped him to weather the inner storm of loneliness that hit him the moment he moved to New York City full time. He soon decided he did not want to be a burden to Annie and started looking for his own apartment. Although he had worked on some lucrative TV commercials, the residual payments were slow to come through and he decided the only way to afford a reasonable apartment was to share.

John joined forces with a group of other young actors he had met at various auditions around the city and began apartment-hunting. Initially, most of the rents seemed to be way out of reach. But eventually they found a half-condemned tenement on the corner of Fifty-Sixth and Eighth Street, in Hell's Kitchen, one of the toughest areas in the city. There was no heating, the elevator was permanently broken and there was a plentiful supply of cockroaches. But it was home. John became the unofficial resident chef and was soon conjuring up panfuls of delicious lasagna and spaghetti.

Meanwhile, Bob LeMond had become more than just an agent to John. LeMond kept his newest client busy by sending him out on regular auditions and he was always prepared to listen whenever John had a problem he wanted to get off his chest.

Years later, LeMond proudly recalled what an excellent impression John gave at virtually every audition he attended. 'John was a dream. He knew how to handle himself, how to walk, how to talk. He had it all from day one.'

Over the next few months, John auditioned and won parts in commercials advertising BandAids, MONY Insurance, Pepsi,

Honda motorcycles, Mutual of Omaha and h.i.s. Slacks, to name but a handful. However, commercials were only one aspect of John's blossoming career at this time. He was also starting to get major roles in acting showcases. These showcases were specifically designed to give actors a chance to be seen in plays by casting directors who were constantly on the lookout for new talent.

John's first off-Broadway showcase was a play called *Metaphors*. He earned $112 a week. His next role was in a revival of a play called *Rain*, based on a W. Somerset Maugham story. The show was produced in New York's Greenwich Village area and John played a gawky young marine called Private Griggs. As always, he found himself best suited to the 'loner' roles.

Also in the cast of *Rain* was an attractive blue-eyed, dark-haired actress called Joan Prather. Although she was a few years older than her teenage co-star, the two became good friends.

John relished every minute of his new career. Here he was, barely out of school, yet working regularly with actors – the kind of people he loved best.

Years later he explained his situation perfectly. 'How do you go back to school and make anybody understand how it was to be with those theatre people watching the sun come up over cigarettes and wine.'

Not that John himself was indulging in any such social pursuits. He has always explained his complete and utter abstinence by insisting that drink, drugs and tobacco never held any appeal for him. However, during that time in New York he was apparently always at ease with other people's habits. He had a great need to accept and be accepted by the people he admired the most.

While he was doing these special showcase performances, John also landed roles in two television soap operas, *The Edge of Night* and *Secret Storm*. Although they were small parts, they gave him an opportunity to work in front of cameras in properly developed dramas. TV commercials were all very well, but they usually took up to three days to shoot a thirty-second segment. On the daytime soaps, the production team spent a day recording thirty minutes of film, which gave John a chance to use his talents as an actor in a very different way.

Unlike many of his colleagues in New York, who were apprehensive after years in theatre, John actually enjoyed being in front of a moving camera. He learned to act naturally and subtly, and speedily when required.

During those early days in New York, John was only turned down for a handful out of the dozens of auditions he attended. His first ever movie audition was for a part in a film called *Panic in Needle Park* in which he read for one of the lead parts as a teenage drug addict. John was actually beaten to the part by Al Pacino, so it was nothing to be ashamed about and he went straight into an audition for h.i.s. Slacks the next day, grabbing a role worth many thousands of dollars in TV commercial residuals.

Throughout all this, John felt he managed to keep his relationship with Denise Wurms intact by regularly returning to Englewood to see her. He even arranged for Denise to go with him to visit his oldest sister Ellen at her ranch for the weekend. It was a plan that was intended to cement their relationship.

But, while John was in Chicago for a short tour of a play, he got a call from Denise, announcing that she couldn't carry on their relationship any longer.

His sister Ellen recalls, 'She told Johnny she wanted to break up with him. He was devastated.'

John was stunned. He had never cheated on Denise and had been assuming that they would eventually marry, once his career was more settled. Now she was telling him it was all over in a brief telephone call. He wasn't going to give her up that easily.

John flew home on the next plane from Chicago and rushed round to the Wurms residence in Englewood the same afternoon. Denise was understanding, but adamant. She expanded on her earlier phone call and told John it was clear his career was the most important thing in his life and not her. John tried to explain that his long absences in New York would slow down once he landed a regular part in a TV soap or series. But Denise would not change her mind.

John returned to Chicago for the evening performance of his play exhausted and crushed. He felt he had been betrayed by Denise. From that moment on, he felt an overwhelming mistrust of relationships and found it difficult to sustain any romances.

John's next big professional break came when he was just eighteen and won the part of Doody in the first national touring production of the musical *Grease*.

On the *Grease* tour, John became good friends with three of the cast – Ellen March, Ray DeMattis and Marilu Henner. These friendships were to last for years afterwards.

The character of Doody in *Grease* turned out to be yet another lonely figure whom John could relate to. He was an awkward, well-meaning kid who yearned to be like the cool greasers around him. He was also naive, tongue-tied and the opposite of a lady-killer. But Doody's saving grace was that he played the guitar (as John did in real life) because he believed it would make him seem more appealing to girls.

Years later, John played the supercool lead role of Danny Zuko in the movie version of *Grease*, but that transformation into smooth star was something that came when his career ascended to much dizzier heights. At the time of the stage tour version, John would never have even been considered for such a hip role.

Leading the gypsy life on the road with *Grease* for nine months was a very important experience for John, even though it was extremely demanding and tiring. In some ways, John was on a high, enjoying the fun of being involved in such a major project, but he was also finding it very gruelling.

He explains, 'To try and have fun for nine months is just as difficult as trying to hold a heavy thought thing going. It can work both ways. You've got to work up a technique to make it look as if you're having fun.'

To break up the demands and occasional monotony of the tour, John began commuting to Los Angeles to appear in episodic television shows whenever *Grease* took a short break. His guest slots included such shows as *The Rookies*, *Emergency* and *Owen Marshall*. His previous experience on TV soaps proved a big help in getting jobs on these programmes. Commuting to LA also gave John an opportunity to make new contacts in Hollywood.

When the *Grease* touring show hit San Francisco, John got a note in his dressing room from former girlfriend Denise Wurms saying she was going to be in the audience that night and would like to meet him afterwards. John's heart jumped. Perhaps she had changed her mind and they could try to mend their broken relationship.

A few hours later, John's expectations came down to earth with a nasty bump when Denise rushed up to him backstage, hugged and kissed him and then announced that she was getting engaged to another man back in Englewood.

His face turned pale in an almost exact replica of one of the classic *Saturday Night Fever* scenes when John's character Tony Manero discovers his girlfriend has another lover. John knew then that his earlier suspicions about Denise were entirely correct.

He later conceded that he had been naïve to expect Denise to wait in Englewood for his eventual return. But the split hurt him deeply and when he discovered she'd been seeing someone else it was a double blow to his self-confidence. Today, Denise lives in Washington with her family. She has actually remained in contact with John throughout his career, mainly because of his close friendship with her brother Jerry.

When the *Grease* tour finally ended, John was offered the chance to play loner Doody in the Broadway version of the show. Actresses Ellen March and Marilu Henner also joined the Broadway cast of *Grease* which helped cement their friendships with John.

Unbeknown to most of the rest of the cast of *Grease,* John and Marilu had started a secret romance. The relationship had developed through those endless nights on the road and the close community spirit that emerges during tours. With a steady income from the Broadway version of *Grease*, the couple decided to get an apartment together in New York City.

John and Marilu were not even out of their teens and yet living together like grown-ups. Nevertheless, the young couple did act in a rather childish manner at times.

On one occasion, when a thick fog drifted through the city, they went into Central Park and acted out a super-sleuth improvisation as if they were a couple of cockneys living in London during the era of Sherlock Holmes. It seemed as if John was obsessed with acting even when he was off-duty.

John and Marilu also became rather partial to his favourite food, tuna-melt sandwiches, and listening to the soundtrack of *Last Tango in Paris*. After the *Grease* run on Broadway ended, John got his second movie offer through Bob LeMond which involved flying from New York to LA for an audition. The film was called *The Last Detail* and it was to star Oscar-winner Jack Nicholson. John was desperate to get the part because it was an opportunity to work with Nicholson. He read for the role of the young prisoner being shown a good time on the town before being handed over to the authorities by his two sailor escorts.

Another actor, Randy Quaid, had already been auditioned for the prized role. In the end, the producers chose Quaid because he had a rougher, less innocent quality than John.

'They thought I acted the part very well, but that Randy *was* the part. I came so close I was kind of hot,' recalled John years later, the disappointment still audible in his voice.

But *The Last Detail* audition wasn't a complete disaster for the young actor because he made a good impression on legendary casting director Lynn Stalmaster, who decided to keep an eye on the handsome teenager.

John – totally unaware of Stalmaster's interest in him – was very disappointed about losing the role, but fortunately another offer of work in a Broadway musical, called *Over Here*, came in just a few days later. It starred the Andrews Sisters, a famed singing trio from the forties who were similar in many ways to the Sunshine Sisters formed by John's mother Helen in the thirties.

John's role, as a character called Misfit, involved a lot of singing and dancing and even the notoriously harsh New York theatre critics loved his performance. He was also appearing alongside Marilu Henner, who had managed to get a major part in the show.

A very healthy regular income of $450 a week from *Over Here* enabled John to start flying lessons at Teterboro Airport, in New Jersey – the same airport from where all those planes used to fly over his little bedroom in Englewood.

Meanwhile, the subject of returning to school had been entirely dropped by the Travolta family. Sam and Helen were now convinced that their youngest son didn't need a diploma to make a decent living.

A young New York journalist who met John in those early days remembers a shy teenager who was completely unlike the supercool character he eventually became. 'He was open and willing to talk,' she recalls. 'But it was obvious he didn't feel totally at ease in social situations, especially those which involved people he barely knew. He was very shy and he spoke in this soft little voice.

'I thought he was very vulnerable but, as a matter of fact, I felt sure then and there that he'd be a big star one day. It wasn't just that he was such a nice person or that he seemed happy to go out of his way to be nice and pleasant and helpful. It was more that he had this incredible charisma, the real stuff of which stars are made.

'John would open those blue eyes and look so innocent! I knew it wouldn't be long before every young woman in America would be dying for a chance to mother him and take care of him.'

But John didn't let those first few acting jobs go to his head. He still felt a twinge of guilt about quitting school and even told one friend at the time, 'If I want to go back to school, I can. And

I know I can do a better job now.' He was refusing to completely close the door on his academic education, just in case it still all went wrong.

After nine months in *Over Here*, John won a part in another Broadway show called *The Ritz*, starring Jack Weston, Jerry Stiller and Rita Moreno. This time the job offered $600 a week. 'That was the most money I had ever heard of!' recalled John.

But agent Bob LeMond was not impressed by the offer because he had other plans for his brightest new client. He believed that John was at a turning point in his career and that staying on Broadway would be a serious tactical error.

'Let's give Hollywood a try and see what happens,' LeMond told John.

The young actor was surprised because it seemed crazy to give up a secure job offer just to go out to California on a gamble.

'But Bob, what's the point? No one knows me there.'

'They soon will, John. I promise you, they soon will.'

Bob LeMond later justified this advice by insisting that he wanted John to grow as an actor, to face new and different challenges, and the only way to do that was to head out west.

'You try to avoid horizontal movement, which is doing something that you've already done and that will not get you anywhere,' was how LeMond explained his tactics. 'We will concentrate on vertical movement.'

This may sound more like a battle plan than a career strategy but it was precisely that to LeMond. He believed every move in his client's career had to be tactically correct otherwise he would never attain the fame and fortune he so clearly desired. LeMond wanted John to move *up* in his career, instead of staying at the same comfortable level. Eventually, it was Helen Travolta who persuaded John to go to Hollywood. On hearing about LeMond's suggestion she immediately told her son, 'Give it your best shot.' That was almost enough to persuade John, but he still had live-in girlfriend Marilu Henner to face with the news. She actually saved him the trouble by leaving before he had a chance to tell her about his plans. Yet another relationship had ended in shreds. John was starting to get a complex about where he was going wrong with women.

His sister Ellen has her own theory as to why he had such problems at the time. 'Looking back on it, I really think that Johnny's softness, kindness and trustfulness aren't qualities younger women appreciate. Those girls were looking for someone tough and macho.'

This was an interesting appraisal since John himself was starting to wonder whether the answer would be to date older women. It often seemed as if his mother and sisters were the only ones who truly appreciated him.

The first stage of John's Hollywood gamble was to say goodbye to his beloved family and friends before heading for California. He was feeling apprehensive about what lay ahead and insecure about whether LeMond's grandiose plans would actually work out.

Partly as a response to his own fears about LA, John persuaded his old schoolfriend Jerry Wurms – brother of his one-time love Denise – to accompany him on this high-risk adventure. Jerry actually turned his back on a career as a drug-enforcement agent in Florida to join his old friend.

Jerry was an enormous help when they got to Hollywood, as he drove John from audition to audition on the back of his motorbike. However, acting roles weren't exactly pouring in. John was immediately rejected on two movie auditions and, as far fewer TV commercials were made in LA, there was much less work from that lucrative direction. By the time he got to his third try-out for a movie, he was starting to wonder if Bob LeMond had been right. John kept thinking about that cosy weekly salary on *The Ritz*, while LeMond kept reminding him that he was only twenty years old, with an incredibly bright future ahead of him and enough time to invest in his career.

John was so depressed by the way his career was going that, in his own words, 'I felt like nothing could work right.'

Bob LeMond kept telling him to be patient. But scouring Hollywood for work had taken a huge toll on the young actor's self-esteem. He started to doubt his own abilities and his in-built self-confidence was faltering.

LeMond was extremely concerned about his young would-be star. He knew just how demoralising it could be on the Hollywood bit-part acting circuit, but he had warned John to expect a rough ride for at least a year. Privately, LeMond thought it might take anything up to five years for him to break through into mainstream acting roles.

As the months progressed and success seemed to become ever more unattainable, John began to have trouble sleeping. He was homesick. The few friends he had in LA only seemed interested in what use he might be to them. He was getting close to quitting and catching the first plane back to New Jersey.

In a bid to cope with his depression, John started seeing an analyst who opened his eyes to some aspects of his life that were undoubtedly making his stay in Hollywood so miserable. The analyst told John that one of his biggest problems was that he was clearly disappointed in himself for 'choosing negative people to be around'.

'I wanted to be more consistent and feel good; I didn't want it to be such a darn roller-coaster ride,' was how John described it many years later.

Another reason for his emotional problems in the early days in Hollywood was his inability to make friends easily. The only person who really kept John's spirits up during those early days was his old school friend Jerry Wurms. Aside from the occasional party, at which John tended to feel completely lost, the young actor spent much of his spare time reading books on planes and pottering around the two-bedroom apartment he was sharing with Jerry, who had become his business adviser.

Jerry compared them both to *The Odd Couple*. 'I was the neat one, John was the slob. He left his socks where they fell on the floor and never put his dishes in the sink.'

In those days, John also had quite a problem choosing sensible clothes. His sister Ellen explains, 'Johnny never got it together with his clothes. His shirts were always short and they stuck out of his pants, his colour combinations were terrible. He actually lived much of the time in a pair of khakis – full of holes – that he couldn't bear to throw out.'

In the midst of all this emotional turmoil, John went to a movie audition for a 'C'-grade horror flick called *Devil's Rain*. To his utter amazement he won the role. *Devil's Rain* starred Ernest Borgnine, Ida Lupino and Eddie Albert and was supposed to be a taut thriller shot entirely on location in Mexico.

John's own shooting schedule wasn't particularly long or strenuous because he had such a small role. But it was a start.

CHAPTER SEVEN

WRONG PLACE, RIGHT TIME

DURANGO, MEXICO, SUMMER 1974

Mexico owes its name to the Aztec tribes which occupied the central tableland and whose war-god was Mexictli. It is a vast country of more than 768,000 square miles (or one-quarter the size of the United States, its northern neighbour). Almost exactly in the centre of this vast hot expanse lies Durango, just above the Tropic of Cancer, which is marked by a white band painted on the high road south of the city. Temperatures in this dusty outpost frequently exceed 100 degrees. Durango is permanently overlooked by volcanic mountains that cast an eerie shadow over it when the sun sets low in wintertime. They roll away into the hazy distance, changing colour as the light changes. The foreground is broken up by organ-cactus, so-called because they resemble the pipes of a huge organ.

This was John's first ever trip outside the US and he was apprehensive. All his friends and family had warned him about the water, the food, the lawlessness. But John's main fear was the movie he was about to embark upon. *Devil's Rain* certainly appeared to be a career move in the right direction, but he had a feeling that this wasn't exactly a five-star production. He'd arrived on a rickety plane from Mexico City after taking a regular airline there from LA. No one had been at the tiny airport to meet him and the accommodation sucked.

His only consolation was that he discovered his old friend Joan Prather had a supporting role in the movie so at least he had one soulmate.

Joan was three years older than John, but neither of them noticed the age gap. Joan's life in showbusiness had started at the age of six when she'd been a skating mouse in the *Ice Capades*. At nine, she was chosen by the legendary Burgess Meredith for a role in Dylan Thomas's *Under Milk Wood* at a theatre in her home town of Dallas.

By the time she was fourteen, Joan was working in community theatre, as well as appearing in two weekly variety shows on local TV and a host of commercials. The only time she ever missed out was when she was not chosen for the finals of the Miss Teenage America Pageant. Small parts in TV shows like *Happy Days*, *Sanford and Son* and *Executive Suite* soon followed.

Out in the sweltering heat of Durango, John and Joan became virtually inseparable throughout the *Devil's Rain* shoot. John was still feeling low about his career and had continued to see his analyst back in LA.

Prather recalls, 'He was in need of friends. He was depressed, as was I, and we were the only two young people there, really. It was a very lonely time for him. The friends he had were using him as a doorwipe, to put it bluntly.'

A couple of years earlier, Joan Prather had become a member of the Church of Scientology. As she and John bonded in Mexico and he poured out his feelings about life back in Hollywood, she produced some of the Scientology books she had brought with her. Initially, John showed nothing more than a passing interest. Then, a few days later, he completely changed his tune.

Joan takes up the story, 'One day Johnny got very ill with the flu. In Scientology we do a thing called a "touch assist", which makes you get better much faster. It's not magic. If you have a broken bone, it'll heal it in two weeks instead of six.

'So I was giving him the assist and, in the middle of it, he looked at me and said, "This is the first time anybody's ever really helped me without wanting anything back for it." I started showing him my Scientology books, and he just couldn't read enough of them.'

Not long afterwards, John joined the Church of Scientology. 'Basically you go into it because you want to handle some problems. It has no barriers on what it is.'

John's recurring bouts of depression disappeared soon after he joined the Scientologists. 'It made sense to me right away because it seemed like a means of self-help. A meter shows you when you're responding to a bad experience in your past. You find the source of pain, acknowledge it, deal with it. That seemed to me very logical, and I was right, I get answers that way. OK?'

He even believed that discovering Scientology meant he would never have to worry about finishing his formal education. 'Now, I'm into Scientology, the science of the mind,' he says. 'This helps you deal with your life better; to understand your own mind and everyone else's.'

Meanwhile, John's movie debut in *Devil's Rain* turned out to be less than memorable. 'I only had a couple of lines,' he recalls, 'but I was so completely disguised by the make-up that I don't consider I really existed in that movie.'

John actually had his face covered by a mask throughout his brief appearance and his two lines were dominated by the use of the word 'Blasphemed'. After that, he mysteriously melted into a pool of liquid.

Not long after *Devil's Rain* wrapped, John won a far more substantial role on a TV show called *Medical Center*, starring Chad Everett. When John's episode aired, a producer named James Komack tuned in. He was casting for a brand new TV series called *Welcome Back Kotter*. Remembering that casting director Lynn Stalmaster had highly recommended a young actor called John Travolta, Komack studied the episode of *Medical Center* and decided there and then that this guy had to play a major role in his forthcoming TV series.

Superstardom was on the horizon for John Travolta. His hard work and persistence were about to pay off in a very big way.

James Komack – executive producer of *Welcome Back Kotter* – had already auditioned at least half a dozen actors for the role of Vinnie Barbarino. Then he called up casting supremo Lynn Stalmaster, who contacted John and set up an appointment for what is known in Hollywood as a general reading.

When John showed up for the reading, Komack talked to him for just two minutes before looking him straight in the eye and saying, 'I want you to play the part of Vinnie Barbarino.'

John stared at the producer in astonishment. There hadn't been a reading. No screen test. No weeks of anguished waiting to hear if he'd got the job.

'Don't you want to test me … or see my list of credits … or something?' John asked.

Komack shook his head. 'Not necessary. I'll work out the contract later.' That was it. The whole thing had happened so swiftly that John couldn't believe he had the part. At first, he didn't even call to tell his family because he wanted to be sure. In fact, he didn't fully accept that he had the part until the day he reported for work on the first episode of *Welcome Back Kotter*.

Programme producer Komack never forgot how surprised John had been when he gave him the news. 'I couldn't convince him that he had the part. He refused to believe me. He even followed me to New York, where I had gone to cast the other *Kotter* roles, pestering me to test him for Barbarino.

'You must be crazy, John,' James Komack told the young actor. 'You've got nothing to gain by it and if you put in a bad test it could wind up costing you the part.'

'But I wanna do it, James,' came John's reply.

Komack shook his head in amazement and then granted the young actor his wish. Fortunately, John tested superbly.

John had been on the West Coast for just four months before breaking into the mainstream with a regular role in a major TV series. Although John was astounded by his good fortune, his family were not in the least bit surprised. They saw his role in *Kotter* as an example of how hard work can pay off. They also believed that John was an incredibly talented young man.

On the surface, John seemed, to people like James Komack, to be a super-cool, brashly confident young performer. But he was actually so terrified that he carried a bottle of Maalox in his pocket to settle his rumbling, nervous stomach. Nevertheless, he knew that playing Vinnie Barbarino in *Kotter* was the biggest break of his life.

'I thought it was a hot role,' John recalls. 'As a matter of fact, I knew it was. Vinnie was an Italian kid who dreamed of one day being a Mafia leader. It was a good role. I actually had a chance to flash a lot.'

John's agent Bob LeMond was equally enthusiastic about the part. 'When I read the script of *Kotter* I knew Vinnie Barbarino could make John a star. You get that feeling about roles. And the size had very little to do with it. So many actors make the mistake of going for big roles. What you should go for are the ones that have the most effect. The ones that show off what you can do.'

The role of Barbarino was especially significant because it marked a change of persona for John. This character was a tough kid from the streets of Brooklyn who was the leader of a group of borderline juvenile delinquents called the Sweathogs. Barbarino was brash, semi-articulate, conceited and the neighbourhood Casanova and can best be described as somewhat akin to The Fonz in *Happy Days*.

Welcome Back Kotter was created by writer Gabriel (Gabe) Kaplan and his friend Alan Sacks. Kaplan had originally been a stand-up comedian who used the world of the Sweathog clan from Brooklyn in his comedy routine for some years. Audiences loved the stories about the teenage street-gang members and Kaplan realised that a story revolving around their antics in, and out of, school could make the ideal popular TV sitcom.

The characters created by Kaplan and Sacks are worth describing in some detail because this series played such a vital part in John's career. There was:

GABE KOTTER (The Teacher): Once a borderline delinquent himself who returns to his old school to take on the challenge of teaching bored, semi-illiterate street kids.

JULIE KOTTER (The Wife): A schoolteacher who is Gabe's sweet and understanding wife. She helps to ease the trauma of dealing with such difficult pupils.

MR WOODMAN (The Vice-Principal): A mean and unsympathetic school administrator who's the butt of many rude jokes and remarks.

ROSALIE: Basically a nice girl and average student, mockingly labelled 'easy' by fellow students. Touchingly vulnerable.

ARNOLD HORSHACK (A Sweathog): A likeable fool with a piercing laugh. The uncoolest, most endearing member of the Sweathog gang.

JUAN EPSTEIN (A Sweathog): Affectionately nicknamed 'The Animal', this Jewish Puerto Rican was voted 'the most likely to kill' by his class.

FREDDIE 'BOOM-BOOM' WASHINGTON (A Sweathog): He's black, beautiful and proud to be a Sweathog.

VINNIE BARBARINO (Leader of the Sweathogs): A swaggering Italian tough who's a wow with women and a zero at academics.

Even before *Welcome Back Kotter* aired, there were a few rumblings about the programme because the idea of promoting juvenile delinquency on television raised several eyebrows. Concerned parents and TV critics claimed that youngsters would be influenced by the antics of the Sweathogs. There were also complaints about the show being set in such an unruly area of New York City. It was pointed out that academic standards were far below acceptable levels at the fictional school. One TV station in Boston actually banned the show on the basis of what they had heard about it on the grapevine.

But James Komack adamantly stuck to the show's original premise and its characters. On 9 September 1975, millions of viewers across the United States tuned into the first episode of *Welcome Back Kotter*.

Initially, the only actor in the show who got any measurable publicity was creator Gabe Kaplan, who also starred as teacher Kotter. Most TV critics mildly applauded the show, but no one expected it to become one of the biggest hits of the TV season, which is exactly what happened. Contrary to the fears of TV censors and executives, the show was far from offensive and the characters were positively endearing, especially the members of the Sweathog gang.

As John's co-star Larry Jacobs – who played Boom-Boom – explained, 'We lightened the show up. We're street smart, but we're not really toughies. We're sort of nice guys. We're not punks. If you met us in an alley, you might think you had a chance.' Inevitably, all the Sweathogs soon became household names amongst kids across America. But it was John's character, Barbarino, who stood out. Viewers believed him to be a gentle kid with a heart of gold beneath a tough exterior. He seemed to combine arrogance with sweetness and John turned into an overnight idol for millions of young people across the country.

Fanmail started to pour in from thousands of women aged eight to eighty. Letters were addressed to John or 'Vinnie'. They called him 'cute', 'cuddly' and 'sexy' and a lot more besides.

Some asked for an autographed photo, while others proposed a date or marriage. After just one year on the show, John's fanmail totalled 10,000 letters a week. Then promoters latched on to his huge popularity. Rapidly, four different posters of John were marketed and sold in millions. Then John's smiling face began appearing on T-shirts, mugs, tote bags, school lunchboxes and dozens of magazine covers. He was twenty-two years old and already the toast of Hollywood.

Even back in Englewood, fans were proving difficult to avoid. Helen and Sam were still living in the same quiet unassuming property and many *Kotter* fans would simply sit on the front lawn. Others would go right up to the house and snitch slivers of the porch and siding to take home as souvenirs. Whenever John returned to Englewood, policemen had to be called to break up the large crowd that inevitably gathered on the Travoltas' grassy front yard.

The Travoltas were so besieged by phone calls that they changed their number to an unlisted one. Barbarino fans would call from all over the country and many of them even reversed the charges.

Helen later recalled, 'One day, I got a call from Washington – the state of Washington. The operator said it was from Ellen so I took it. It was just some kid.'

Other young girls phoned the Travoltas to profess their undying love for John and some of them proudly told his parents how they had been stalking him in Hollywood. At the time, Sam and Helen accepted all the attention as something they would have to live with. After all, they had encouraged John to seek fame so they could hardly complain about it when it happened. And there was no way they would move house.

The Travoltas never missed a *Kotter* episode. But they got mightily fed up with being asked personal questions about their son by complete strangers in the local supermarket.

Sam Travolta explained, 'My wife used to get so mad because people would ask if John was the Vinnie Barbarino character –

meaning, was he a dumb kid? I wouldn't say he was a brain, but he was no *dope* either.'

In Englewood, Travoltamania spread like wildfire and there was even a proposal to hold a 'John Travolta Day' at Dwight Morrow High School. John was particularly surprised by this accolade as he had left the school without even graduating.

Everything John did suddenly became big news. He appreciated it at first, as it seemed to represent approval from his audience – the general public. But then all the attention began to scare him. On one occasion, he went to Joe Allen's restaurant in Hollywood wearing glasses, a hat and a fake beard. It looked ridiculous, especially as Joe Allen's was a favourite hangout for young actors.

John sat at a back table and drank his coffee in complete silence. Eventually he was recognised by two pretty young girls who immediately asked for his autograph. Soon after, other people came over, as word of his appearance spread throughout the restaurant and John ended up signing autographs until his hand hurt. Then he excused himself by going to the restroom. Soon afterwards, he sneaked out of the back door and went home.

John tried to take all this sudden fame in his stride, but he did not like having absolutely no control over it. The strangest aspect of it all was that he wasn't even the main star of *Welcome Back Kotter*. He actually spent very little time on screen. In that first series, he averaged a total of about five minutes per episode and appeared in only ten out of every thirteen shows.

By the second year of the series, John was even confident enough to admit, 'I've seldom been on this past year. My schedule is very light. I could almost do it in my sleep. I work about three or four hours a day, then do dress rehearsal on Mondays and tape the show on Tuesdays. It doesn't bother me that I'm not prominent on the show each week or that I'm not paid a great deal. The series has been good for me, and I'm crazy about Kaplan. In fact, the whole group is like one big happy family. Sometimes I come to the show in the worst mood imaginable, but I snap right out of it being with the guys.'

Other cast members of *Welcome Back Kotter* insisted there was no resentment about John's swift rise to fame. Actress Ellen March had become a close friend and confidante since their days together in the theatre and she said, 'John doesn't have an enemy in the world and he never says anything nasty about anyone.'

Certainly on the surface, John was the perfect gentleman. However, he was always careful not to show his ambitious streak in front of his colleagues on the show.

In public, John continued to tell anyone who would listen what great people he worked with. 'Everybody is really great on the show. The guys hang out together, like a team effort. Nobody upstages anyone else. And believe me they're all pros. Every week I get an acting lesson.'

John spent a lot of time outside the studio with his fellow cast members organising events like mini-basketball games with Gabe Kaplan and Larry Jacobs. He even briefly dated Julie Strassman, the sister of Marcia Strassman, the actress who played Kotter's wife. But none of his brief encounters with females seemed to lead to anything permanent and John was growing increasingly paranoid about the motivation of women who made it clear they wanted to date him. Fame certainly had its drawbacks.

CHAPTER EIGHT
TRAVOLTAMANIA

WELCOME BACK KOTTER SET, ABC-TV STUDIOS,
CENTURY CITY, EARLY 1977

Everyone was walking around with their heads bowed, barely able to raise a smile or a hello for their colleagues. The cast and crew had just been given the news that John's friend comedian Freddie Prinze had committed suicide. John was devastated.

Later that day, he broke the icy atmosphere by talking to his two Sweathog co-stars Robert Hegyes and Ron Palillo in a corner of the set. One-time stand-up comedy star Prinze's death had shaken them badly. Prinze was considered, like John, to be an up-and-coming star.

Palillo later recalled, 'Bobby and I were sitting around the table with John and we all vowed that we wouldn't let something like that happen to us. We pledged to call one another if we ever got so depressed that we might be on the point of suicide. We all recognised that what happened to Freddie could happen to any of us.'

The memory of the anti-suicide pact that the three young

actors agreed upon that day stayed with John for the rest of his life and actually prevented him from considering the ultimate escape in later years, following some very tragic occurrences.

Despite Prinze's death, John continued to pump his relatively minor role in *Welcome Back Kotter* for all it was worth. He deliberately played up to the audience with a swing of the hips or a twinkle of the eye. At the start of the first series, his character Barbarino had seemed very one-dimensional, but John gradually introduced a whole new range of feelings to the part. He knew that *Welcome Back Kotter* was a showcase for his talents and if he wanted to make it big then he had to put all he had into the character of Vinnie.

The show's producer James Komack was full of admiration for the way in which John moulded the role. 'In the beginning of the series, Vinnie was very slick and tough. But Johnny has a likeable, sweet, and even soulful personality. He has a spiritual attitude, so we made Barbarino a devout Catholic. He then made him an even more appealing and vulnerable character.'

Within one season of *Kotter,* John got extremely restless about his part in the series. He wanted to try something new and told his agent Bob LeMond to push harder to find him a movie. However, there was a problem; John's contract on *Kotter* pinned him down for a further two years. He had already lost out on starring in one film called *Days of Heaven* because of that work schedule and he was desperate not to sacrifice any more meaty movie roles.

The producers of *Welcome Back Kotter* were so worried that John might quit for bigger and better things that they tried to give the show an added ingredient by hiring a young actress as the first female Sweathog.

Melonie Haller was an ex-model and TV-commercials actress discovered by producer Komack when she was standing at the back of the *Kotter* rehearsal room one afternoon. She was rapidly cast as Angie, a girl who aspired to join the all-male Sweathogs.

Melonie's role lasted only a few episodes because the show's millions of fans found a female Sweathog completely unacceptable and sent hundreds of thousands of protest letters to the producers. However, Melonie did manage a few romantic dates with John off the set and the two remained close friends for much longer than her part lasted.

Meanwhile, John, in a typically diplomatic move, made it clear in public that he had no intention of walking out on his *Kotter* contract. He acknowledged that the show had helped his career immensely, but he did tell a number of journalists that he expected his role as Barbarino to be kept to a minimum and he was determined to continue pursuing his movie career.

Reflecting on his role in *Kotter*, John says, 'It enabled me to do what might have taken twelve years otherwise. I never knock Vinnie. He broke me through the sound barrier and gave me a lot of credibility in the business.'

Nevertheless, he did not hesitate to turn down an approach by ABC Television for him to do a series based on the Barbarino character. He confided to a friend that *Kotter* 'would be my first and last TV show'.

Unlike his TV persona Vinnie Barbarino, who aspired to be a Mafia leader but never had the drive to achieve his dream, the real John Travolta had all the dreams, but also had the energy to achieve them. He would never be satisfied to stay at the same level and was constantly in search of new opportunities.

Around this time, John became close friends with actor Henry Winkler, who played The Fonz in *Happy Days*, a show that many thought *Welcome Back Kotter* was based upon. A camaraderie developed between the two actors as they tried to help each other to, as John later said, 'keep our heads together'.

Winkler and John were both learning to cope with fame under very similar circumstances. Despite tabloid gossip that they were fierce rivals, they have actually remained friends to this day.

Said John, 'Henry and I are good friends. Our paths have gone in different directions, that's all.'

And Henry Winkler added, 'John and I will always be good friends.'

John even managed some wholesome praise for Winkler's performance as The Fonz. 'I really loved Henry in that part. He was excellent.' Inside Hollywood the media continued to claim that John ripped off some of the Fonz character traits for his own TV role as Vinnie Barbarino. But, as John pointed out, 'Fonzie's cool and tough. He hits one note. You wouldn't be surprised if Vinnie cried, but you would if Fonzie did.'

During that first season on *Kotter*, John managed to get another movie role, this time on the horror flick *Carrie*, directed by Brian de Palma and co-starring Sissy Spacek and Nancy Allen. John played Billy Nolan, who teams up with girlfriend Nancy Allen to play some really dirty tricks on Sissy Spacek, a strange girl with mysterious powers. John enjoyed working with de Palma, and *Carrie* went on to become one of the highest-grossing horror films of all time.

Career-wise, John broke through as a movie performer thanks to his role in *Carrie*. It was a significant role because John was playing the opposite of his wholesome favourites. In *Carrie*, John's language would have made the Sweathogs blush and there were some raunchy sex scenes with actress Nancy Allen.

But John's worst moment during filming came when he had to bludgeon a pig to death in order to get its blood and use it to smear all over a girl's dress at the prom the following evening. He was terrified of the pigs and became convinced they would bite him. But he got through it in the end.

Nancy Allen recalled that both of them smelled of pigs for days afterwards. Meanwhile, John kept a low profile in public; the most daring place he ever visited was the local takeaway hamburger joint.

John's biggest problem at that time was his incredibly busy schedule. He was starting to find himself neglecting the people who really mattered in his life: his parents, family and handful of friends. He had the occasional date with girls, but these were rare outings and he didn't even have time to pursue his favourite hobby – flying.

By the spring of 1976, John had become one of the most overexposed young stars in America, all because of his role in *Kotter.* Besides the hunky-looking posters, there were cut-outs, colouring books and a host of other souvenirs of Vinnie Barbarino. There were also dozens of requests for personal appearances, most of which had to be turned down.

On one episode of *Kotter* John did a fun, scat version of the Beach Boys' classic 'Barbara Ann', only it came out 'Bar-bar-arino' on the show. His fans adored it.

One of them, a thirteen-year-old girl called Kim, happened to be the niece of Bob Reno, president of Midsong International Records, an RCA-owned record label that produced stars like Melanie and the Silver Convention. Little Kim called her uncle to tell him about John's singing debut on television.

Bob Reno decided to watch the *Kotter* show himself and immediately afterwards phoned John and asked him to do a demo track to see if he really could sing.

John told Reno about his musical background and all the singing he had done in *Grease.* Then he mentioned that he had recorded a little-known record called *Over Here* to accompany the show he appeared in immediately after *Grease.* The Andrews Sisters dominated most of the disc, but John did sneak in one big number called 'Dream Drummin'. It was by all accounts an uncomplicated musical arrangement and the song is said to be the best thing John ever recorded. On the strength of that performance, Bob Reno signed John to a record contract immediately.

John described this latest development in his showbusiness career as 'a chance to share my vocal festivities'. He insisted on helping to choose the specific numbers that would be featured on his debut album. There was to be his own version of the Elvis hit 'Big Trouble', in deference to the master. There was also a whole range of contemporary songs that read like a *Who's Who* of John's favourite music at the time – Neil Sedaka, Eric Carmen, the

Rascals. In addition there were three original songs by actor Michael Lembeck, John's old friend from his *Grease* days. Another song on the album, 'Let Her In', was chosen to be released as a single because everyone thought it had hit potential. But the most important song to John was the last one cut on the album, 'It Had To Be You'. It was his mother's favourite tune from the days when she used to sing it with the Sunshine Sisters. On the back of the album, John even dedicated that track to them. The single alone sold more than 800,000 copies and reached the number-five spot in the Cashbox Top One Hundred chart.

The album – simply entitled *John Travolta* – had to be put together at high speed because of his incredibly busy schedule. There were also demands from the record company to get the record into the stores quickly to capitalise on John's ever-increasing popularity. John was unhappy with the end product and even admitted a few weeks after its release, 'I was at one-quarter of my ability.' *Time* magazine said the record was 'a bland rock album tailored to sub-teens'.

But, despite all this, the album sold like hot cakes. Many fans bought it just because of the cover photos of John which were expertly taken by Jim Fridley, a fashion photographer then married to John's sister Ellen. His family's ranch near Palm Springs became a favourite bolt-hole for John.

On the front of the album was a full-colour shot of John in pale-blue turtle-neck sweater to match his eyes. On the back was a sexy black and white photo of John in tight hip-hugging jeans and open shirt, with a smouldering expression. Many inside the music industry proclaimed that the record would have sold even if John had simply hummed the tunes through an old tin can.

Predictably enough, 'Let Her In' became a hit single almost immediately, and John was named as 'the new pop male vocalist of the year' by *Billboard* magazine.

In September 1976, John appeared alongside the guest performers at the second annual Rock Music Awards, broadcast live from the Hollywood Palladium by CBS-TV.

A year later, John did another album called *Can't Let You Go*. It was a marked improvement on the first, although it was still hammered out at high speed under intense pressure from the record company. Two songs – 'Whenever I'm Away From You' and 'Slow Dancing' – did well in the singles charts. But John's handsome features and skin-tight trousers did more than anything else to help sell those records.

John was upset by the critics' reaction to his career as a pop star. He felt he had worked hard at his singing and was bitterly disappointed that he was not being taken more seriously as a vocal performer. However his middle-of-the-road musical choices didn't exactly help.

Despite all this, John's agent Bob LeMond took full advantage of his star client's latest career move by taking out full-page advertisements in movie-industry publications like *The Hollywood Reporter* showing the sexy album covers complete with a note congratulating John on his newfound success as a pop star. One ad read, 'His face is his fortune.' That just about seemed to sum up John's musical career. Many showbusiness observers were surprised by the bragging tone of the advertisement. Some critics also resented the fact that John, who had never been known as a singer, could get a record produced because he was a teen TV idol, while so many talented singers were unable to get their careers off the ground.

John was deeply hurt by the jibes. Throughout his life he found it difficult to accept any criticism. This was partly due to his position in the Travolta family as the youngest child who usually got his own way. It may also have been partly because he had found showbusiness success so swiftly and at such a young age.

At such moments he tended to turn to the Church of Scientology for comfort. He explained at the time, 'It makes my life simpler by helping me to understand the other person. This past year has been so frustrating that it could have made me go bananas if Scientology hadn't kept me sane.'

But all the sniping comments from music critics had no effect whatsoever on the general public. When John started making a number of personal appearances to help promote his records, the response was positively overwhelming. At one Cleveland record store he was rushed by 5,000 fans and at the world's largest indoor shopping mall in Schaumburg, Illinois, an estimated crowd of 30,000 mobbed him. But there was worse to come.

KORVETTES RECORD STORE, HICKSVILLE, LONG ISLAND, MAY 1976, 10 AM

The main floor of the store in the town's Mid-Island Shopping Plaza was packed with thousands of girls waiting for their hero to appear. Suddenly word got out that he had been whisked by freight elevator to the roof because of the overflow crowd that had started gathering outside at 6.30 am that morning.

'There he is,' screamed one of the 10,000 desperate females.

'It's him.'

John looked down at the crowd from the roof and waved.

'John! John!' they gasped.

John was overwhelmed and just a little scared by what he saw. But all this extraordinary adoration also gave him a surge of adrenaline. On a sudden impulse, he swivelled his hips and the crowd sighed.

John turned to two burly security men who were on the roof with him. 'Hold me, guys.'

They then held him by his belt buckle as he began his Vinnie Barbarino dance routine on the edge of that roof. Below, his fans were cheering ecstatically. For three or four minutes he twisted and gyrated like Tom Jones. They adored every second of it.

A few minutes later, John – disguised in a local policeman's uniform – was taken in a squad car to the local precinct 'for his own safety and that of the crowd', a breathless officer told local newsmen afterwards.

During the near riot that followed, three teenagers suffered from what police termed 'heat prostration'. When a police helicopter carrying a medical technician hovered overhead, the crowd, thinking that it was coming to take Travolta away, refused to make way for it to land. The three teens were later treated at a nearby hospital in Syosset.

The mob scene at the Hicksville shopping mall was witnessed by town resident Cathy Jameson. She recalled, 'It was exciting but kinda scary, too.'

But that wasn't the end of it by any means. The younger fans – predominantly female – got so angry when store security announced that John had gone and wouldn't be signing autographs that they broke the windows and wrecked the record store in what can only be described as a scene of Beatlemania-type hysteria.

The crowd went literally wild with anger. 'We bought three of his albums with our hard-earned money. They should have let him do autographs,' screamed fourteen-year-old John R. Gruendl, who had visited the store with his mother and two sisters to see Travolta in the flesh.

Another angry shopper, Barbara Cook, of nearby Tallow Lane, Levittown, said, 'I'm burning my Korvettes charge card and I plan to tell my friends to do the same. It was a mob scene. My two youngsters, who love Barbarino, were up at seven and getting ready. But they got nothing. Now I have two crying little girls on my hands.'

John himself was terrified by what he witnessed at Hicksville and suffered from nerves for days afterwards. He wondered if there was a safer, easier ways to sell records. He also feared that his acting would suffer as a result of all these rather unpleasant diversions.

Not long afterwards, John was sorely tempted by an offer from a rock promoter to form a live singing act and take it on tour. There seemed to be the potential to make an exorbitant amount of money. As John explained at the time, it would have been enough 'just to go on and sign autographs … they didn't want my abilities, they wanted my presence'.

And there lay his biggest dilemma. John saw himself as an

artist, not a personality. He also feared that if he went on live concert tours he would risk losing his reputation as a singer. (No one at the time had the courage to say that he didn't exactly have a very serious reputation to lose.)

His heart was primarily in acting. As he told a friend at the time, 'It's more long-lasting. I don't want my career to be over tomorrow.'

With mounting pressure being exerted on him from every direction, John surprised many Hollywood observers by turning his back on a highly lucrative third record album deal as well as countless TV acting offers. Instead, he did a summer touring production of the play *Bus Stop*. It was his way of telling the world that he believed he still had to learn a lot more about his chosen craft. He earned less than $1,000 a week on the tour, but for the first time in years he actually felt fulfilled by what he was doing.

John was effectively risking his career and his fame. But he wasn't worried. He had made his decision and he would stand by it, no matter what. The *Bus Stop* tour was a completely different proposition from his earlier experiences on the road. To start with, he was constantly being chased to commit to other projects even though he was still contracted to appear on *Welcome Back Kotter*.

At one stage, ABC-TV called John to say they would not release him from his long-term contract to pursue a movie career. Then, after much haggling, they agreed to only if the movie company chasing John to appear in a film called *Days of Heaven* would buy out his contract at enormous expense (approximately $500,000). But the movie company wouldn't pay out that kind of money and John eventually lost the part to a young actor called Richard Gere. There were to be many future battles between the two young stars for major movie roles.

The *Bus Stop* tour itself was constantly marred by the enormous number of teenage girls in the audiences. John lived like a recluse in his dressing room, only talking to his two older sisters who had small roles in the play, and co-star Anita Gillette.

Gillette recalls, 'Johnny never dated while we were on the

road. He just had his family. He never made any overtures to me, either.'

John's interest in older women – Gillette was in her mid-thirties – came later, even though he had to kiss her full on the lips every night and she spent much of her time on stage dressed in high heels and fishnet stockings. Meanwhile, the audience continued to get completely steamed up during the *Bus Stop* tour. At one performance in New York's Westchester County, state troopers had to be called in to hold the girls back. Gillette explains, 'These screaming teenagers started leaving in the middle of the third act so they could be the first in line at the stage door. They didn't care about the play. They only cared about getting a picture or an autograph from Johnny.

'So one night when I came off stage, I screamed at the management, "You tell those kids that they'd better sit in their seats for the entire third act or I won't let John appear." Finally, the management was forced to make several announcements before every performance, one of which I've never heard in a theatre before or since: "Do not pop your gum during the show." I swear that's what it said.'

Beneath the surface Anita Gillette and many of her fellow professional actors were getting increasingly annoyed by the chaos that ensued at virtually every performance. 'It was a very frustrating experience because we couldn't go to work, we couldn't do the play.'

It certainly didn't help matters that John's single, 'Let Her In', was a Top Ten hit throughout the play's run that summer. Most nights John had to leave the theatres by specially devised secret methods.

The scenes during the *Bus Stop* tour took John full circle. He had decided to do the play to escape the drudgery and fame of TV, but the crowds at the theatres had proved to be just as bad as those in the record stores. There were a lot more people who were interested in his presence rather than his talents. The shadow of Vinnie Barbarino loomed over him.

At this point, John was living a relatively quiet personal life because he genuinely believed he needed to conserve his energy for his work. He was also remarkably careful with money. He made a point of begging his parents not to sell their house in Englewood because he still got a tremendous kick from arriving home unexpectedly, flopping down in his favourite rocking chair and allowing Helen Travolta to pamper him.

He had splashed out on a classic 1955 Thunderbird and a small Aircoupe two-seater plane so he could indulge his favourite hobby of flying, but that was it. He'd also moved to a modestly priced $500-a-month apartment in a high-rise block on South Doheny Drive on the borders of West Hollywood and Beverly Hills.

John was deliberately saving money so that he would never again have to take roles purely for financial reasons. He wanted to be the kind of actor who ended up with parts he adored, rather than taking jobs just to pay the rent. As he told a friend at the time, 'I don't want to have to take anything that comes along, just because I need the money.'

John was fully aware that, as a TV star, he could not simply rest on his laurels. His next ambition was to be a movie star.

CHAPTER NINE

THE BOY IN THE PLASTIC BUBBLE

HOLLYWOOD, AUGUST 1976

One of the roles John believed would help move his career forward was the lead in a TV movie called *The Boy in the Plastic Bubble*. John was to play a teenager forced to live shielded from the world by plastic because of his congenital lack of immunity from disease.

TV director Randal Kleiser and producer Joel Thurm never had any doubts about casting John. The difficult part was to find the right supporting actors to help him carry off this sensitive role.

Selecting the actress to play John's mother was a virtual elimination contest. A number of women were initially considered for the part. One name on the list was Diana Hyland, who was a member of that know-the face-but-can't-quite-place-it school. The blonde, blue-eyed one-time high-school cheerleader was what is known in Hollywood as a good pro. After auditioning her, Thurm and Kleiner decided to pick Diana for the role because of her experience and the depth they hoped she could bring to the part.

Meanwhile, all Hollywood eyes were on how John had managed to secure one of the largest ever fees for a TV movie.

Daily Variety reported, 'John Travolta negotiates a smashing breakthrough as a serious actor.' John was actually paid $700,000, the third-highest salary ever for a TV movie.

But what also put *The Boy in the Plastic Bubble* on the map was that, during the making of the film, John fell in love with his co-star Diana Hyland.

Diana – a Grace Kelly type – who had earlier been cast with Paul Newman in Broadway's *Sweet Bird of Youth* and even played the minister's alcoholic wife on TV's *Peyton Place* was the last person one would expect to fall for a teen idol like John Travolta. There was a nineteen-year age gap between them. She was almost forty-one years old and he had just turned twenty-two.

Even though she played his mother in the TV movie, there was an immediate spark between them, and John would eventually find himself embroiled in a relationship that would be more emotionally wrenching than anything he had ever experienced before.

For her part, Diana was totally charmed by her co-star's boyishness and impressed with his thoughtfulness and with the gentle rapport that sprang up between him and her four-year-old son Zachary Goodson. The presence of Zachary actually helped cement the relationship because John seemed so at ease with the little boy.

John even made a remarkable pledge about Diana to sister Ellen: 'If I go into this relationship, I'm going in all the way. I'm just so scared. I don't want to be hurt again.' He was clearly referring to what had happened with Denise Wurms.

Sam and Helen were understandably apprehensive when they first heard about their son's affair with a woman old enough to be his mother.

But then Ellen explained to them how wonderful Diana was. 'And don't forget,' she told her parents, 'Johnny's been a very lonesome boy. This woman is making him happy.'

Ellen recalls, 'That was very true. Diana was so classy, so dynamic, so good! She was everything Johnny ever dreamed a lady could be. No one ever loved him the way she did.'

The problem was that their love for one another was doomed from the start.

To understand and appreciate why John Travolta fell passionately in love with a woman almost twenty years his senior, one has to recognise the major influences in his life. His mother Helen and his three older, strong-willed sisters convinced him that a man without a wise female stood little chance of real happiness in life. At least, that's what he believed when stardom first struck in his early twenties.

John insisted to friends at the time that age was irrelevant and he was attracted to all types of girls. But the bitterness and disappointment he suffered when his first love Denise Wurms ditched him for another man definitely soured his attitude towards younger women.

He even had a handful of highly erotic, but rather impersonal, one-night stands which he later proclaimed to have been 'most unsatisfactory'. He kept these brief, cold encounters secret from everyone at the time, and they had the effect of making him even more careful about whom he dated.

Here he was, single, handsome, rich and famous yet very unsure about whom to trust. He should have been enjoying himself playing the field, giving any girl a whirl on the basis that he was young and unattached and it didn't really matter. Yet what John really craved was a combination of the real love he felt for his first ever sweetheart Denise and the close friendship he had with his mother and sisters. In Hollywood, such a relationship is very hard to come by.

As his role in *Welcome Back Kotter* brought him increasing amounts of media attention, he began to find himself less and less attracted to the type of girls his fans expected him to date. Certainly, he was seen with quite a number of young actresses, and the Hollywood paparazzi regularly photographed him with various attractive budding stars on his arm. But John was actually more interested in older women. He found them more humorous, less inclined to be obsessed by the material things in life and far more knowledgeable. They were also much better at communicating.

As John conceded at the time, 'I don't go for looks. Sure, it's nice to have, but I don't put total weight on it.'

He went on, 'A good personality is far more important than a pretty face. Sometimes even girls who are at first unattractive become very pretty when I get to know them. I don't want to miss out on someone special just because she might not have all the physical attributes we're taught to look for. If you have an affinity for a person, you can overlook physical imperfection.'

John found himself swept up by Diana Hyland, his co-star in *The Boy in the Plastic Bubble*. She was certainly attractive in a very serene way, but she came with more baggage than most twenty-something actors could handle.

John was intrigued by Diana because she was strong-willed and completely unimpressed by his new-found fame. She also wasn't afraid to tell him within hours of their first meeting that she found him attractive. John was certainly not the old-fashioned type of male who gets put off if a woman makes the first move.

Writer Suzanne Munshower encountered the star during his *Kotter* days and shortly after his romance with Diana Hyland began. She explains, 'He's happiest if a woman tells him what she feels, rather than waiting for him to ask her first. John's certainly no male chauvinist! He firmly believes that all is equal in love.'

She continues, 'But, by the same token, John is not passive either. He'll gladly seize the initiative and go after someone who appeals to him.'

Diana Hyland was convinced that they were two people with a real passion for each other. The most unusual aspect was of course the age difference, which was unfortunately a serious concern for John's closest advisers. They feared that if news of his romance leaked out it could seriously damage his appeal to the millions of young girls who watched him on *Kotter* and then went out and bought every souvenir, record and poster of him that they could lay their hands on.

Here was John Travolta, the ultimate teenagers' sex symbol, going out with a woman who was old enough to be a grandmother. His attitude to Diana also highlighted the fact that John simply did not appreciate just how big a star he had become. He still didn't consider himself as a sex symbol and was genuinely puzzled by what was happening around him.

When girls aged eighteen and under were banned from the ABC studios where *Kotter* was taped, because their screaming interfered with the programme quality, John was more surprised than most.

Meanwhile, Diana Hyland took it all in her stride. She had been an actress for almost as long as John had been alive and she had the ultimate satisfaction of knowing that the man adored by millions of women only had eyes for her.

Ironically, when they met she had just played the part of The Fonz's girlfriend in *Happy Days*, the show (and character) that John was supposed to be such a rival to. Other cast members on *The Boy in the Plastic Bubble* immediately noticed how John and Diana would go off between takes and talk quietly together.

Few knew it at the time, but Diana was fighting a battle against cancer. She had already been forced to have one breast removed to stop the disease spreading, and she believed she had beaten the illness. Thanks to careful breast reconstruction, no one on the set of the TV movie was aware of her brush with death, even though she had a number of scenes in which she only wore a negligée.

Diana Hyland hid none of this from John. In any case, he would have found out all about it from his sister Ellen, who had been a good friend of Diana's for some time.

But the relationship between John and Diana did not turn into passion overnight. During those first few weeks on the set of *The Boy in the Plastic Bubble* they became close friends and confidants but little more in physical terms, even though they had definitely started to fall in love.

What really brought them together were some of the

remarkable parallels between their lives. They had both grown up determined to be actors and they shared an intense desire to work.

Diana was born in Cleveland Heights, Ohio, on 26 January 1936. Just like John, she wouldn't settle down to a comfortable life in her home town and eagerly moved on to New York City. After six months of trying, she landed her first professional acting job as the lead in *Robert Montgomery Presents*, a popular TV anthology show of the time. The year was 1956, just two years after John's birth.

Various theatrical assignments were then followed by a starring role in a New York-based TV soap opera. Then the call came from Hollywood and Diana starred in a number of movies including *One Man's Way* (1964), followed by *The Chase* (1965) with Marlon Brando, Jane Fonda and Robert Redford and *Smoky* (1966). But she was best known as Susan Winter in TV's *Peyton Place*.

Not only did Diana share John's compulsion to act; by a remarkable coincidence, her favourite hobby was also flying.

At the wrap party to celebrate the end of the shooting of *The Boy in the Plastic Bubble*, they 'admitted not only a friendly attraction, but a sexual one', explained John. 'The intensity of it was new to both of us.'

And director Kleiser noticed, 'They did stay longer at the party than most. There must have been a full moon that night.'

They kissed passionately at the party and then went their separate ways – John to a much-needed break with his family while Diana went off to prepare for her role in a popular TV sitcom called *Eight Is Enough*.

John was in a state of emotional turmoil because he knew the press would give him a hard time for having a relationship with a woman who was so much older. He decided that didn't matter. But there was also the matter of her illness, although that made him feel an even stronger loyalty to her.

John turned increasingly to Scientology because he genuinely believed it would enable him to come to grips with the 'what' and 'why' of his feelings for Diana. He recalls, 'There was something about her, a quality I can't define even now, that I found so appealing. It exceeded anything physical. She had every colour I ever imagined in a person.'

A few weeks later, John returned to Hollywood from his vacation and they started getting heavily involved. The press interest was intense, but John seemed able to brush off all the nasty innuendoes attracted by such an age gap. In fact, John's relationship with Diana paved the way for a gradual change in the attitudes of the general public towards the 'older woman younger man' syndrome. Nowadays such a liaison would not provoke any comment at all. But that wasn't the case twenty years ago.

One time, a reporter asked him outright what he thought of the fact that Diana was old enough to be his mother.

'I don't know about that,' answered John in his most matter-of-fact voice. 'My mother is sixty-five.'

Unfortunately, Diana found it harder to cope with the non-stop media intrusion into their relationship. Her mother, Mary Gentner, explains, 'Diana thought too many people put too much emphasis on their ages. As for John, Diana told me, "Mother, he's ageless."'

Once John and Diana's families knew how serious the couple were becoming, they gave the relationship their full blessing. However, John wanted to avoid further public revelations about them so they tended to stay at home on the west side of LA. Most nights she would curl up on the couch beside him, feet tucked under her legs, an elbow resting on the arm, palm turned up to support the side of her face. John would pour his heart out to her about his life, his career, his future, and she would listen avidly.

When it came to criticism, Diana did it in a way that was meant to help, not tear anything down. She was never cruel in pointing out flaws. If it was called for, she sometimes relied on gentle needling to get her point across. She didn't think it was fair to toss a negative out without making a constructive suggestion at the same time.

Diana was especially concerned about John's tender emotions. Her mother Mary Gentner recalled, 'She was always telling Johnny he was too sensitive. He sometimes let things upset him that she thought shouldn't. She told him he had to learn how to take some of the unpleasantness of life better. He had to learn to get his back up, get a shield up around him so he wouldn't be hurt so often. That's what Diana had learned to do in Hollywood.'

Eventually, John became psychologically stronger thanks to Diana. He learned from her to show stamina and strength of character, to fight back in a subtle, effective way.

Diana also encouraged John to shed some weight. All those years of candy and chocolate bars had taken their toll. He had become flabby and they both knew that, in order to be a successful young male lead actor in Hollywood, he needed to be super-fit and slender.

But there was another problem which few people were ever aware of: John had a very low energy level. He tired easily and there had frequently been times when he had fallen asleep right in front of people at a dinner party or at home in front of the television.

At that time, John actually feared that he might not be able to handle any major roles because of this problem. But Diana convinced him that, with the right kind of exercises, he could cure himself and he did.

Diana herself was a great dancer and she would frequently turn on the radio in the bedroom of her home and dance away for as long as an hour. Usually they'd end up in hysterical laughter before collapsing on the bed.

Diana became enthralled by her power to mould John into a big star. She watched him push himself further and further and was delighted by the effect she was having on him. His efforts were a tribute to their love for one another.

By the fall of 1976, John began to believe that his love affair with Diana might be the real thing. He even told reporters at an

LA movie première, 'This is very serious.' John's relationships with Denise Wurms and later Joan Prather and Marilu Henner seemed unimportant compared with the level of passion he felt for Diana.

Diana's parents learned to appreciate what their daughter saw in such a young lover. Her mother Mary Gentner said, 'After I got to know Johnny I understood why Diana and he didn't have a problem dealing with each other on this. Johnny often seemed more like a man of fifty than a boy in his twenties. He was so mature about some things.'

At one stage, Diana and her son Zachary virtually lived at John's rented high-rise apartment in West Hollywood, which was described as a 'cell' by one visitor and 'drab' by another. The sparse furnishing was a definite throwback to John's less affluent days. In his bedroom was just a plain divan covered by a tatty cotton spread and a portable television sitting on top of an overturned trunk. In his closet, were dozens of unopened and half-completed model aeroplane kits. John admitted being a slob and that he tended to leave things lying where he had dropped them. But Diana didn't seem to mind one bit.

The couple talked about marriage, children and buying a home together. But, more significantly, they 'came out' as a couple and started attending parties and premières and dining at well-known restaurants. The 12 November airing of *The Boy in the Plastic Bubble* further fuelled the rumours. Five days later, at the première of *Carrie*, more public attention was heaped on them and by the end of that month they had attended their first black-tie Hollywood event as a couple. They also agreed to do a *People* magazine cover story about their romance.

Meanwhile, John's performance in *Bubble* brought him critical praise. Pauline Kael commented in the *New Yorker* that he 'gave the character an abject, humiliated sensitivity that made the boy seem emotionally naked'.

November 1976 was a good month for John. He had been acclaimed for his acting abilities and he was in a happy, solid relationship. What more could he ask for?

CHAPTER TEN

COWGIRL IN THE SAND

PALM SPRINGS, CALIFORNIA, WINTER 1976

During the early days of their romance, John and Diana would regularly head for Palm Springs, a two-and-a-half-hour drive from Los Angeles. In the summer, temperatures often soared to 120 degrees and Palm Springs took on the appearance of a ghost-town. Restaurants and shops closed down, as the intense heat drove most people away. The town's survival was (and still is) dependent on the winter migration of vacationers and tourists from colder parts of the state. They swell the population from 32,000 to 64,000, filling everything from dingy, nondescript motel rooms to sprawling California ranch houses adjoining any one of twenty-nine golf courses.

Palm Springs had once been a virtually private community reserved as a playground for the very rich and the most successful members of the movie industry. Clark Gable and Carole Lombard travelled there for weekends. Studio chiefs and agents conducted business at the poolside. The young Howard Hughes liked to plot industrial takeovers there.

In the 1970s Palm Springs still attracted the very wealthy but it was also visited by many ordinary citizens hoping to get a look at the likes of Bob Hope and Frank Sinatra who had houses in the area.

John Travolta's original reason for visiting Palm Springs was that his sister Ellen had moved to the eighty-acre ranch owned by her husband's family on the outskirts of the city. The young star would frequently drop in on his sister and her family. He found life on the ranch far more relaxing than the Hollywood bustle that surrounded him at that time.

John liked to just talk and read whenever he visited the ranch. He wasn't particularly athletic so he never once went out and saddled up any of the horses. But he sometimes liked to walk around the ranch at sunset, alone with his thoughts.

John's love of cowboy boots started when he first visited the ranch shortly after arriving in Hollywood as a penniless and friendless teenager determined to make it to the top. His sister Ellen's father-in-law Harry Fridley took him into Palm Springs to buy his first ever pair of cowboy boots after he almost got bitten by a snake while walking round the ranch one evening.

'He turned to us for a lot then. He didn't have much money, so we even trucked some things to LA to help him furnish his little apartment. He appreciated every little thing that was done for him,' recalls Harry.

Soon after making it on *Welcome Back Kotter*, John began flying his tiny Aircoupe plane to the desert to see his family. Often unannounced, he would fly into the small private-planes-only airports of either Bermuda Dunes or Banning. One time he rode his motorcycle all the way to Palm Springs from LA, but the family begged him not to try the trip ever again as they worried about his safety on the freeway. Flying seemed a better option.

When Diana Hyland came into his life, Palm Springs was still top of John's list of perfect weekend retreats but, because he did not want to impose on his sister's family, he took Diana to hotels like the Hot Springs Spa in nearby Palm Desert and the respected Ingleside Inn in Downtown Palm Springs.

The Ingleside Inn hosted dozens of celebrities, like Cher, Marlon Brando, Sylvester Stallone, Tom Selleck, Robert Wagner and Goldie Hawn, to name but a few. Owner Mel Haber was immensely proud of his twenty-eight individually designed suites, offering everything from a steam bath to fresh flowers and even matches imprinted with the guest's name. No paparazzi were permitted anywhere near the hotel and if a guest wanted to check in under an assumed name none of the hotel staff would raise an eyebrow. It was the perfect retreat for John and Diana.

On 19 December John was nominated for the coveted, but little-known, Golden Apple award as 'Best New Star of the Year' given out by the Hollywood Women's Press Club. He and Diana decided to attend the awards luncheon together.

John looked smart in an open-necked shirt and dark velvet blazer and kept close to Diana, with her long blonde curls gently falling to her shoulders and her antique blue shawl perfectly complementing the deep blue of her eyes.

John eventually lost out in the voting for 'Best New Star' to Nick Nolte, who'd just hit the big time with the ABC mini-series *Rich Man, Poor Man*. But none of that mattered to John and Diana. They smiled broadly for the cameras and left arm in arm, as the motordrives buzzed and the flashlights popped.

Later that week, the couple even looked at a huge mansion in Bel Air which they wanted to purchase. John had no doubt that he was involved in the most serious relationship of his life.

LOG CABIN, BIG BEAR SNOW RESORT, CALIFORNIA, LATE DECEMBER 1976

Just east of Palm Springs, this popular mountain resort has become a regular destination for many members of Los Angeles' upwardly mobile middle class. In December 1976 it also offered John and Diana the chance to host a real family Christmas.

John was not earning huge amounts by any means. Most of

the $1,500 he was paid each week on *Kotter* went towards paying his lawyer, press agent, business manager and manager. He was lucky to clear $300.

So, with a restricted budget, John got his sister Ellen to find them all a large cabin to rent in Big Bear for the Christmas week. The one she found was perfect; it had a fireplace in the living room, ample space for piles of Christmas gifts, peaceful views of the surrounding snowcaps, plus a nearby toboggan course, ski trails and a frozen lake for ice skating and ice sailing.

Diana was particularly excited about the vacation because it would provide John with a proper opportunity to cement his relationship with her young son Zachary. She was keen for John to become a big brother/father figure to the child.

Within hours of their arrival from Los Angeles in John's classic T Bird, the rest of the Travolta gang turned up: Sam and Helen flew in from New Jersey along with John's Aunt Mildred. Ellen travelled over for the day from her ranch near Palm Springs, bringing John's nephew and niece, Tommy and Molly.

Diana told all John's relatives how she and John planned to take a romantic trip by Concorde from New York to London and then to Rio in the spring. She even persuaded him to go and buy himself a brand new white suit for the trip.

However, during that Christmas break, Diana became seriously ill with continual nausea. At first she thought it was just a nasty dose of flu. But there was also a nagging backache. On her return from Big Bear she went to see her doctor.

Two diagnoses were forthcoming. Diana was suffering from a mild form of pneumonia, but, worse, her cancer had moved into her spine. She was immediately sent back to the radiation-therapy and nuclear medicine department at Los Angeles' Cedars-Sinai Hospital. Specialists quickly pronounced that the cancer was inoperable, but there was a faint hope that radiation therapy might result in a regression of the spreading tumours.

Over the next month, Diana faced an endless round of hospital visits, as her health seriously deteriorated.

John – away filming in New York – was almost as exhausted as Diana because he started making regular trips back to visit her in California. He was in a state of almost continual jet lag. The couple both tried to make these brief reunions as relaxed as possible, but there was an underlying knowledge that she was in extreme pain and inching closer to death.

John never forgot one plane trip when he broke down because he couldn't get any aspect of the past seven months with Diana out of his mind. He rejected the stewardess's offer of a meal. He tried to read a newspaper. That was no good so he tried a book. That proved even more fruitless.

He looked out of the port-hole at the sky and clouds all around him. He looked up towards heaven and thought of their fun trips to Palm Springs, their candlelit dinners together, playing games with little Zachary. His face was pressed up against the window of the airliner so that none of the other passengers would notice the tears streaming down his face. He wanted to appear strong, but it was no good; he felt like a broken man.

Another time, John was so stressed about seeing Diana that he felt a lump on his scalp and said to her, 'What if this is a tumour? What if I have cancer, too?'

Diana looked up at her young lover and smiled sweetly. 'Well honey, if you do, you're going to have to deal with it.'

John looked at Diana with tears in his eyes. He realised then just how much she was dealing with, every single minute of every single day. Death was in her face, yet she dealt with it. From that moment onwards John dealt with every problem as it came along because nothing mattered that much.

Diana found it agonising even to walk and was literally bent over in pain much of the time. Her forehead was full of lumps and she was taking vast quantities of painkillers just to keep going. She held on for a few more days, but then agreed to be admitted to hospital. She had lost all her hair and ordered a wig, but she preferred to simply wrap a scarf over her head. She wasn't eating. Her life was ebbing away.

By the time she went into hospital in the last week of February 1977 the tumours were all the way down her spine, with the biggest one at the base. People who visited her found it difficult to hide their shock at the change in her physical appearance.

Throughout all this, Diana had kept her condition a secret from the cast and crew of *Eight is Enough*, the TV sitcom she was starring in. But when her friends from the show turned up at the hospital one morning she finally decided to come clean. It was a heartbreaking moment.

Her mother Mary Gentner recalls, 'They were all gathered around her bed. The doctor came in and stood next to Diana. She looked up at him and said, "Doctor, tell them how long I have." He said she had three to six months. As he said that, tears the size of quarters fell from Diana's eyes. Then she put one hand to each eye and brushed them away. Diana regained her composure quicker than anyone else in the room.'

Diana actually went through a period of wildly mixed emotions about her young lover John at this time. She loved him. She wanted to see him again, to hold him, to be held. But she also couldn't stand the thought of him suffering because of her pain.

Diana's conflicting feelings sometimes created turmoil when they talked. At one stage, she told John not to return to her. He was devastated at first, then he realised why she was saying these things and took no notice.

When she was slipping away from life, John made sure he was at her side. Diana knew she was going. She'd hold on for him. But she wanted to get out of that hospital. Her mother Mary recalls, 'Diana wanted to die at home.'

On the morning of 26 March, Diana – weakened by the trauma of blood transfusions – was transported by ambulance back to her beloved home at Midvale Avenue, in the West LA district of Westwood. Inside, she was made as comfortable as possible in her bedroom. A nurse was in constant attendance and oxygen tanks were placed strategically by her side.

When John walked into the house, his eyes were glistening, but he covered that up with a wonderful crooked smile. The moment he saw her he said, 'My angel, you are just as beautiful as ever.'

They talked quietly and ventured outside for a short walk in Diana's beloved garden. They meandered through the flowers and bushes. She pointed out the half-completed playhouse that was being constructed for Zachary.

They stopped and he held her close, cradling her with a tenderness usually reserved for the handling of newborns. They had only a short time left. She looked up at him and smiled gently, the lines creasing her haggard face. She was unrecognisable as the beautiful woman he had met and fallen in love with such a short time before. But he still loved her. 'I'm going now,' Diana whispered. 'But you are going to have this work.'

The tragedy lay in the timing. Just a few weeks earlier they had been standing on the brink of incredible personal and professional success. Together for only seven months, their dreams were just beginning to be fulfilled. Then all this happened.

Back in the bedroom a few minutes later, Diana began fading in and out of consciousness. John was young and had a fantastic future ahead of him. She made him promise not to stop. He mumbled his agreement and tried to stop himself crying.

Then Diana made a will for the first time. It was a struggle but they managed it. However, there was a problem.

'The most important thing in the will,' recalls Diana's father Ted, 'was that Diana wanted Zachary to be with Johnny. There was no legal way that could be done if Zachary's father wanted him, but Johnny and Zachary adored each other. Johnny would have loved to take him. Unfortunately, I guess neither of them was thinking too clearly at the time. Johnny signed the will as a witness and, since he was also named as a beneficiary, that made the will invalid in California.'

Out of consideration for Zachary, John decided not to pursue the will after Diana's death. But he has made strenuous efforts ever since to maintain the relationship with her son.

Not long afterwards, Diana received the last rites from local priest, Father Robert Curtis. There were a number of prayers spoken out loud, followed by the anointing of the body with blessed oils. Diana was not well enough to participate in the ritual. The only other person in the room was a nurse.

Father Curtis recalls, 'John held her in his arms while I anointed her. I'm sure Diana knew what was happening to her. She had reached a point of acceptance and was being held by someone who meant a great deal to her.

'When I left the room, it was just John holding her. It was a very private thing between them, so I left them alone. Being able to die in someone's arms is a very lovely thing. It is not an experience many people are fortunate enough to have.'

John still recalls the precise moment that his lover died, as he sat on the edge of the bed cradling her in his arms. He held on to her tightly as she gently passed away.

Diana's breathing slowed, then her feet went very cold and John felt the heat just fading away up her legs. It happened very quickly. Moments later she died in his arms. He didn't panic but quietly sobbed on her shoulders.

John stayed straight and strong, trying to retain control of his emotions despite his inner turmoil. Not long afterwards, the other family members assembled by Diana's bedside. Only the rumpled clothes and tousled hair gave away the full extent of what her long-impending death had done to him. John tried to speak to them but not a sound would come out at first. Then he told them, 'I felt the breath go out of her.' That was it. There was no more to say. She had died at 7 pm that evening.

Outside the ebbing moon of 27 March 1977 marked the passing of another day. It also marked the end of a romance that had taken John Travolta to hell and back.

John immediately and maturely assumed responsibility for making the call to the funeral home. The most basic of services was ordered: cremation and a simple container for the ashes. John also planned a memorial service for Diana.

Her ashes were scattered at sea just off her favourite stretch of beach at Santa Monica. But that wasn't the end of John and Diana's relationship. 'I will always feel she is with me – I mean, her intentions are. Diana always wanted the world for me in every way,' he said. Those feelings were to return to him frequently, even after finding emotional stability and happiness.

After Diana's death, John felt like Kris Kristofferson did when a reporter asked him about Janis Joplin. Kristofferson murmured, 'I don't like talkin' 'bout Janis now, it's like grave robbin'.'

John did not publicly comment on the tragedy until an interview with David Frost a year after Diana's death. 'It was a relationship which filled so many of my needs. I hope again I may find a relationship to fill these needs. It doesn't happen that often in anyone's life, so the idea that it has happened once already to me is pretty good. If it happens again, that would be really special.'

At Diana's memorial service, John wore the white suit he had bought for the trip they had planned to Rio.

The service itself was due to be held on a stretch of beach at Santa Monica which was the site where William Randolph Hearst's mistress Marion Davies had lived in a mansion called Beach House. The house had long since pulled down to make way for a public beach, which had become a favourite spot for Diana to take Zachary for afternoon strolls.

Unfortunately, word of the service leaked out and before dawn that day a crowd began assembling. Reporters and photographers took their positions and waited for the circus. When John was informed, he immediately rescheduled the service and notified every guest to come to Diana's house instead.

Throughout, John remained calm and clearly in control of the proceedings. But that all-white suit certainly caused a few raised eyebrows until John explained to the mourners why he was wearing it. He told the story of how he and Diana had planned their trip to Rio and how Diana had persuaded him to get a white suit. 'She said it was what they wore down there,' he said in an almost childlike way. It was as if he was talking about his mother. John had purchased the suit on his way to the service, after remembering that conversation with Diana.

Those at the service later said that John wore the suit like a suit of armour in defiance of her death. Instead of seeking the comfort and sympathy of the guests, he moved amongst them offering his sorrow.

'He handled himself far better than I think I could have at his age,' recalled family friend Bill Blinn. 'Nobody wanted a circus funeral for Diana, least of all John. He did it with class. He was much more of an adult than I thought he would be.'

The only release from John's anguish was his work and he threw himself into it with a vengeance. Yet, beneath the surface, John felt emotionally torn to shreds. 'I have never been more in love with anyone in my life,' he insisted to one friend just days after Diana's death. 'I thought I had been in love before, but I wasn't …'

John insisted that he would have married Diana had she lived. He appreciated that he had to get on with his life because that was what she wanted. He even acknowledged to close friends that he could see himself marrying and having his own family in the future. But he also told people that the woman he married would have to be very special and he wasn't entirely certain if such a person existed.

John's mother Helen was extremely worried about her son's state of mind during that difficult period after Diana's death. She explained, 'Diana was so generous. She told John before she died, "I want you to pursue your career, and don't mourn over me."'

But John couldn't help feeling the pain of loss. For more than a year following Diana's death, he found himself at the centre of constant press attention over what many gossip columnists considered the most heartbreaking story to come out of Hollywood since Clark Gable lost his beloved Carole Lombard in a plane crash during the Second World War. One newspaper even went so far as to offer huge sums of money to several members of the *Welcome Back Kotter* cast for their inside stories. The payments were refused, in some cases, in rather indelicate language. Even a book entitled *John and Diana* was published. Written by Mary Ann Norbum, it sold hundreds of thousands of copies.

In California, John continued to encounter increasingly pushy fans at virtually every street corner and had to hire two bodyguards. Each time he left the *Kotter* studio it was akin to a presidential visit.

John explained at the time, 'It takes five men around me to walk me to my car. I still love my fans but I resent having to live like a prisoner now. I've become a fugitive. It's reached the point where I don't like people to know where I am.'

In Englewood, things were going from bad to worse. During a public appearance near his home town, John was followed back to his family's house by hundreds of fans. When police finally cleared them away from the Travolta doorstep there was a knock on the door. It turned out to be the police wanting John to autograph twenty-five photographs for their children.

John just wanted to be left alone to grieve in private. But his advisers knew that, despite the tragedy of Diana Hyland's death, he was on the verge of superstardom.

CHAPTER ELEVEN
THE BALLPARK

HOLLYWOOD, WINTER 1976 – 77

John suddenly found himself at the centre of a remarkable tug-of-war over his services as a movie actor. The buzz around Hollywood was that he had definite box-office appeal and the right kind of vehicle could turn him into a superstar. The man who finally won him over was Australian entrepreneur Robert Stigwood who, mainly on the strength of his own extraordinary charm, persuaded John to sign a three-picture deal.

Stigwood was a Bermuda-based multimedia entertainment magnate whose interests included Eric Clapton, the Bee Gees, the stage version of *Jesus Christ Superstar*, the movie version of *Tommy*, two hit television series licensed to TV producer Norman Lear and several long-running theatrical productions in London.

By 1976, 44-year-old Stigwood also had his own record label (RSO) and two potential smash-hit movies in development – *Grease* and *Sergeant Pepper's Lonely Hearts Club Band*.

John's association with Stigwood was sparked by his role as Vinnie Barbarino in *Kotter*. He'd been spotted by Allan Carr, personal manager of such stars as Ann-Margret, Peter Sellers,

Marisa Berenson and composer Marvin Hamlisch. Carr was interested in producing movies with his friend Robert Stigwood so they bought an option on the long-running Broadway musical *Grease*. Carr called Stigwood and told him to watch *Kotter* and see what he thought, although at that stage they intended to approach John's arch professional rival, Henry 'The Fonz' Winkler, for the Danny Zuko lead.

But when Stigwood watched John on *Kotter* he immediately decided that he would be a better bet for *Grease*, even though he had no idea of John's previous connections with the stage show. A meeting was arranged and, within a few weeks, John had committed to a three-picture deal, the first of which was to be *Grease*.

However, the option on *Grease* had a clause which stipulated that the movie version could not be released before the Easter of 1978 because the producers of the Broadway show did not want any competition. Stigwood didn't want to wait that long to launch John. He needed to find another project for his new protégé as quickly as possible.

Back in Hollywood, many of John's colleagues were expressing concern that things seemed to be going too quickly for the young actor. James Komack, executive producer on *Kotter*, commented, 'I just worry about his ambition. It's massive. He knows he's good and he knows he's hot. There's the danger, as a result, of his going the way of David Cassidy and the Monkees, of hitting it big and then fading fast.'

John totally disagreed with such opinions. He insisted, 'I feel we're all here to have an effect on life. The reason you want to act is that you need attention. In this industry many people belittle the artist.' From the way he talked in such intense terms about his career, it was clear that he was taking it incredibly seriously.

The publicity surrounding the Stigwood deal brought John's potential superstardom to a head, even though he hadn't actually begun to work on a movie for the Australian yet. The deal itself guaranteed him more than a million dollars in fees for three movies plus a share of the profits. These contractual terms had been skilfully hammered out by agent Bob LeMond and his partner Lois Zetter. Instead of opting for a contract that paid everything up front, they gambled on the success of the Stigwood projects and decided to go for a percentage share of all the profits. It was a canny move that would eventually help make John one of the wealthiest stars in Hollywood history.

However, at this early stage, every aspect of the deal was entirely hypothetical. John could be a millionaire within the next two years, but if none of the movies was made he would walk away with nothing.

Stigwood was convinced that John *would* be a huge movie star so he refused to just sit back and wait until *Grease* could be made. Instead, he looked around for another project with a similar music-based theme and came up with *Saturday Night Fever* after reading an article in the 7 June 1976 edition of *New York* magazine. The piece, written by British journalist Nik Cohn, was called 'Tribal Rites of the New Saturday Night'. It told the allegedly partly factual story of a group of young people in working-class Brooklyn who spent their entire week working at dull jobs, until Saturday night when they went dance crazy at the local disco.

'The new generation takes few risks. It goes through high school, obedient; graduates, looks for a job, saves and plans. Endures. And once a week, on Saturday night, its one great moment of release, it explodes,' wrote Cohn.

Cohn claimed he created the character of Vincent – who became Tony Manero in *Fever* – from a composite of three of the young men he met while researching the story. Vincent was 'the very best dancer in Bay Ridge – the ultimate Face. He owned fourteen floral shirts, five suits, eight pairs of shoes, three overcoats and had appeared on *American Bandstand*. Sometimes music people came out from Manhattan to watch him, and one man who owned a club on the East Side had even offered him a contract. A hundred dollars a week. Just to dance,' wrote Cohn.

A month after reading the magazine article, Stigwood announced he had bought the rights and wanted John to star in it.

But what has never been disclosed before is that Londoner Cohn actually based his disco king Tony Manero on a one-time villain in the Goldhawk Road, Shepherd's Bush, West London, whom he'd known in the sixties, with the name and accent transposed. Cohn was so worried about this fakery he became convinced John would spot it the moment he read his article. Cohn had taken it for granted that John was a Brooklyn native himself and would pull his article to bits when they met.

In fact, the opposite occurred. John told Cohn he was deeply impressed by the story and did not doubt for a minute that the characters were real.

John recalls, 'I thought that, if it could ever be a film, it could be very powerful. It had images and values that were very strong.' But he did have one fear: 'I wondered if I could ever come across as strong.'

At the beginning of October 1976, John began pre-production work on *Fever*. He had until the middle of the following February to prepare himself for the role of nineteen-year-old disco champion Tony Manero. The first thing he did was start getting himself into good physical condition with a vigorous exercise routine. John also took dance lessons for three hours every day.

But there were problems looming; John was worried he might lose the *Fever* role because of the tight *Kotter* schedule. He arranged to spend all day on the *Kotter* set and all evening rehearsing for *Fever*. Most of the actual shooting of the movie was carried out during a hiatus in the *Kotter* schedule. John knew he had to honour both commitments and it was made clear to him by the team at *Kotter* that he could find himself embroiled in some serious legal problems if he tried to walk away from his contract with the show.

Eventually, a number of incidents occurred which led to a breakdown of the previously good relationship John had enjoyed with his TV bosses. Firstly a segment of *Kotter* that featured Barbarino in most of it began rehearsal without its star because John didn't appear. A stand-in replaced him for the day's work. It then emerged that the sitcom's producer James Komack was in negotiations with John's lawyer Fred Games. Soon everyone else in the cast became aware that there was some kind of problem between John and the producers.

Finally, after missing three working days, John showed up just in time to tape the show. The scene he had missed rehearsals for had to be drastically rewritten because he hardly had any time to learn his lines. The message was very clear; John wanted his role as Barbarino to be kept to a minimum. He simply did not have the time to work a forty-hour week on the *Kotter* set.

Each evening after his *Fever*-training dance lessons, John would visit discotheques in the Brooklyn neighbourhood and 'try out my stuff'. He would go in alone and frequently find himself surrounded by young girls who had spotted his resemblance to Vinnie Barbarino.

John actually became completely obsessed with the character of Tony Manero. He wanted to eat, breathe, sleep, talk and walk like him. Whenever he was asked about the character he made it sound as if he were alive and kicking rather than a fictional creation.

'The kid is the best disco dancer in the area,' he breathlessly explained to one showbusiness reporter. 'But he's got family problems, friend problems and future problems. He wants more out of life than his surroundings offer him. He knows he has the potential to go ahead, but he doesn't know how. He has a fear that his life is crumbling.'

John knew there were similarities between Tony Manero and his *Kotter* character Vinnie Barbarino, but he believed he could go beyond his previous limitations as an actor and turn Tony into someone really special.

He recalls, 'I knew I could play it well, give it a depth and dimension that would be interesting to a different public. The character strikes so close to home. Watching Tony, I saw loneliness, frustration; I saw everything people deal with in real life. There's nothing glamorised about his personality. He's neither macho nor withdrawn, heroic nor anti-heroic. He's universally identifiable. It's almost like Vinnie would be if he grew up. It's the next step, definitely an expansion of that character.'

There was also a strong element of John's own character in the role. It was tempting at the time to speculate that he might have turned out like Tony Manero if he had been brought up in a different environment. Naturally, John denied any connection, but the fact remained that he *had* to use some of his own character to make Tony so believable.

Something else that is little known, despite all the legends that have built up around *Fever*, is how Tony's clothes were chosen. John himself was responsible for the sensational look that contributed so much to the movie's eventual success. He insisted to the film's producers that he should wear clothes that were at least three or four years out of date.

The short leather jackets, the tight flared polyester pants and shirts were actually the 'in thing' in 1972 – 73. John and his wardrobe department went all over New York City searching for the right clothes in thrift stores. Finally, he stumbled on a shop in Greenwich Village and another shop out in Brooklyn. Then came the hair; that would be a combination of what John was familiar with back east before he'd hit Hollywood, plus what he had observed on the young people in Brooklyn who were all wearing their hair blown straight back at the time. The mannerisms, the walk, were all created simply by watching the kids on the streets of Brooklyn.

John found himself drawing on memories of his older brother Joey when he started trying to pin down the ritualistic behaviour of his character Tony Manero. He explained, 'Joey would dress up on a Saturday night and go out with a group. He even had his own dressing ritual before walking out with a girlfriend to a dance at the community centre.' But when the first draft script of *Fever* was sent to John he was worried that the Tony Manero character was far too similar to Barbarino after all, and he feared he could not give Manero the depth he needed.

Desperate for other opinions, John asked friends to read the *Fever* script. Their verdict was unanimous.

'Baby,' one very close friend shouted. 'You are going to be great in this! This Tony, he's got all the colours! First he's angry about something; he hates the trap that Brooklyn and his dumb job are. There's a whole glamorous world out there waiting which he feels only when he dances. And he grows, he gets out of Brooklyn!'

All John's friends and advisers went on like this. 'He's *miles* from what you've played, and what isn't in the script, you're going to *put* there!' another one insisted.

But, despite all this enthusiasm, John still wasn't entirely convinced. He was worried that Tony was a better dancer than he could ever be, although everyone assured him that he would learn.

The next version of the script by writer Norman Wexler impressed John far more. He was also pleased with the cast being assembled by director John Avildsen. His two leading ladies were strong performers: Donna Pescow was to play the pathetic Annette who has a desperate crush on Tony Manero and Karen Gorney – who had made her name as Tara on the daytime soap *All My Children* – was cast as the stronger Stephanie.

However, it gradually emerged that Avildsen – who had just been nominated for an Oscar following his superb work on *Rocky* – had certain ideas that were not entirely in line with John's or Stigwood's vision of *Fever*. The week before the shoot was scheduled to begin, Avildsen was dismissed by producer Stigwood after a heated disagreement about the way the film was going to be shot.

Stigwood made a muted statement to the press: 'I am sorry that I had to fire him on the day he was nominated for an Oscar. John Avildsen is a very nice and talented man, but he wanted to make a different movie from the one I intended to make, and different from the one John Travolta wanted to make.'

John later explained, 'John Avildsen wanted to make more of a love story concept for the film. More like *Rocky*. I like Avildsen very much, but I'm glad we didn't go his way and instead went back to what the writer Wexler intended. People get caught up in wins. If something wins for you, you're going to go with it. Avildsen was in the height of his success with *Rocky*. He needed to sit with the success of that picture. Maybe if he'd had one in between *Rocky* and *Saturday Night Fever* it would have worked.'

In many ways it did work for Avildsen because he got the Oscar for Best Director that April. But John Travolta also got his way because new director John Badham agreed to make the movie that both the star and producer believed was going to work – a tough, hard-edged and hard-talking film that looked at the underbelly of the so-called glamorous disco world.

Just before filming got under way, in February 1977, John leased an apartment from Carly Simon and James Taylor and started commuting to locations in some of Brooklyn's toughest neighbourhoods. The apartment was in one of the city's most elegant older buildings on Central Park West in Manhattan. Looking across the street from his living room, John had one of the most tranquil views in the whole of New York: Central Park blanketed in snow as the joggers made their weary way along the many paths that criss-crossed the wide open spaces.

Back on *Fever*, John and director Badham both believed in lengthy rehearsals. John even told one friend, 'I can't create a lot until I'm actually rehearsing with the actors I'm going to be working with – I don't know until then what they're going to do in a scene, or what I'll get from them to react to.'

The young actor also had an immense influence on certain aspects of the script and asked for dozens of changes. But Badham and writer Norman Wexler did not seem to mind. They believed that John's involvement could only improve the vital fine-tuning of the project. John was not the type of actor who demanded revisions just for the sake of establishing his personal power over the production. So they were surprised when – just before shooting commenced – John presented an attaché case full of changes to producer Robert Stigwood. He was particularly concerned that there was no dance solo in the original script. John genuinely believed that there should be a forceful, sensual visual presentation that would say more about Tony's character than a hundred words of dialogue.

Initially, John went in hard on Stigwood. 'You spent all this money on training me, and you're not going to let me do a solo dance? That's what the kids who are good do.'

Stigwood wanted to do it his way. But John would not give in and kept insisting the dance solo should be put in the movie. Eventually, Stigwood backed down and the scene was written into the screenplay.

After that, John pressed again because he didn't agree with Stigwood filming the solo dance sequence to 'Stayin' Alive'. He wanted it to be shot to 'You Should Be Dancing'. Once again John was eventually victorious.

But he wasn't finished yet. John then decided to tell Stigwood how the cameraman should shoot the dance solo scene. 'Tight close-ups and head-and-shoulder shots would work perfectly,' he said, adding, 'Please let's really show how this guy could clear a dance floor.'

There were other examples of subtle dialogue changes in *Fever*:

> *Tony Manero is trying out a new step with his ideal dance partner, when she asks him a question.*
>   *'Did you make that step up yourself?'*
>   *'Yeah,' says Tony proudly. 'No. I saw it on television . . . then I made it up.'*

The modification, and the contradiction, were changes made by John on the set of *Fever*. They perfectly reflected Tony Manero's stubborn pride and restless insecurity.

John got his way on all counts in the end and the dance solo scene, as it appeared in the film, was the ultimate vindication of his judgement. The potency of his solo was completely unexpected, and the throbbing music, pulsating lights and gyrating dancing exploded out of the screen. When the movie was released, even Fred Astaire raved about the style and content of that particular scene and much of it was down to John Travolta himself.

He had learned just how important it was to have an attitude when it came to his own career. He was master of his own destiny and if that meant insisting on changes to a script then so be it. The buck stopped with John.

CHAPTER TWELVE
DISCO FEVER

BAY RIDGE, BROOKLYN, FEBRUARY 1977

They instantly called John 'The Man' when he turned up for his first day on location work for *Fever*. It was a name which stuck. It pleased John in an uncomplicated way. The name was actually a spin-off from Vinnie Barbarino in *Kotter*.

But 'The Man' wasn't always happy. On one of the earlier shoot days, *Fever* director John Badham had expected him to strip naked for one of the movie's most controversial scenes when he virtually rapes Stephanie, the independent chick who is so goddamn cool.

Before shooting even began, John had already warned director Badham that he couldn't do the scene naked after seeing it referred to in the original screenplay. Badham decided to ignore his star on the basis that, once he got into the character of Tony Manero, John would understand why his brief appearance in the nude was so vital to the movie. But John had actually grown even more determined not to strip as the shooting of *Fever* progressed. When it came to the all-important scene he stuck rigidly to his guns.

Eventually, a compromise was reached whereby John offered to sit up in bed in black bikini briefs and 'adjust himself'. His reasoning was simple. He knew perfectly well that the *Fever* producers wanted to titillate their audience and that was why they had wanted him to strip, but he believed that to give the audience just a hint was far preferable to complete nudity.

'I think it helps to get people excited but not too much,' is how he explained his attitude a few months later.

But the truth about certain aspects of the infamous opening sequence of *Fever* is far more remarkable. It showed Tony Manero walking down the street, moving to the rhythm of the disco music in his head. His body and a can of paint he is holding swing to the beat of the Bee Gees' 'Stayin' Alive'. In the following ten seconds it becomes clear that the character on the screen owns the street and the territory around it. More important, the actor on the screen completely captures the attention of the audience. Travolta Fever has begun.

Director John Badham – who put a lot of time and energy into getting that scene right – explains, 'This gay lives for the time he can go to the disco. This is a boring day job. It's only in the evening when he can come alive. So, when thinking about this sequence, we needed to understand what he was wanting to do, and how could we show that in an interesting cinematic way?

'The idea came in a flash – let's look at his feet. Let's see him in a way we have never seen before. How can we get the camera down to the ground so that we can see his shoes ...

'His mind was in his toes, the soles of his feet, in his heels and how they impacted with the ground. The dilemma of the movie is satellited in this particular shot. This is a fella who can do much better in life, yet he is stuck in a dull, mundane ordinary world which he wants to break out of.

'He looks like he owns these streets. It is his world. He is in control. He has a magical charisma the first time we see him.'

Then Badham revealed for the first time that the opening shots were achieved without John. They weren't his feet. The director went on, 'John had all those personal problems in his life at that time and had to go and deal with that and we were left without an opening.

'We did it with his double called Jeff Zinn and I asked Jeff to walk like John would walk to the song. He ambled down the street in a rather boring way. My assistant, a dancer, made him do it in a more interesting way.

'Then John came back and I said to him, "John, here's what we had to do while you were gone. But John says, "I don't walk like that."'

'I know you don't, but can you kinda imitate the walk?' asked Badham nervously.

'No, I'm not doing that. I don't walk like that.'

'I thought to myself, "Oh my God, what are we going to do?"'

It wasn't until Badham was editing the movie that he decided to use the stand-in's sequence instead of the real John Travolta's.

'The legs and feet strutting down the street in the movie's opening sequence belonged to Zinn,' says Badham.

And he pointed out the irony of the situation. 'It was ten seconds of raw film-making and it probably did more than anything else to launch John Travolta as a Hollywood superstar. But it wasn't even him.'

In the middle of all this pressurised movie-making, John was also having to deal with Diana's illness and, eventually, her death.

Fever director John Badham recalls, 'The poor guy was like a zombie. But John didn't want people to feel sorry for him. After the funeral he had the hardest scenes in the movie still to do, the scenes with the family. But he was very professional. The entire cast and crew felt terrible.'

Everyone on the *Fever* set was so deeply affected by John's situation that they made a large donation to the Damon Runyon Cancer Fund. Both cast and crew became extremely protective of John during the remainder of the filming. John later described it as 'the hardest time of my life'.

Manager Bob LeMond ensured that John was surrounded only

by people he liked and trusted. Even the young actor's chauffeur Larry offered to work a seven-day week because he worried that the other driver might not be taking enough care of his star boss.

Diana's words of encouragement were still ringing in John's ears when he returned to the *Fever* set after her funeral. As director John Badharn explained, 'He put his attention to the work and overcame his emotional feelings. Some of the best scenes in the movie were done during that period.'

The scenes Badham was referring to were the family scenes as well as the emotional scenes with Stephanie and Annette, the girls Tony Manero gets involved with. John saw his character Manero as 'being far more sensitive than any of the people around him, and he had a lot more going for him'.

John closely observed the extras used during filming in Brooklyn so that he could keep adding fresh dimensions to his character. Sometimes they'd invite the young star into their homes after work for a drink or a meal. John watched carefully and memorised the magical moments that he wanted to use when he got back on the film set the next morning.

Other, more risky aspects of the script John insisted he conveyed simply by acting. There was the excessive drug-taking and drinking, not to mention the non-stop swearing, neither of which had ever been on John's social agenda. 'I just acted all that.'

John also produced one of the most emotional moments in the movie – by accident. This was when Tony and Stephanie were seated on a bench facing the Verrazano Bridge. He tells her all the statistics about how the bridge was built, because that bridge is his only means of escape from a life of drudgery. It's his way out. None of this is revealed in dialogue. Instead, Tony's secret yearning for freedom comes out in floods of tears. Those tears were not in the script and John later admitted they were as much of a surprise to him as anyone else. But they made the character of Tony Manero real to the audience. They made everyone care.

John's mother Helen had taught him early on in life how to add his own emotions to a situation and conjure up the perfect scene. And he deliberately injected quite a number of spontaneous moments into the movie by allowing himself to bounce off what other actors were feeding him. John kept each scene – with family, friends or the woman he loved – flowing naturally and dramatically.

Diana Hyland's legacy was to help him conjure up those special moments by thinking about her during such scenes. He gave it all away when he travelled to see Diana's mother a few weeks after Diana's death and found the elderly lady weeping.

'I don't like anyone to see me like this, but I cry every day,' she told John.

'So do I,' he replied gently.

His lover's death had made John Travolta grow up incredibly fast and develop a maturity far beyond his years. 'I feel like I'm an old spirit in a young body' was how he put it at the time. 'I feel like I know a lot, like I've been around and lived a lot.'

On the set, during the final few weeks of shooting *Saturday Night Fever*, John refused to allow doubles to be used during a highly dangerous fight scene after his fitness trainer Jimmy Gambina told him it would look phoney. Gambina then showed the actors, including John, how to make authentic-looking swings at their opponents.

But John did use his double Jeff Zinn for certain scenes. Zinn thus became an overnight minor celebrity and would sign autographs for dozens of women every week. His favourite message was: 'To be saved in case of stardom. Love, Jeff Zinn.'

Another major influence on John's performance in *Fever* was disco dancer Deney Terrio, who was responsible for all the 'out-front' disco dancing that became John's trademark on the big screen.

'I took John through a hundred different steps and the ones he fell into the easiest and looked the best, I kept,' explains Terrio.

The dance sequences were considered so important that Terrio had a notebook in which he wrote down the best moves for later use by John. He reveals, 'Like the knee drops and the splits, the Russian leaps that he did – I got that from watching an ice skater.' For many of those dance sequences, John became so dependent on Terrio that he insisted the disco dancer accompany him for every shot.

John used a stand-in called Jinx Hodges for the racier dance routines to save the embarrassment of his female co-stars. Hodges' job must have been the most sought after in America, as all she had to do was grind up against the country's number one sex symbol!

Throughout the gruelling *Fever* shoot, John would get up at five every morning and not get home until past ten in the evening. And he constantly kept up his dance practice.

The dance interiors themselves actually ended up being shot in the real 2001 Odyssey Club in Bay Ridge, Brooklyn, which had featured in Nik Cohn's original article in *New York* magazine. It was a location around which many legends would grow up.

CHAPTER THIRTEEN
SPACE ODYSSEY

2001 ODYSSEY CLUB, BAY RIDGE, BROOKLYN, NEW YORK, MARCH 1977

The one-storey white-washed building was thirty years old and located in a half-commercial, half-residential area. At the entrance three kinds of identification had to be presented to burly doormen. Then steps led down into a hallway where red and black shag-pile carpet and fake wood panelling covered the walls. There was also a black and white checked carpet on the floor. On the right was a bar where large green and yellow plastic balls hung from the ceiling. Through the hall, there was a dance room on the left. At the back of the dance room were three balconies, divided by tiers and white wrought-iron fences. On the balconies were chairs and tables with red and white checked tablecloths. The entire room seated about 750, and the dance floor in the centre would hold about fifty. There was also an elevated stage and the DJ's booth.

The whole place was ideal for filming, with only a few extra touches and props needed to make it the perfect location. Paramount, the movie's distributors, installed a dance floor that lit up and projected different colours on all the dancers. This alone cost $20,000. Then they put in a dry-ice machine which churned out fog while the dancers were grooving. A specially designed eighteen-inch mirrored ball was ordered and hung from the ceiling over the dance floor. Spinners and floodlights were also added for more light variation, and the walls were covered with shiny paper in silver, green, red and yellow. The room looked perfect – a wonderful combination of gaudy seventies style and Hollywood glitz. Enter John Travolta and the *Saturday Night Fever* crew.

When the kids in the area heard the news that John Travolta was at their neighbourhood disco, all hell broke loose. On the first day of filming at the 2001 Odyssey, a crowd of more than 4,000 people – mostly kids who had skipped school – packed the area in front of the club. Some overenthusiastic boys and girls even broke down police barriers to try and get a closer look at their idol. Things got completely out of hand when one gang of youths tried to overturn John's mobile home under the mistaken impression that it might force him to come out and greet them. He wasn't in it at the time.

Inside the 2001 Odyssey things were only slightly calmer. Several club regulars were used as extras in the movie and a handful even got to meet their idol John Travolta. One dancer called Patrick breathlessly told anyone who would listen, 'John was real nice. When he came to the disco, he'd turn around and wave and smile to the crowd outside. And he was kind of shy too. It was funny. You didn't expect this guy who plays a real cool disco king to be shy, but John was. I liked him a lot.'

John's relentless training also seemed to have paid off. Many of the seasoned dancers were soon in awe of his talents and he was nicknamed 'the hot fox' by many of them.

John even made an effort to get to know some of the locals who had been hired as extras, especially the nineteen-year-old Italian from Bay Ridge around whom Nik Cohn claimed he had centred his New York magazine article. His name was Vinnie and

John was impressed by him from the outset, although he was little different from what he had expected. No one of course realised that Vinnie's character actually amounted to only a very small percentage of Tony Manero.

'He was a much milder guy than the article made him out to be,' explains John. 'He was a kid dressed in a three-piece suit and high heels, a blond Italian – I thought he'd be dark. He was very cool. He was working for his father in some capacity. I sensed more of a maturity in this guy; he was not like the other guys in the discotheque. I know what it was about him: I didn't sense the anger in him that I had expected from the article.'

In fact, Vinnie's only anger centred around the director's decision to use the 2001 Odyssey as the location. 'This place is going downhill fast,' he told John. 'Why are you filming here? This place isn't where it's happening.'

John sympathised as best he could, but he really didn't have time to worry about Vinnie's opinion on such matters right then.

Throughout the filming John continued to hang out at real discos in Brooklyn and Manhattan. He especially concentrated on the young men and their carefully synchronised dance movements.

'I studied them and how they worked their bodies, as well as how they danced. Tony Manero is a total entity that I created by observation,' he explained.

John fully appreciated how important dancing was to these people. 'They feel great when they're doing it. If you love music and you can move, it makes you feel better. I think dancing is those people's basic search for excitement. It's a release, an escape from daily living. In Tony Manero's case, he got such great validation from it that when he went out, it was not only a great feeling, but it was also an ego thing ...'

In May 1977, the *Saturday Night Fever* roadshow finally ended. The movie's success now depended on the skills of the director and his editor. John flew back to Los Angeles to return to *Welcome Back Kotter*. It would be several months before he knew how the public and the critics would react to his portrayal of a character who was very different from Vinnie Barbarino. John was excited, scared and hopeful. Anything could happen now.

In order to cope with his life at that time, John turned increasingly to the Church of Scientology's philosophy which had given him strength in the past. But would it help now?

What had shattered John most of all about Diana Hyland's death was that he had no control over it. He had grown up in charge of his own destiny and he had been lucky enough, until that point, never to lose anyone that close to him.

Michael Lembeck, an actor, composer and one of John's closest friends, explains, 'Scientology gave John a deep strength. He could never have handled himself so well without Scientology. It virtually saved his life.'

At the time of Diana's death, John even sent for a Scientology counsellor or 'auditor' to fly in to New York to help him get through the gruelling work on *Fever* that still lay ahead. The auditor drafted special sessions for John intended to help him overcome his misery. The sessions worked, and John was able to complete his work.

A Church of Scientology session consists of a series of questions devised by the auditor and directed at a subject. During the questioning, the subject is hooked up to an E-meter, a device which monitors the body's electrical energy. By observing a needle on the E-meter, the auditor can discover what questions cause the greatest stress, and then focus on specific problems. The E-meter becomes a kind of therapeutic lie detector. It helps measure the 'state of the spirit' while monitoring the subject receiving counselling.

John underwent several of these sessions and gradually came to terms with Diana Hyland's death. The successful auditing sessions refuelled his interest in Scientology and he even began examining the history of the Church to try and get a better understanding of its role in society.

Founded in 1950 by L. Ron Hubbard, the Church describes its teaching thus: 'Scientology is an applied religious philosophy. Its goal is to bring an individual to an understanding of himself and his life as a spiritual being and in relationship to the universe as a whole.

'Scientology provides mankind the means to attain a comprehensive understanding of the human spirit and to achieve the traditional religious goals of spiritual enlightenment and salvation. This spiritual path is the result of almost fifty years of extensive research by the Founder L. Ron Hubbard. The millions of Scientologists and others who benefit from L. Ron Hubbard's discoveries regard him with great respect and admiration.'

The reason behind John's conversion might have been just as simple as the fact that he craved a sense of belonging. Movie critic and screenwriter Michael Medved reckons that artists and entertainers need 'a community, a tribe, a place where they can fit in'. He also explains, 'Part of being in the arts has to do with rejecting whatever the conventional wisdom is.'

Beverly Hills psychologist Dr Eugene Landy who has treated some of Hollywood's most famous names, explains, 'Religion is just one of those things celebrities turn to. The need for structure in every life, but especially in a celebrity's,' declares Dr Landy, 'is one of the basics of all basics.'

The Church of Scientology itself has always insisted that it is not concerned about the number of famous people who have joined its ranks in recent years, but there is no doubt that celebrities such as John do serve a useful purpose. Scientology is the only religion that offers a church exclusively set aside for professional performers.

That church, called the Celebrity Center, is located in the middle of Hollywood. The Church of Scientology claims it was originally established to satisfy the need of artists and other professionals in Hollywood for a quiet place for them to attend religious services without the disruption celebrity sometimes causes. That desire for privacy meshed well with Scientology founder L. Ron Hubbard's belief that artists were important to the well-being of a society.

John himself admitted that the Scientologists had helped him learn how to handle problems better. He told one reporter, 'Scientology is a very personal thing to me, but it's really helped me through the good and the bad. It's taught me to be more consistent. Now I know how to handle problems for myself. No more outasight highs and deep lows.

'You always have the fear, "Success is terrific now, but will it last forever?" When you hit it quickly you don't know where to go. Never let yourself be a flash in the pan. Scientology makes it all a lot saner.'

John also went on record as claiming that Scientology was a tremendous aid for an artist. 'There is a need for Scientology in helping artists. It is essential for actors to understand communication. The basic Scientology course of communication is very valuable. It's important for people to be able to communicate and that's what Scientology is all about.'

The Church of Scientology was becoming like a second family for John in California. He regularly took people like Scientology member actress Karen Black, her husband Kit Carlson and John's personal Scientology minister out to dinner at famed LA restaurant La Maison.

Others in Hollywood were somewhat baffled by the position of the Church when it came to the raunchy roles played in movies by some of its members. But a Scientology official offered this statement: 'Scientology allows individuals to decide what they do rather than us dictating to them. John has his own choice of films. He may discuss his movies with a counsellor. But again, it is his own self-determination – his choice alone.'

Intriguingly, it seems that the Scientologists make very few demands of belief or absolute morality and the Church certainly does not pass judgement on people's decisions and actions.

Having found it so helpful to have a counsellor on hand during the second half of the filming of *Saturday Night Fever*, John decided to try and do the same on each movie he made. He also helped the Church raise funds to buy more property in the heart of Hollywood. John started spending at least six hours a week studying the writings of founder L. Ron Hubhard, particularly the Scientologists' bible, *Dianetics – The Modern Science of Mental Health*.

When *Fever* finally hit the screens of movie theatres across America, the reaction, even amongst the critics, was extraordinary. Frank Rich said in *Time* magazine, 'John Travolta is a revelation ... he floors the audience ... his carnal presence can make even a safe Hollywood package seem like dangerous goods.'

David Ansen, of *Newsweek*, pronounced, 'For Travolta, it's a triumphant starring debut ... you can bet the film makers knew they had a good thing going when they turned on the music and let Travolta loose!'

Ansen summed it all up when he added, 'In a less engaging actor's hands, Tony could have been insufferably arrogant and dense. But Travolta's big slab of a face is surprisingly expressive, revealing a little boy's embarrassment and hurt as well as a stud's posturing. Travolta understands Tony with his whole body – needless to say, he can dance up a storm – and you can't keep your eyes off him. It's a fresh, funny, downright friendly performance.'

If the critics had any reservations at all about John's performance it was that he was perhaps too good. Some wondered if he hadn't been typecast, especially since Tony was not that unlike Vinnie Barbarino. But John's biggest fan turned out to be the fearsome critic Pauline Kael, who insisted, 'At twenty-three, he's done enough to make it apparent that there's a broad distance between him and Tony and that it's an actor's imagination that closes the gap.'

John was so touched by Kael's words that hers became his personal favourite of the hundreds of reviews for *Fever*. He even kept the 17 December 1977 issue of the *New Yorker* in which it appeared. 'Travolta gets so far inside the role he seems incapable of a false note; even the Brooklyn accent seems unerring ... There's dedication in Travolta's approach to

Tony's character; he isn't just a good actor, he's a generous-hearted actor.'

John was so proud of that review that his assistant handed out copies of it to reporters interviewing him for months after the release of *Fever*. He described Kael's critique as 'an actor's dream' and felt indebted to her ever after.

On the opening night of *Fever* – 12 December 1977 – people queued for up to a mile to be the first to see John do his stuff. At the première party at the Tavern on the Green Club in New York City, crowds tried to jam into the building because they knew John was inside.

In Los Angeles, 2,000 guests attended a *Fever* party that cost Paramount $150,000. Amongst the guests were Sam and Helen Travolta, who were driven to the party by stretch limousine. Other guests included Cher, Lily Tomlin and the entire cast of *Kotter*. Helen – who'd had a $50 hairdo for the occasion – even managed a dance with *Fever* producer Robert Stigwood.

Sam Travolta's main recollection of the evening was 'this guy who followed me around all night with a tray of drinks. "What's going on?" I asked him. And he said, "I was told to take special care of you."' Sam always smiled at the memory.

One of the most notable spin-offs from the success of *Fever* was that disco dancing suddenly became a national epidemic. It seemed that movie-theatre audiences were leaving cinemas with an irresistible urge to dance. As a result, disco-dancing schools and discotheques popped up all over the States.

At the 2001 Odyssey Club, in Brooklyn, attendance increased dramatically – along with the entry fee – and visitors started complaining that it didn't seem as nice as in the movie. But the crowds kept coming. One man from Canada travelled all the way to Bay Ridge just to ask if he could buy a chunk of the dance floor put in by the movie company for the *Fever* shoot. 'John Travolta Dance Contests' were held for kids aged twelve to sixteen every Saturday and Sunday afternoon from 1 to 5 pm with a $3 admittance fee. One of the dances, called 'the robot', was especially inspired by John's performance in the movie and was a firm favourite among the teenagers. The walls of the 2001 were also adorned with posters of John in *Fever*.

On the recording front, an incredible nine million copies of the *Saturday Night Fever* soundtrack were sold. It became the biggest-selling record in history, beating such dinosaurs as Carol King's *Tapestry*, Peter Frampton's *Frampton Comes Alive* and Fleetwood Mac's *Rumours*. Bee Gee songs from the movie, 'Stayin' Alive', 'Night Fever', 'More Than a Woman' and 'How Deep is Your Love?', remained on the top ten singles charts for months.

The Bee Gees themselves were as surprised as anyone. Said band member Barry Gibb, 'It's funny. We wrote the songs for *Saturday Night Fever* without ever knowing what the movie was really about. Robert Stigwood dropped by one day while we were on vacation in France and asked for five or six songs for the movie. We worked at top speed and within two weeks we handed him the songs.'

The huge soundtrack album sales for *Fever* also helped the careers of singers like the Tavares, who sang 'More Than a Woman', and Yvonne Elliman, who sang 'If I Can't Have You', both songs having been written by the Bee Gees. John Travolta had the golden touch as far as dozens of people were concerned.

Outside the States, *Saturday Night Fever* proved just as successful. In Britain, the queues were as long and the passion for the music spread to thousands of pubs and clubs across the country. It was much the same story in Europe and the rest of the world.

In April 1978, Travoltamania reached new heights when John was featured on the cover of *Time* magazine, indicating that he had become a figure of national importance rather than a flash-in-the-pan pop hero. The cover was dominated by a vast banner headline reading 'Travolta Fever'.

Next came the inevitable spin-offs from the successful movie. One TV show, *Joe and Valerie*, debuted in the spring of 1978, just a few months after *Fever* was released. Then John's brother

Joey was asked to play a Tony Manero-type character on a TV show. He turned down the offer in the end because he feared it might offend his younger brother.

There was also the hit TV show *Stayin' Alive*. A disco movie entitled *Thank God It's Friday* became the first in a long line of imitations to hit the big screen.

The downside to all this fame and fortune was still the harassment from fans. John found it virtually impossible to enjoy a quiet meal at a restaurant without someone trying to steal the fork out of his hand. Then he was banned from his beloved flying because neither Lloyds nor any other insurance company serving Hollywood would agree to give him insurance cover if he flew. He even had to stop using his Honda 350 motorcycle.

John's old school buddy and confidant Jerry Wurms was still living in his apartment on Doheny Drive, along with *Fever* co-star Donna Pescow, who was trying to take advantage of the buzz surrounding the movie by staying in Hollywood to be available for any work offers. The apartment was still dominated by a pool table, a big-screen TV and yet more model planes.

Despite his temporary 'ban' on flying, John then bought himself a thirty-year-old twin-engined DC-3 with seats for at least fifteen people. It was a dream purchase for him.

Amongst his other close friends at that time were English-born actress Kate Edwards (whose mother Joan Edwards started working as John's secretary in 1976) and ex-girlfriend Marilu Henner. It was definitely women who showed the most concern for John's well-being following Diana Hyland's death. A group of them would take him out for an evening at his favourite Japanese restaurant on Sunset Strip. The problem was the constant interruptions by autograph hunters, who usually received a friendly greeting from John, but no autograph.

His patter for signature-hunters usually went as follows. 'Autographs are sort of impersonal,' he would tell them, extending his hand, 'but I'd like to meet you.' The fact that a lot of his fans were young and extremely pretty was 'not relevant', according to John at that time. He even confessed to a friend some time after Diana's death that he was afraid of having a relationship and found that his feelings about women 'were much more exciting in my fantasies than reality'.

It was almost as if he was holding himself back, trying to express passion in his thoughts rather than his actions.

During the months following the release of *Fever*, John gradually pulled out of the public spotlight altogether. He had just been through a weird twelve-month roller- coaster ride of emotions, from the success of *Kotter* to the joy of getting the lead in *Fever*, down to the death of his beloved Diana and up to the incredible reaction to the release of *Fever*. Now he had to get back to reality and start considering the future. His next move was going to be just as important as his last

CHAPTER FOURTEEN
SEXUAL FEVER

HOLLYWOOD, 1977

Thanks to the success of *Saturday Night Fever*, John was in close contention with such distinguished actors as Fernando Rey and John Gielgud for the prestigious New York Film Critic Circle Awards. He also got the Best Actor Award from the National Board of Review, in addition to being nominated for a Golden Globe Award, given by the Hollywood Foreign Press.

One of the most intriguing aspects of the success of *Fever* was the way in which people from all walks of life and sexual preferences hailed John as their hero and were touched by his performance as Tony Manero.

Actress Lily Tomlin told journalists at the time that she was 'knocked out' by John's screen presence and plans were already under way before *Fever* was released to find a project for both of them to star in together.

And Tomlin wasn't the only bigtime actress trying to net John for a money-spinning vehicle. Barbra Streisand and Liza Minnelli were discussing movie deals with him, and Streisand even enjoyed a couple of dinner dates with John. Although their relationship never really took off on a personal level, they were certainly happy to profess their undying love for each other in professional terms.

Meanwhile, *Fever* distributors Paramount insisted on paying John $50,000 a year – for doing absolutely nothing. The only condition was that he did not work on a movie for any other studio.

Back in Englewood, New Jersey, John's childhood home, life hadn't really changed much, despite the presence of yet more autograph and souvenir hunters.

Mr and Mrs Travolta even got into the habit of passing out glossy photos of their youngest son to any fans loitering near the house. Down in the bright-red basement recreation room, there was a large bulletin board crowded with pictures of all the kids. Here the superstar received equal billing with his siblings, and his photo smiled out among shots of Ellen, by then thirty-seven, who was acting in pilots for both NBC and CBS; Annie, twenty-nine, just married and acting in New York City; Joey, twenty-seven, who was once a teacher and had taken off for LA with a gift of $5,000 from his kid brother and the promise of a screen test; and Sam Jnr, thirty-four, who had worked for years as a shipping clerk at Fabergé but, hooked on showbusiness, was learning to play the guitar and trying to get his own band together.

Margaret, thirty-two, by then the mother of two children, was making $80,000 a year doing voice-overs and TV commercials in Chicago. Annie found parts in summer productions of various plays thanks to John. She also had a one-line appearance in *Fever* in a pizza parlour: 'How many slices?'

Even mother Helen had a tiny walk-on part in *Fever* as a customer in the paint store where Tony Manero worked. John certainly believed in keeping it in the family.

Then there was Joey – the older brother who seemed permanently in John's shadow even though he was considered by those inside the family as the 'outgoing kid'. Joey wanted to make it in movies on his own terms, but with a name like Travolta that was going to be tricky. He wrote a script based on his experiences teaching emotionally disturbed and retarded children. He'd also been a singer and had even been allowed to write one tune for *Fever*.

On the surface, Joey appeared to have complete confidence in what he was doing. 'Films don't intimidate me. I learned from Ma that you may have to deal with people who aren't nice, but you don't have to be like them. And I learned from my father that you can deal with anybody and just be yourself – Dad's the same way he is wherever he is.' Nevertheless, Joey did concede that he 'probably was' a little afraid of following in his brother's footsteps.

When John was allowed to pilot his twin-engined DC-3 by Paramount, he used it like a taxi to drop off various family members in Chicago and New York. The inside of the plane had been refurbished to look more like a living room than a small airliner. Every time they stopped to refuel, caterers would come on board with lavish spreads of fresh food.

John took Sam and Helen Travolta to Hawaii, as soon as he started earning real money on *Kotter*. Helen was delighted by the experience. As she explained, 'John thinks of everything on his plane. I fell asleep for a while and, when I woke up, Johnny was gone and the two pilots were sitting in the cabin. I ran to the cockpit, and there was Johnny flying that thing, and singing and looking so gorgeous in a white turtleneck and a scarf – it was just like a movie.'

In fact she was so surprised to see John at the controls that she reacted like a concerned mother who'd just discovered her small son in the garage sitting behind the steering wheel of the family car.

'You *can't* fly this,' she said.

'Come on, Ma,' smiled John. 'I'll give you a lesson.'

Helen took the joystick nervously and the plane suddenly veered up towards the sky. In the cabin everyone blanched.

Then John came on the loudspeaker: 'Nothing to worry about,

folks. Just keeping this beauty on course for our next destination.'

Inside Hollywood there was speculation about how John could afford to run two planes at such an early stage in his career. He explained it by saying, 'I sat down and had a long talk with myself and I said, "Hell, John, you're allowed to change with your success. Your fans want you to change. If not, what are you working so hard for?" So, instead of a house, I bought an airplane. I thought, John, you now deserve to buy yourself something.'

Flying offered the perfect release from the non-stop pressure of moviedom. John also felt an enormous sense of nostalgia when he got behind the controls.

On the ground, fame had already become a trap from which there seemed no escape. In his plane, far from the madding crowds, he could plan his future and find the time to figure out what his past had taught him. Some weekends, he'd spend more than ten hours – and a fortune in fuel – flying around the country thinking about the next movie offer or whatever.

John explains, 'I get romantic on airplanes. I'm honest on a plane ... There's something about the timelessness – you're suspended in time. I get real relief on a plane, all my pressures get suspended. There's always something important and dramatic about those engines going pfft – it's like the whole world is watching you. I get the same feeling when I'm piloting. Once you're away from the airport and trimmed out, you have plenty of time to daydream. It's glorious.'

The Christmas after *Fever* was released John rented a mansion in Connecticut so that the whole family would be together for the holidays. He constantly showed great generosity to his family.

Sam and Helen also went to London with John when *Fever* opened to a rapturous welcome in Britain. That was followed by a rented villa in the South of France. Sam was appalled by the price he had to pay in London for his favourite cigars and decided to ration himself. John had to tell the hotel manager to send up boxes of cigars, and then he checked daily to see that his father was smoking them.

Meanwhile, Helen Travolta was so overwhelmed by the price of an American breakfast in one European hotel that she ordered one breakfast and split it between her and Sam. John was amused and then tried to explain to his parents why the money just no longer mattered.

'Think of this money like Monopoly – the studio's paying.' Then he sat and watched them eat, worried that his mother wasn't getting enough nourishment. 'Spoil yourself a little, Ma,' he'd say.

Helen later recalled, 'All in all, we'd have been happier in a small second-class hotel; that's where people like us belonged. But that would have hurt Johnny's feelings. Johnny deserves all this fuss. I hadn't done anything to deserve this.'

Saturday Night Fever continued to fill movie theatres wherever it played. In its first sixteen weeks, *Fever* grossed a staggering $81 million, about eleven times its break-even figure – and that was only in the United States. It eventually became the third-highest-earning adult-rated feature film in history, with worldwide grosses of $350 million; its soundtrack sold over twenty-five million copies.

By the spring of 1978, word was spreading through the Polo Lounge, Beverly Hills, and Elaine's restaurant (the Polo Lounge East) in New York that John was beholden to no one – not even Robert Stigwood – when it came to his career decisions; that he was Svengali to his own Trilby; that *he* chose his roles; that, while he was close to his manager Bob LeMond, it was John who said yea or nay to everything, right down to which of his publicity stills were used and where and when he made any personal appearances. He had become increasingly selective about the interviews he granted to journalists. But he still insisted that ABC-TV – producers of *Welcome Back Kotter*- answer all of his 10,000 fan letters that arrived each week. He even asked Bob LeMond and his staff to research fanmail-answering services, but found the least expensive one charged 25 cents per answer, or $17,500 a week, or $910,000 a year – a ludicrous figure by anyone's standards.

In many ways, John was still finding life in Hollywood very alien. He tended not to socialise with anyone outside his small band of close friends, and he preferred it when his family came to visit.

Perhaps one problem was that his apartment was not exactly inspiring. The walls were a non-descript orange and brown, the carpet a forgettable green, and the Spanish-style furniture looked as if it had been borrowed from a Holiday Inn.

There were dozens of model planes piled on top of a pinball machine in an unused bedroom. Many of them were vintage airliners like the ones he used to see soaring above his home back in Englewood, New Jersey. There were old Lockheed Constellations, with their distinctive twin tails and British Britannias. But pride of place went to the sturdy little DC-3s, the workhorse aircraft of the previous four decades.

Helen and Sam frequently responded to SOSs from their son and flew down from New Jersey. Helen still considered John to be her baby and both parents were well aware that beneath that brash exterior was a sensitive, shy soul who only really came alive in front of a camera.

In LA, Helen would stock John's refrigerator with hamburgers, pies and frozen pizzas. He loved her to prepare a meal for when he got home. She worried about him. Was he eating enough? Who was doing his cleaning for him? Helen feared that he had been through much too much for any twenty-four-year-old to deal with.

Sometimes John longed for his mother to treat him like a child. Often, after a vast dinner and an hour in front of the TV set, John would retire to his bedroom, get his pyjamas on and then call out, 'Tuck me in, Ma.'

Helen would go running into his bedroom to make sure her 'little baby' was comfortable before giving him a big kiss on the cheek. 'Good night, Johnny.'

It was only then that John Travolta – the young performer named the most popular movie actor in the universe in 1978 by the World Film Favourite Awards – went to sleep. Whether he had sweet dreams we will never know.

Outside, most of Hollywood was buzzing with excitement about the young star whom many considered the biggest sex symbol since Rudolph Valentino.

The creation of the legendary Great Lover was perfectly described by Valentino himself when he talked about how he broke through in Hollywood:

'And so, once again, I was in a new place, starting on a new career, without money. If I had known, while waiting outside the studio gates in Hollywood, the obstacles that lay ahead of me, I would never have had the courage to batter my way in. Fortunately, there is a destiny which drops a curtain over the future.'

Those words could have referred to John Travolta in the late seventies.

CHAPTER FIFTEEN

THE PRICE OF FAME

JOHN'S APARTMENT, SOUTH DOHENY DRIVE, BEVERLY HILLS, SUMMER 1977

Director Randal Kleiser presented himself to the concierge who told him to go right up to Mr Travolta's apartment because the actor was waiting for him. Kleiser, the 31-year-old director with whom John had worked so effectively on the TV movie *The Boy in the Plastic Bubble*, took a deep breath and headed for the elevator. In the nine months since they had last met, John had been through it all: an affair with Diana Hyland, followed by her death, and having to cope with the overwhelming pressures of Hollywood stardom. Now Kleiser had been hired to direct John in *Grease*, his follow-up movie for Robert Stigwood. He was visiting John that hot and sticky day to discuss the role before shooting got under way.

What Kleiser found was a broken young man. The combination of Diana's death and the emotional downs that he'd been expected to reflect in his role as Tony Manero in *Saturday Night Fever* – which had only just finished shooting – had drained him of energy and enthusiasm.

Kleiser and John got on to the subject of Diana almost immediately. The young actor kept referring to her as 'my loss'. He seemed to want to talk about her endlessly, continually recalling his love for her and how good she had been to him. Kleiser was very concerned. Here he was, about to start shooting a light-hearted musical, and his main star was in the midst of a deep, grieving depression.

'I want to make *Grease* into a real party atmosphere movie, John,' said Kleiser in the hope of lifting John's spirits.

The actor barely responded.

'We want to keep the atmosphere light, to make sure everyone has a good time,' continued Kleiser. 'It's going to be a fun event. I think that's the right mood to have during the production, don't you?'

John looked up as if he'd just awoken from a trance. 'Sure, Randy. Whatever you say.'

Kleiser did not know how to react. His meeting with John ended shortly afterwards. But there was no turning back because John was contractually locked into the role. Kleiser just hoped that, when pre-production work on *Grease* began a few days later, they could all pull together to get John out of his dark mood.

When John got to the Paramount lot to start work on *Grease*, he had come full circle. Instead of playing the nerdy Doody as he had in the earlier stage version, he was slated to star as heart-throb Danny Zuko.

Grease seemed like a natural follow-up to *Fever*, even though it would be many months before *Fever* was actually released in movie theatres. Producers Robert Stigwood and Allan Carr had absolutely no doubt that *Fever* would be a huge success and their priority was to keep Travoltamania going for as long as possible. In any case, they would have got John to star in *Grease* before *Fever* if it had not been for that complicated contract with the stage show's producers which stated that *Grease* could not be released as a movie until the middle of 1978.

Immediately after completion of *Fever*, a lot more cash was injected into the budget for *Grease*, bringing it up to the $6 million level. Then, just as pre-production work on *Grease* seemed to be going smoothly, John astounded the movie's producers and director by announcing that he did not want to do it. Everyone went into immediate panic mode.

'I'm concerned about the crossover from the play to the screen. I don't know whether it'll work,' he told production staff. They all kept wondering why he had never mentioned his reservations before. But he really hadn't had time to think about *Grease* until then.

There were other reasons behind John's change of heart. He genuinely feared he was in danger of being permanently typecast. First there had been Vinnie Barbarino in *Kotter*, then that role in *Carrie*, followed by Tony Manero in *Fever* – all working-class punks, even though John had managed to characterise each role in a unique way.

John would only agree to continue with *Grease* if it was done his way. He wanted to make Danny Zuko softer, to prove to the audiences that he could play a different kind of character. He also felt under pressure because he had just signed a contract to star alongside Lily Tomlin in a more sensitive movie called *Moment by Moment*.

The producers urgently ordered screenwriters to perform extensive 'surgery' on the *Grease* script. They juggled it around, rewrote huge chunks and added a new musical score.

John eventually gave the screenplay his approval. He then told one reporter in serious tones, 'I thought, What's wrong with doing a light musical? Brando did a musical, *Guys and Dolls*, very early in his career. There aren't that many musicals around to do. Who knows when I'll ever do another? So I thought it was a good move for me.'

Besides John's initial misgivings about *Grease*, producer Allan Carr faced a good deal of resistance to bringing the movie to the big screen. Studio executives at Paramount kept insisting it was out of date. 'Who wants to see a musical about a leather-jacketed fifties greaser and some goody-goody girl?' they asked. But Carr kept plugging away. When he first started pushing the project he actually saw Elvis Presley and Ann-Margret in the leading roles. But a lot of years had passed since then.

Then Carr went after Henry Winkler and Susan Dey, from *The Partridge Family*. But 'The Fonz' turned down the project because he felt it was too similar to his TV role in *Happy Days*. By the time John came on board, producer Carr had only been impressed by two of the dozen or so other actresses tested. They were Marie Osmond and Deborah Raffin. Carr then approached Olivia Newton-John and asked her to undergo a screen test with John. Luckily, they immediately built up a close rapport. Olivia explained, '*Saturday Night Fever* wasn't out yet and I didn't even look at John as a huge film star. None of us knew what to expect and he was as sweet and encouraging as can be.'

The decision to cast Olivia did pose one problem for the film makers. What were they going to do about her distinctive Australian accent? They thought of giving her dialect lessons, but that would only have made her more uncomfortable in her movie debut. So director Kleiser simply had the script altered so that Olivia's character Sandy became a recent import from Australia.

In the movie, the prim Sandy – who at seventeen was twelve years younger than Olivia's real age – tries to win back John's love by drastically changing her image. No more conservative dresses for her. She comes on in skintight pedal pushers, with a low-cut blouse, sexy red heels and a cigarette dangling from her mouth. The Pink Ladies, her friends at school, love it. So do the T-Birds, the raunchy group of greasers led by John.

John found the fifties setting of the movie quite difficult to get a handle on. He started calling director Kleiser in the middle of the night to seek reassurance about which take had been the best the previous day. 'When he thinks he isn't perfect, he's very frustrated. He can be depressed a whole day about it. He doesn't have any objectivity as to how good he really is, and, because of that, he comes across so well,' recalled Kleiser.

John also insisted in public that *Grease* was some kind of social statement about life. He claimed, 'The fifties didn't have a lot of great causes. Everything was more dull, bland and complacent. And in a lot of ways, that's the way things are today in the seventies. I think audiences can relate to that.'

Grease co-star Jeff Conaway says that working with John on the film was 'fun – and very trying'. Conaway had actually been cast as Danny Zuko in the stage version of the show when John had played a secondary character. And Conaway admitted he became agitated when it came to shooting some close-ups with the 'over-keen' John during filming Conaway explains, 'I had a close-up and John had an off-screen line. Afterwards, he came running up, asking, "Think that line was all right?" I said, "John – it was *my* close-up!" But that's OK. He's twenty-four. When I was that age, I was paranoid, too.'

Even John's agent Bob LeMond admitted, 'John worried about every take in the movie. He worried whether the avocados were going to get ripe in the trees. It comes from being a perfectionist. But his sensitivity and vulnerability are exactly what makes him a big star.'

John himself knew he had, up until then, been a difficult actor to work with. He wanted to lighten up and he explained, 'It was like whoever's darker or more neurotic was the more talented. What the fuck does that mean? When I decided to drop it all, I started to do well.'

But it was the musical numbers that were the heart and soul of the *Grease* production and great care was taken to see that the atmosphere on the set was sufficiently musical. Producer Allan Carr kept the set open so that the sounds flooded the entire Paramount Studios lot on Melrose Avenue, Hollywood. Champagne parties on the set were common occurrences, although John never touched a drop of alcohol himself.

For John, *Grease* seemed to represent a new beginning for his personal and professional life. For the first time since Diana's death, he learned to be more sociable. Inevitably rumours about hot new romances began to surface.

John's image as a Hollywood hunk seemed to inspire just about every hopeful starlet to claim they had shared his bed. His photo was in virtually every newspaper and magazine in America alongside some 'conquest' or other. At the time he said, 'I see pictures of myself dating girls I've never met, giving out interviews I've never given and being turned into the biggest carnival freak of any guy I can recall.'

The truth was that there was no one special in his life and he told anyone who would listen that he was concentrating on his career. He occasionally hung out with old pals like Marilu Henner and Joan Prather, both of whom had been his lovers in the past. But those relationships were entirely platonic. All the non-stop press interest in his love life actually had the effect of turning John into an even more shy and reserved person. He didn't trust women he didn't already know very well, but he didn't want a relationship with any of those past lovers. He was in a very difficult situation.

Hollywood gossips made it worse by continually referring back to John's relationship with Diana Hyland and even the young star himself unintentionally encouraged this by telling one writer that young girls were not his type. 'After Diana, I'm more interested in older women.'

On the set of *Grease*, director Randal Kleiser instituted a complete ban on any members of the cast or crew talking to John about Diana Hyland for fear it might upset him.

When *People* magazine published a huge front-page story stating that John was rich and famous but none of that mattered because of the tragedy of Diana's death, everyone on the set tried desperately to keep the magazine away from John. Then he spotted it.

Randal Kleiser takes up the story: 'John had been in a good mood before, clowning around and anxious to get going with the rehearsal we had fixed for that morning. When he saw the magazine cover, he got morose. From then on, everyone kept that kind of publicity away from him.'

Inevitably, many observers started to speculate that John was only interested in having a mother-substitute as a girlfriend. Then, in the middle of all this, rumours of an affair between John and his *Grease* co-star Olivia Newton-John surfaced in Hollywood. Talk about the relationship began at one of the parties producer Allan Carr gave for the *Grease* cast during the early stages of production. John was being interviewed by reporters about Diana Hyland's death when tears filled his eyes as he recalled his love for her. Olivia reached out and took his hand. That tender moment was all the gossips needed. Within a day, John and Olivia were being hailed as Hollywood's newest romantic couple.

Both instantly denied the romance. Olivia was then living with her British manager Lee Kramer. But the rumours continued unabated. The legendary gossip columnist Rona Barrett reported on 19 July 1977, during her *Good Morning America* slot, 'Good news for die-hard movie-buff romantics who remember the good old Hollywood days when the actors and actresses met on a movie set and fell in love as the whole world looked on. My sources say it's happening again on the set of *Grease*, where stars John Travolta and Olivia Newton-John came together first as co-stars, but are now discovering each other personally and liking what they see. Insiders say it's already hand-holding time on the set, and it appears that romance is back in movie-making, behind the scenes at least.'

Rona Barrett's piece summed up the situation. Romance or no romance, everyone wanted a glamorous Hollywood couple and John and Olivia fitted the bill perfectly.

Olivia's manager and lover Lee Kramer was philosophical about the situation at the time and insisted, 'That's just a rumour put out by the movie's publicity people. It simply isn't true.'

But today Kramer admits that it was a romance the world

wanted. 'I was very hurt by the suggestions of a relationship with Travolta.' Kramer – who split up with Olivia, professionally and personally, many years ago – has recently been told a different version of events: that John and Olivia *did* have a real-life affair. 'Maybe they did not reveal it at the time so as to protect me. I always thought they were just genuine friends.'

Kramer claims Olivia was encouraged to be seen with John because it was great publicity for *Grease*. In the newspapers, there were almost daily reports of John and Olivia sightings. One rag claimed that John had spent a few days at Olivia's ranch in the Malibu Hills. They were spotted relaxing by her pool and later horse-riding. Lee Kramer confirms that John did indeed visit the ranch.

Olivia insisted, 'The hand-holding and kissing are for the cameras only. We've just become very good friends. And that friendship is working to capture the love we must show for the cameras. I have my own love life after work, and I try to keep that out of the spotlight. Travolta and I are not an item.' When pushed to describe her relationship with John, she added, 'He was as sweet and encouraging as could be. We sometimes went out for a meal or drinks after a day's work. But that was all there was to it.' The press claimed that Olivia had actually split up with Lee Kramer, but they were together throughout.

Meanwhile, John occasionally let slip his sexual feelings about other women. He admitted to *Playboy* magazine that he sometimes had fantasies about Jane Fonda. He told them, 'I don't necessarily like to think of Jane Fonda's sex life, but I may like to think of *having sex* with Jane Fonda.'

There was a protective wall surrounding John. His advisers, managers and hangers-on, all of whom believed they knew what was right for him, completely isolated him from the outside world. Their number-one priority was to keep him happy while they were trying to film a musical comedy – it wasn't easy.

The *Grease* production continued smoothly and on schedule into late August 1977. The entire film had to be shot at

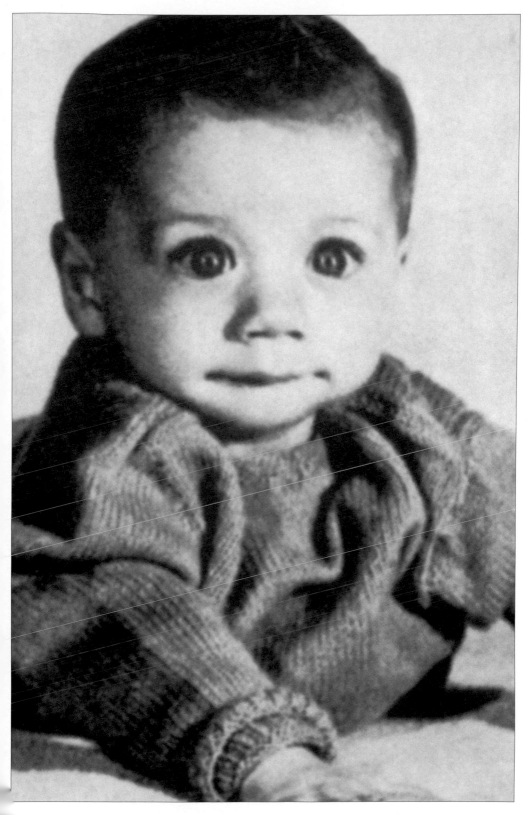

At six months old, baby Travolta already has signs of his famous dimples.

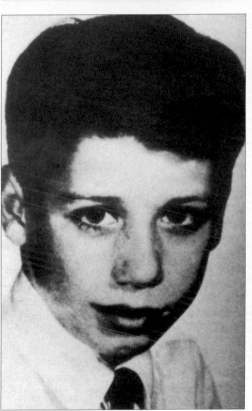

Above left: John's oldest sister, Ellen, always looked out for her younger brother.

Above right: John's childhood home. His family lived in this home in Englewood, New Jersey, for more than forty years.

Below left: At the age of six, John took to the stage as he followed his love of acting.

Below right: At home preparing for a friend's rock 'n' roll birthday party.

Above: While still a teenager, John ventured to Hollywood with his acting career and moved to this apartment block on Crescent Heights, West Hollywood. The same block was later home to director, Quentin Tarantino, and, coincidentally, the pair had a meeting here prior to *Pulp Fiction*.

Below left: John's love for planes and flying has escalated over the years. After his first TV success, he bought this $3,500 Aircoupe single prop plane.

Below right: The supercool superstar poses alongside his '55 T-Bird, another purchase following his early success.

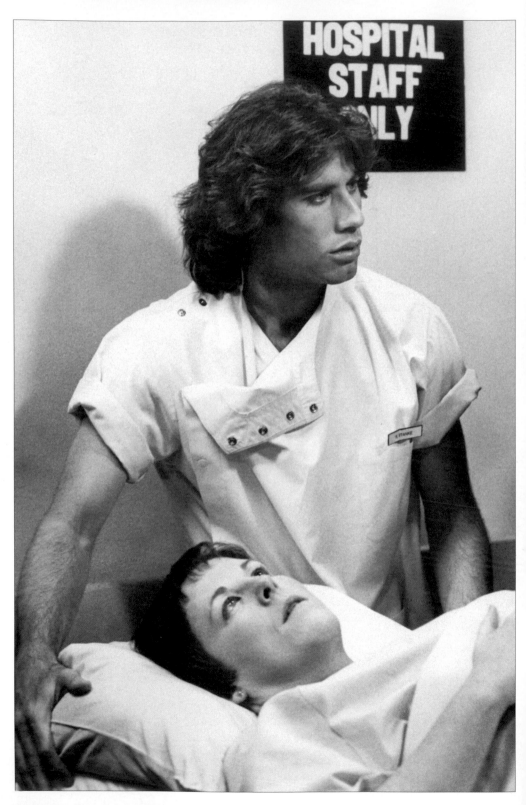

John's big breakthrough came when he landed a starring role in the TV series *Welcome Back, Kotter*.

Above left: John with Diana Hyland in a rare public appearance after her illness was diagnosed.

Above right: On the up … as his career soared, John soon moved to a penthouse apartment in Beverly Hills.

Below left: The suite at the Ingleside Inn where he spent one of the last romantic nights together with Diana.

Below right: The owner of the Ingleside Inn, Mel Harber, helped keep John and Diana's visits to the hotel discreet.

John showing off his now legendary dance moves as Tony Manero in *Saturday Night Fever*.

Above left: Travolta attends the premiere of his film *Saturday Night Fever* with his good friend Kate Edwards.

Above right: Olivia Newton-John landed the sought-after role of Sandra Dee in the hit film, *Grease*, opposite John.

Below: Performing the famous 'Greased Lightnin'' song and dance routine.

Above: John with his proud parents Sam and Helen at one of his glittering film premieres.

Below: In 1980, he starred in *Urban Cowboy* as an unworldly country boy who moved to the big city of Houston.

breakneck speed because John was contractually committed to return for a third season of *Welcome Back Kotter.*

When *Grease* premiered in June 1978, John's fans seemed just as interested in seeing him singing as they had been to see him dancing and acting 'straight' in *Fever.* Even the *Grease* soundtrack album sold at the same pace as the *Fever* record. John's rapidly released solo number 'Sandy' had just as big an impact.

At the vast televised opening night party for *Grease,* John drove up with Olivia in his own classic '55 Thunderbird. He seemed extremely relaxed and happy with life for the first time in more than a year. Out of the giant speakers, Frankie Valli sang, 'Grease is the Word' from the song Bee Gee Barry Gibb had written for the movie.

Grease ended up doing almost as well as *Fever,* taking $150 million worldwide, even though the critics gave the movie a definite thumbs-down while still hailing John's performance.

'His animal magnetism is such that every time he appears on screen as . . . the punk with a heart of gold, it's impossible to watch anyone else,' wrote Robert Martin in the *Toronto Globe and Mail.* The best moments in the film were not dialogue, but shots of Travolta reacting, suddenly becoming macho when he realises the gang is watching him talk to his girlfriend or smothering a giggle after accidentally elbowing Olivia Newton-John in the breast.

Stanley Kaufman commented in the *New Republic,* 'John Travolta ... sings pleasantly, and he does more vivid phallocratic dancing as in *Saturday Night Fever.* He's not really *good,* but that's not his fault – there's no part, just a lot of twaddle. His appeal doesn't yet work head-on, it works sideways, obliquely, through tensions, like Cagney's and Bogart's ... But his power is truly powerful, and he should thrive.'

On the alleged romance front, actress Nancy Allen, the twenty-one-year-old brunette who played John's evil girlfriend in *Carrie,* was linked to him. She was reported as saying that she and John were in love. 'He was terribly lonely after Diana died, and called me from New York to visit him. I flew there, and we fell in love – for the second time.'

Nancy Allen insisted that her affair with John had been kept out of the spotlight because they never went out in public and spent cosy evenings at his apartment instead.

John said absolutely nothing about his supposed affair with Nancy Allen. But, when he was linked with his *Fever* co-star and dancing partner Karen Gorney, a truckload of publicity, including a controversial cover story in *People* magazine, was sparked off. John denied that romance as well.

But Karen was happy to talk about her feelings for 'JT', her nickname for John. 'I did love him; I do love him,' she insisted. 'We dreamed about each other a lot. I just melted every time those icy-diamond eyes of his looked at me. The way it is in the film is the way it is.'

John seemed bemused by Karen's outburst. 'Where do these people get these stories?' was all he could say about his supposed romance with her.

Karen later conceded, 'I guess I blew it by being too shy.'

British actress Kate Edwards remained close to John throughout this period. They went on a skiing vacation together, but there was never a romance between them. She says, 'He was a kind, warm, well-meaning guy, but we simply never dated. It just wasn't that kind of friendship.'

During a trip to London to do some promotion work for *Fever*, John briefly dated beautiful thirty-year-old socialite actress Marisa Berenson, who starred in *Barry Lyndon* and *Cabaret*.

In an uncharacteristic admission, John said, 'She's beautiful. Her face is like a painting. She has a museum quality about her. You just want to look at her for hours.'

Unfortunately, not long after their brief romance, Berenson suffered facial injuries in a car crash and had to undergo extensive plastic surgery. But a brief friendship with a beautiful woman thousands of miles from home was not enough to fill the 'gaping hole' left by Diana Hyland's death. John admitted, 'I'm very alone. But there's a difference between loneliness and alone. I don't feel lonely I just feel alone. This may sound ridiculous, but at twenty-four I've lived a very fulfilled life. I've always been able to achieve many of my goals, but there will always be new goals.'

At the time, John was deeply concerned about the prospect of marriage. He hoped to one day emulate the marriages of friends like Paul Newman and Joanne Woodward. He genuinely believed that fidelity was the key. He had seen how it had worked for his parents, but he didn't think he was ready to handle that kind of responsibility.

He admitted, 'It's hard not to be tempted because you are always being stimulated, working with the most talented, attractive people. But, if you can keep it together, it's very admirable.' Even romance related to work as far as John was concerned.

John was more irritated by the number of people who took advantage of him. Every time he took his cars or planes in for repair he seemed to be charged four times the normal rate just because he was supposedly rich and famous. 'When they see me coming, the price of parts goes up. They're not even subtle about it. They just rip me off overtly.' Such was the price of fame.

Back at his modest $500-a-month apartment on South Doheny Drive, in LA, the walls might have been filled with memorabilia from his recent, highly successful past – posters from *Over Here* and *Grease*, magazine covers – but John was spending most of his time alone. Both Jerry Wurms and *Fever* co-star Donna Pescow had moved into their own places. He needed something more substantial in his life. Christmas was just around the corner so he decided to try and make an effort.

CHAPTER SIXTEEN
HANDLING IT

HUGHES CONVENIENCE STORE, BEVERLY DRIVE, LOS ANGELES, CHRISTMAS EVE 1977

John moved down the aisles of the store as if he was Tony Manero swaggering between the shelves of paint at the hardware store from *Saturday Night Fever*. Word soon got around the store that a star was on the premises. By the time John turned up at the check-out till clutching a small plastic Christmas tree and a basket of goodies, most of the women in the vicinity were gaping open-mouthed at the celebrity in their midst.

A few minutes later, John swung his silver-blue Mercedes 450 SL into the underground parking lot of his high-rise apartment block home just around the corner and headed for the elevator. For the first time in months he felt reasonably upbeat about life. He unlocked the front door to his modest apartment and immediately unpacked all the decorations he had just bought, hanging them on the plastic Christmas tree and around various points in the sitting room.

Later that evening, John's close friends Jerry Wurms and Kate Edwards showed up to swap dinky $2 gifts with John. One of the presents he received was an ornamental pair of tiny dancing shoes, a reminder of his starring role in *Fever*.

John, sprawled on a plush, thick white rug, half under the Christmas tree, laughed. 'Wow. D'you think they'd still fit me?'

The others giggled.

John then jumped up to demonstrate the twists and twirls he had so easily executed on the big screen. It was hard to imagine that just one year earlier John had not had the foggiest idea how to disco dance.

It was inevitable, following such extraordinary success, that John Travolta would become a target for criticism and jealous backbiting. Hollywood itself was split between the old guard who considered him a dumb hunk and the younger studio execs and agents who recognised that he was actually up-to-date and *very* cool in a wide-lapel-and-flares sort of way.

John was sensitive to such unwarranted cruelty and had a very hard time dealing with it. 'I was very vulnerable and open to everyone and I kept feeling the blows whenever anyone did something covert.'

Amongst these 'covert' operations was the circulation of a rumour suggesting that he was extremely hard to work with. A so-called colleague from the *Kotter* series anonymously told one publication, 'John's a very enthusiastic boy with a great, healthy sense of self. Sometimes too healthy. Occasionally, because of his looks or the fact that he got more attention and more fanmail, he would act up and become a bit surly and pompous.'

There was probably a grain of truth in this report because John had come from nowhere in a relatively short period of time. He had his own business manager, agent, publicist, secretary, lawyer, financial adviser and record producer. He was a virtual mini-industry and that also made him an easy target.

Some critics inside Tinseltown claimed that John was a power-crazy character determined to exploit his own fame. He certainly had a reputation. It was said inside Hollywood that the most valuable piece of furniture in his house was his mirror. The truth was (and still is) that John cares about how he comes across to the public. Sometimes people misinterpreted that as vanity.

When interviewed by the *New York Times*, he said to the reporter, 'May I ask you a question? What kind of impression do I give when I'm with you right now?'

'Charming and relaxed,' came the reply.

'Good,' said John. 'I'm relieved you have that impression because I was worried that maybe there was something bad I projected. People always seem to think I'm cocky, and I try so hard not to be. Maybe I should just stop trying.'

During his final days on *Welcome Back Kotter*, some of his co-stars teased him unmercifully about losing his hair. Eventually John began to believe them. Running his fingers through his thick, dark hair, he would ask anyone who happened to be passing, 'Hey, take a look. Am I really losing it?'

When John was interviewed on a TV network news show to promote *Fever*, he was accompanied by manager Bob LeMond and his publicist Michele Cohen, who were allowed to read the introduction to his interview before taping of the show began. They were offended by a certain part of the script which read as follows:

'John Travolta was first seen in the role of Vinnie Barbarino on the television show Welcome Back Kotter. *Now he is being seen for the first time in his new movie,* Saturday Night Fever ... *Even though some of the critics are being less than kind in their appraisal of Travolta's latest effort, Paramount Pictures is counting on the film being a box-office smash. And John, at the ripe old age of twenty-three, seems to be about to set a record for the journey to superstardom.'*

LeMond immediately objected to the reference to the bad reviews, which he felt implied that John himself had received poor notices. That was totally untrue, but the producer of the TV show refused to change it. There followed a dispute about which film clip should be shown to accompany the interview. Eventually, LeMond was so unimpressed that he, British publicist Cohen and star John walked out of the studio. It was an unfortunate incident which further fuelled stories about John being difficult. One columnist even suggested that John believed he could control what the media said about him. Actually, bad press became part and parcel of John's increasing fame.

He didn't exactly help to dampen those rumours when he began insisting on having right of veto over any photographs of himself to be used in magazine and newspaper articles. Hollywood reporters began muttering that John was becoming too wrapped up in maintaining his sex-symbol image and only chose photographers that made him look his best.

The main reason for John's attitude at this time was the fact that he was surrounded by people praising his every move. He was drowning in a sea of advisers who felt it was their job to protect him from virtually every aspect of his life.

During this period John even began comparing himself to other Hollywood legends. In one interview he made a serious point of saying, 'Lots of people tell me I look either like Joe Namath or Warren Beatty. From one angle I look like Beatty and, from the other, Namath. I think my eyes and teeth resemble Beatty's, while my nose and chin are similar to Namath's. And then there are some people who say my eyes are like Paul Newman's.'

When one admirer told John he looked similar to a young John Garfield, the *Fever* star snapped back, 'I've only seen two of Garfield's movies and I didn't really care for them.' To his critics, such comments were further proof of John's excessive egotism.

And John's weight became the easiest way of attacking him. Commentators referred to his 'persistent paunch'. The problem was not helped by him testing out every chocolate-based dessert in any restaurant he happened to be in at the time. John's apparent lack of concern about his personal appearance was reinforced by his habit of appearing in public with several days' stubble on his face. What few people realised was that he actually suffered from a recurring skin rash which was a result of frequent shaving.

John was also accused of cutting himself off from his old friends. But as one of them, Ellen March, pointed out, 'When you're as busy as he is with interviews and films and TV and reading scripts there is just not much time.'

John's incredibly busy schedule had prevented him from making any good friends inside Tinseltown. He also did not share any of the social habits like drug-taking, boozing and womanising which helped one *connect* more easily in LA. In many ways, John was too clean-cut for the Hollywood of the late seventies.

Sometimes it seemed as if he was getting the worst of both worlds. Everywhere he went he was mobbed, yet he certainly wasn't living the glamorous, decadent lifestyle that most Hollywood heroes enjoyed.

On a trip back to Englewood, New Jersey, he visited his brother Joey at a lounge bar where he worked near the family home. 'He said it was one of the best times he'd had in a long time because nobody treated him like a star,' recalled Joey.

Back in Hollywood, John found himself continually turning to his older sister Ellen for a shoulder to cry on. At this time only the other members of the Travolta family realised just how lonely he was.

ACADEMY AWARDS, SANTA MONICA CIVIC AUDITORIUM, LOS ANGELES, APRIL 1978

John was close to losing his cool. It was the Oscars' fiftieth birthday and excitement was at fever pitch. Richard Burton sidled drunkenly up next to John and muttered the immortal words, 'If you take it from me, big boy, I'll bust your beautiful chops.'

Burton was favourite to scoop the Best Actor Award for his

performance in *Equus*. It was generally felt that the Welsh actor merited the coveted gold statuette simply because he had been a candidate seven times in the past and failed on each occasion at the last hurdle.

The contrast with John Travolta could not have been greater. Yet many there that night believed John should have been the favourite for his performance in *Saturday Night Fever*. People were talking about him being the next Marlon Brando, James Dean and Sylvester Stallone all wrapped up in one.

Despite critical acclaim and a wave of Travoltamania across America within days of the release of *Fever*, the esteemed old guard at the Academy of Motion Picture Arts and Sciences displayed absolutely no interest in the movie which they deemed to be a piece of youth-orientated schlock. It was going to be extremely difficult to muster enough votes for John to win an Oscar. According to CBS-TV movie critic David Sheehan, out of the 3,500 members of the Academy who voted for Best Actor, many did not even bother to see eligible movies and performances. A lot of votes were actually cast purely on the basis of loyalty, personal friendships and publicity.

Sheehan insisted, 'I know that certain members voted either for *Fever* as Best Picture or Travolta's performance as Best Actor on the basis of seeing my commentaries on CBS-TV news, along with the clips from the film that were included.' But a lot did not.

When John had been nominated for the Best Actor category a month earlier, he'd been surprised because he knew that the Hollywood old-timers were hardly his most avid fans. But at least there was a dearth of young male actors at the time. The major star closest in age to John was Stallone, but he was already thirty-two. There was a feeling that up-and-coming stars like Richard Gere would eventually give John a run for his money, but they hadn't truly arrived by this stage.

Even the biggest names in attendance that evening demanded introductions to the young star. Jane Fonda walked up and asked him what success felt like. She had read John's earlier confession in *Playboy* magazine that he harboured sexual fantasies about her and she wanted to meet him. There was a definite sparkle between them but neither followed through. Fonda was in any case happily married at the time. But she was so taken by John that she tried to buy his dance suit from *Saturday Night Fever* when it was auctioned the following year. She was eventually out-bid by a movie critic.

Back at the Oscars that evening, dozens of other stars introduced themselves to John. Typically, John had already worked out his stock reply before he even entered the auditorium. 'I view success with less intensity than the people around me. When you get it, it sort of mellows you out.' John was so scared of nervously blurting out something unintelligible he learned that line off by heart hours earlier.

On a serious work level, John believed that his career was about to enter an entirely new phase. 'Now I can do parts that I want and act with other actors I admire,' John told one reporter on Oscar night. He felt he was in the driver's seat and no one was going to remove him.

John was also extremely flattered to find himself competing against the likes of Burton, Woody Allen, Marcello Mastroianni and Richard Dreyfuss for the Best Actor Oscar that night.

Just before the ceremony, John had actually taken the plunge and formed his own company, John Travolta Productions. He immediately signed his company and himself to a two-picture deal with Orion Pictures with a projected fee of $1 million per movie plus a percentage share of the profits. The normally reserved *New York Times* reported the deal as a genuine news item representing it as the bizarre practices of 'new Hollywood'. They wrote, 'The fact that Mr Travolta is able to negotiate million-dollar deals for himself is commentary on the way Hollywood works in 1978. Thirty years ago, Mr Travolta would have been an employee of Paramount. He would have started the second year of a seven-year contract under which the studio – but not he – would have the option every six months of cancelling. If the contract were not cancelled, it would provide him with small rises each year.'

But the opinion of the *New York Times* did not bother John. He was more concerned when he was pipped at the post for the Best Actor Oscar by Richard Dreyfuss. Burton went away a broken man. At least John believed his day would come.

Immediately after the awards ceremony, Paramount announced that they were planning to star John in *The Godfather III* as the grown-up son of Al Pacino and Diane Keaton, and the grandson of Marlon Brando, who starred in the first two parts.

Then *American Gigolo* was mentioned. *Taxi Driver* writer Paul Schrader was to be the director. It was a challenging role for John because he would be playing a lead character who was obsessed by sex. Schrader said that John was his first choice for the film because 'his sexual electricity is a given. With many other actors, you would have to spend half the movie imbuing them with sexual appeal.'

For his part, John was pleased that he was being offered such roles because it meant he was no longer being typecast as just another Vinnie Barbarino in everything he did.

Meanwhile, he was doing everything in his power to end his association with *Welcome Back Kotter*. But the producers of the show were rigidly insisting that he stuck to his three-year contract. John recognised that the show had helped give him amazingly rapid Hollywood credibility so he continued to turn out for the smallest number of programmes possible. It helped ease his guilt and prevented any nasty legal battles from flaring up.

John's three-picture deal with Robert Stigwood had been a gamble which paid off handsomely. The final movie in his contracted trilogy was to be *Moment By Moment*, co-starring Lily Tomlin. While John only received $1 million for all three movies, he knew he would eventually get a windfall, from the profit-share deals that he signed in relation to the sales of the movies and records. But that would take years to materialise.

Meanwhile, John was telling people that his $1 million basic salary was not a lot of money, all things considered.

'Don't get me wrong,' he told one associate on Oscar night. 'But, man, that's for three films! That's a whole lot of time and work. I spent six months on the dancing for *Fever* alone. A third of a million is not much compared to what some stars are getting per picture and, like they say, you have to strike while the iron's hot.'

On the movie front, no one was particularly surprised when John turned down a $2 million fee to star in *Summer School*, the planned sequel to *Grease*.

Moment By Moment with Lily Tomlin was released at Christmas 1978. John played the role of a younger man falling in love with an older woman. And, not surprisingly, the critics and his adoring public immediately assumed that much of his performance was based on his real-life experiences with Diana Hyland.

John was actually so sensitive about being accused of cashing in on his relationship with Diana that he insisted Paramount did not refer to the younger man/older woman aspect of the movie in any promotional material. As a result, the ads publicising the movie said only: '*Moment By Moment* – a romance where every second counts.'

Back in the real world, John's family continued to be concerned about the young star's personal life – or rather lack of it. His brother Joey told one writer, 'My kid brother is very lonely. He's gone from sixteen to superstardom at the age of twenty-four and it's hurt. He's always around people who want to talk about his career, and not about other things in his life. When you're in a situation like that you're divorced from people, because you're afraid to go out in public. There's a barrier there, and it's very lonely. It's the price you pay.'

Diana Hyland's spirit was still very much alive as far as John was concerned. When she was posthumously awarded an Emmy for her performance in *Eight is Enough*, John accompanied her parents to the ceremony and accepted the award with them. John even walked on to the stage to say 'thank you' on behalf of the woman he had loved above all others. He paused a moment before speaking, holding the Emmy aloft. Instead of saying, 'Thank you,' he shouted, 'Here's to you, Diana, wherever you are.' It was his way of showing gratitude for her love and for what she had done for him.

By the time John celebrated his twenty-fifth birthday in February 1979, he had become the biggest star in the world. He even told *Time* magazine rather arrogantly, 'My theory is that, if you have millions of fans right now, you'll keep at least ten per cent of them for all time. There's really no need to cool off.'

And John's vast army of fans was becoming legendary. While the women continued to swoon, the men aped his walk and his style. Clothing manufacturers couldn't keep pace with orders for *Saturday Night Fever* lookalike white suits. In Britain, there was even a monthly magazine exclusively devoted to stories and pictures of John Travolta. Meanwhile, John kept close to his family and also, touchingly, remained in contact with Diana Hyland's parents, Ted and Mary Gentner, as well as Diana's son Zachary, who had moved back in with his father. In July 1978, John wanted to help Zachary celebrate his sixth birthday by inviting him to a specially organised party at his rented house by the beach in Malibu. Diana's ex-husband Joe Goodson appreciated the offer, but managed to persuade John to have the party at their family home instead.

Privately, John wished that Diana's bedside will had been valid because he would have loved to bring up Zachary himself. In some ways he preferred the idea of being a father to trying to sustain a 'friendly uncle' relationship. Zachary was his secret 'adopted son' in many ways. John felt a responsibility for the boy and has continued to encourage and support him ever since. He still regularly sees Zachary who is now in his twenties.

'It's a relationship that has been kept completely out of the public eye. John adores Zach and vice versa. They are friends for life,' explains a friend.

John's own parents were naturally proud of his achievements. But, because they had been such elderly parents in the first place, they both felt saddened in some ways. Sam Travolta explained, 'I wish all this could have happened earlier, when I was a younger man, so I could look forward to enjoying Johnny's success longer.'

The biggest-selling single of 1978 was 'You're The One That I Want' by John Travolta and Olivia Newton-John. That year, three popes were elected at the Vatican, but only one survived. Rock star Bob Geldof of the Boomtown Rats ripped up an Olivia and John poster on the British TV show *Top of the Pops* when his band finally knocked 'Summer Nights' off the number-one chart spot. But none of this mattered to John. He had other things on his mind as the year came to a close.

CHAPTER SEVENTEEN
MOMMY DEAREST

LOS ANGELES, WINTER 1978/79

At the Oscars earlier that year, Helen Travolta had found sitting through the five-hour award gala excruciating. John, alert to his mother's pain, spent hours during the ceremony massaging her numb knees in front of the 3,000 guests, grinning all the time for the cameras. He tried to persuade Helen to leave the auditorium and was prepared to go with her; but nothing would induce her to abandon what she hoped would be John's victory.

Nobody at that awards ceremony, not even John himself, realised that Helen was seriously ill, although a lot of people had noticed how frail she had become over the previous few months considering she was still only in her mid-sixties.

The Travolta family had chosen to protect John and not tell him that she had contracted cancer. Helen had been so ill when John took her to Paris for the European première of *Saturday Night Fever* that she'd had to be flown back home to New Jersey. But the family insisted to John that it had just been caused by the strain of travelling.

Towards the end of November 1978, her condition worsened and the family were forced to tell John the truth. He immediately organised special healthcare for Helen in LA.

His mother had always been his most valued critic. And she had undoubtedly been the primary driving force behind his remarkable rise to stardom. John saw Helen as the source of the spark, the charisma and the fire that illuminated his work.

Helen, just sixty-six years old, was rushed to Cedars-Sinai Hospital, in Los Angeles, after a relapse, and died peacefully in her sleep in early December 1978. John was once more left feeling extremely vulnerable.

Helen's death had a profound effect on her youngest son; he lost all his love of life, which he had so successfully projected in his movies. In fact, Helen's death was such a blow, coming so soon after Diana's, that John couldn't perform to the best of his abilities in the next few movies he was to star in.

He consoled himself with the thought that at least Helen had been with him at the Oscars that year. (She sportingly told one reporter that she was in some ways glad that her son did not win: 'If he'd done it then he wouldn't have had anything to look forward to.')

John made sure Helen's funeral was a dignified affair by not revealing his mother's death to the press until after the burial had taken place. A few days later, at a news conference to help publicise his latest movie *Moment By Moment*, John and co-star Lily Tomlin almost walked out because he was unsure if he could cope with any questions about his mother's death. Eventually he agreed only to answer some very basic questions about the film itself.

Later, John revealed his true feelings about the tragedy. 'I had a real dichotomy in which I had great success and at the same time great sorrow and tragedy. A lot of people got frustrated when my grief and tragedy got publicised. They were saying, "Because you're famous, suddenly your loss is more important than our loss."'

John's mother had been particularly compassionate to her son when Diana Hyland died but never mentioned that she herself had been secretly suffering from cancer for years.

Close friend and one-time *Welcome Back Kotter* co-star Marcia Strassman says, 'Helen wanted John to be such a success. I am sure that was a problem with John for a long time, but he adored her. And when *Saturday Night Fever* happened, it was like Helen took a deep breath and said, "OK, I can die happy. I've seen him get what he deserves."'

Helen Travolta had always been John's guiding light. Even after he moved to California, she would call him to make sure he was getting enough sleep; call him to see if he was eating his vegetables; and initially even to make sure he was wearing a warm sweater, until John gently pointed out that cold weather was not a regular occurrence in Los Angeles.

After his mother's death, John fell into a period of deep depression and, despite months of preparation that included French coaching and etiquette lessons, he seriously considered withdrawing from his next scheduled movie, *American Gigolo*.

John called up Michael Eisner, at the time President of Paramount, and begged him to let him pull out of *American Gigolo*.

'Look, my mom's just died. I'm not very happy about that and I'm not very happy about *Moment by Moment*. I beg you to let me out of *American Gigolo*,' John told the studio chief.

'You're out,' came the reply.

But next day, Eisner called up John with a suggestion to compensate for his decision to pull out of *Gigolo*.

'How about you owe us one movie and you give us another one?'

'That's cool.'

And that was how John got saddled with *Urban Cowboy* and later *Staying Alive*.

Just six months after Helen Travolta's death, John's father Sam remarried, amid some initial friction from all his children. John was confused by the speed with which his father had decided to find a new wife, but his public reaction was a selfless one: 'I just absolutely want him to be happy,' he told *Rolling Stone* shortly after the surprise wedding.

The new Mrs Travolta turned out to be a youthful-looking 55-year-old called June who had been Helen Travolta's nurse during the final few months of her life. The children were surprised, but as time passed they started to understand why their father had married again.

John publicly said, 'June is a very nice lady. I knew for a couple of months they were thinking about it.' And he repeated, 'I just want my dad to be happy.'

Sam and June moved into a comfortable house in Los Angeles which was bought for them by John.

On Thanksgiving Day 1979, less than a year after Helen's death, John and the rest of the Travolta clan attended a special luncheon at Sam and June's home. By this time, John had even managed to get Sam Jnr – the only one of his siblings not in showbusiness – a job at Paramount Studios in the special-effects department.

There were rumours at the time that John had fallen out with his brother Joey whose style and mannerisms so greatly resembled John's. But Sam Travolta insisted, 'It's not true. When Joey got married recently, John paid the whole family's way out to New York for the wedding and put us up in hotels. Johnny would go all-out for any member of the family and vice versa.'

Whether or not there was a rift, Joey certainly continued to feel in his brother's shadow.

In October 1978, John was invited to dinner at the White House by then President Jimmy Carter. Apparently the Carters' youngest daughter Amy was a keen fan. John flew his own DC-3 up to Washington. En route he even found time to stop in Natchez, Missouri, to say hello to Muhammad Ali, on location for *Freedom Road*, a four-hour NBC special in which Ali starred as slave-to-senator Gideon Jackson. Naturally, there was much talk – all of it completely unsubstantiated – that John and Ali would be teaming up on the big screen at some time in the future.

If there was any doubt that John had truly arrived as a star it was erased when he became the latest in a long line of American celebrities to be attacked by East Germany's Communist Government as an insidious influence on youth. 'Travolta tries to make capitalistic daily life seem harmless,' claimed the Government-run youth newspaper, *Junge Welt*. In West Germany, it was claimed that the anti-Travolta barbs were 'obviously aimed at dampening Travolta's rising popularity behind the Iron Curtain'.

John was then discussed in connection with the leading role in a screen adaptation of Anne Rice's *Interview With The Vampire*. The movie did not actually materialise until sixteen years later, with Tom Cruise in the role that John had briefly been considered for.

John remained very sensitive about his looks and demanded that only certain people should be permitted to take his photograph to accompany press articles.

Meanwhile, *Moment By Moment*'s monumental failure at the box office provoked some movie critics to predict that John was finished in motion pictures. Certainly, he was on a downward spiral for the first time in his career. He was just about handling his personal tragedies, but, when his work seemed to die in front of his eyes, it seemed as if everything was falling apart.

Some, like critic Rex Reed, tried in vain to defend *Moment By Moment*, by saying, 'It is not a great film, but it's too modest to be demolished with the kind of hysterical venom it's been getting. To make so much out of so little, well it's like using a bazooka to blow up a butterfly.'

Deeply upset by the reaction to *Moment By Moment*, John hid himself away from the Hollywood mainstream and told his agents he did not want to read a screenplay or consider any offers of work for the foreseeable future. There were even claims that John had quit the movie industry for good and was about to retire at the grand old age of twenty-six.

As if to give credence to the rumours, John paid $1.5 million for an isolated ranch near Santa Barbara, almost 100 miles north of Los Angeles. He locked the gates behind him and decided to have a long, hard think about life.

RANCHO TAJIGUAS, SANTA BARBARA, SPRING 1978

Hollywood lay nearly 100 miles to the south; further up the coast loomed San Simeon, where William Randolph Hearst and Marion Davies threw their legendary movie parties. Nestled in a canyon just above this picturesque coastal resort was John Travolta's own Spanish-style Xanadu, set amongst seventeen acres of paradisiacal real estate, dotted with lemon groves and avocado trees. Bougainvillaea draped the garage where a Jaguar XJ12 stood parked at an angle. A fountain gurgled in the courtyard which led down to a swimming pool and a murky pond full of carp.

One section of the five-bedroomed property was one of the oldest dwellings in California, having been built by a Spanish nobleman in 1800. Unfortunately a rash of break-ins at the house meant that the place had to be guarded twenty-four hours a day by a private security force. But, with two guesthouses on the property, John liked to think he could invite friends up for the weekend. His guests were a bizarre mixture, including Muhammad Ali and Jane Fonda's then husband Tom Hayden. Visitors were encouraged to play tennis, watch movies in the private screening room and swim in John's pool.

John insisted that he only bought the vast property because 'I was looking to get a place where I could keep a small plane right on the premises.' However, in the end, he settled for a tiny airport fourteen miles away because he couldn't build a long enough landing strip.

But on this particular day, in the winter of 1978, John was all alone at the house. His quiet seclusion was broken only by the chattering gulls winging inland from the nearby Pacific Ocean.

Lounging beside the pool was a sad-eyed and bearded John Travolta. He had never once swum in the pool because he'd hated swimming ever since he'd broken his nose diving into a pool when he was a kid.

John had been reading much of that day, breaking off only occasionally to wander down through the orange groves to talk to the young men and women cultivating the fields of a nearby Brotherhood of Sun commune in the adjoining farm. He looked exactly as he felt – a tired, overworked, emotionally drained movie star nursing the wounds he'd suffered from the loss of the two women who meant most to him.

John took a puff on the first cigar of the day. It was a newly acquired habit, but he found it calmed his nerves. Nearby, a Mexican servant lit the standing candelabras as the sun set low over the nearby Pacific Ocean and cast a warm, orange glow over the house. Over the mantelpiece hung a colourful portrait of John painted by artist Paul Jasmin and given to the young star by *Saturday Night Fever* producer Robert Stigwood.

John stayed two whole days and nights alone at the house, smoking cigars and watching movies. He even spent an entire day just watching Bertolucci's 1900. His own company seemed preferable to anyone else's. He hadn't even taken the time to shave for more than a week and he rather liked the thick, bushy beard that had sprung up as a result. He'd eat by himself, wander up to his private screening room and do what the hell he wanted.

Being alone seemed the only release from his depression. The trauma of those two deaths had been followed by his father suffering a near-fatal heart attack. *Moment By Moment* had been universally slated. Nervous exhaustion had driven him into a corner of anxiety from which there seemed no escape. He was trying to escape the flack, but everywhere he looked there was someone rubbing yet more salt into his wounds.

Just as the decade that had been John Travolta's was drawing to an end, the fairy tale of untold wealth and absolute acceptance ended, too. Everywhere, it seemed, there were reminders of his situation.

WITHIN ONLY A YEAR OF HIS GREATEST SUCCESS IN *SATURDAY NIGHT FEVER*, THE WORD FROM HOLLYWOOD WAS THAT JOHN TRAVOLTA WAS FINISHED, ran the headline in one magazine.

The article continued, 'Rumours abounded that he'd become a hermit, was seriously ill and would never act again …' And so it went on. The only semi-truthful part was that he had become a hermit, albeit a temporary one.

Other headlines like WHAT HAPPENED TO JOHN TRAVOLTA? simply intensified John's confusion and depression.

He stayed in exile until August 1979, when he agreed to play the lead in *Urban Cowboy*. It was a brave move because he knew the whole world had virtually written him off. But it really was a case of now or never.

John was to play a young Houston chemical worker who spends all his nights at a bar, 'the largest honky-tonk in the world'. By day he is an ordinary enough figure, but at night he lives out a cowboy fantasy, complete with Levis, Stetson hat and even an electronic bucking bronco. The story detailed his battle with a real cowboy who steals his wife (played by Debra Winger) and then built to a climax centred around the bronco machine.

In many ways, John saw himself as a modern-day Howard Hughes, isolated from the real world but fascinating to millions. In an ostentatious display seldom equalled since Hughes' heyday, John travelled to his first day on the *Urban Cowboy* location in Houston, Texas, in a magnificently appointed club railway carriage once owned by Hughes himself. The private section of the train featured two bedrooms, its own kitchen, dining room and saloon.

Within days of starting the movie in Houston, press stories began emerging about John's unpredictable behaviour. Even his time-consuming efforts to perfect the Western swing dance steps for *Urban Cowboy* were ludicrously blamed for the movie's budget rocketing to more than $11 million.

Others claimed that John created an atmosphere on the set reminiscent of the Nixon White House, surrounding himself with a loyal palace guard who protected him from all enemies, including a hostile press. He even informed the movie's producer Robert Evans that he didn't want a single journalist on the set.

Everyone, including *Urban Cowboy*'s director James Bridges, was forced to acquiesce to John's gagging order. Bridges even cancelled a dinner party when he heard that one of the guests was planning to bring along a reporter friend.

More than 600 extras used in the dance scenes inside the honky-tonk saloon, which played a central role in the movie, were told they would lose their jobs if they approached John on the set or talked to journalists.

Co-star Scott Glenn summed it up when he explained, 'I've never seen a location where they won't allow you to talk to the press. The film's publicist walks around feeling as useless as tits on a bull.'

John behaved in an erratic manner. He could be co-operative or recalcitrant, generous or selfish, trusting or paranoid. He certainly liked to have his fragile ego soothed by certain members of his inner circle.

When old friend Marilu Henner visited the set in Texas to try and keep John's spirits up, she insisted to newsmen that he was in mint *Saturday Night Fever* condition. Henner tried to make John laugh and even helped defend him from the hordes of onlookers who seemed to watch his every move.

But, despite the brief support of Marilu Henner, things went from bad to worse on *Urban Cowboy*. Reports reaching Hollywood suggested that there were arguments on the set and that veteran producer Robert Evans had threatened to close down the production permanently.

Evans later insisted the difficulties had nothing to do with John's temperament. However he did concede, 'I don't know what his personal problems are, but he is scared to death. Not only of the press but of anything that might make him look ridiculous.'

The conflict between John and Hollywood maverick Evans revolved around the big black beard which John had grown in the months before he started shooting *Cowboy*. Evans ordered his star performer to shave it off, but John and his manager Bob LeMond refused.

In one classic outburst, the producer exclaimed, 'I'm making one Travolta picture in my career and I want him without the beard.'

John had originally kept the beard after his English setter dog took a chunk out of his upper lip back at his ranch in Santa Barbara. The dog bit him on the upper lip in front of friends, covering his face with blood and terrifying his guests. It took ten stitches to close the wound and the dog was shown the door. The attack left a small scar which John and his manager LeMond were afraid would show.

But battle-weary producer Evans told John, 'You're not leaving the beard on.'

John replied tersely, 'I'm leaving it on.'

Evans: 'I'll close the picture down then.'

The two men then stormed off the set in opposite directions. Evans went straight to Paramount and pleaded, 'Don't let Travolta do this picture if he wears a beard.'

The row only subsided when the movie script was rewritten so that John got to wear his beloved beard for the first ten minutes of the film and then shaved it off on-camera as part of the film's plot.

Evans still firmly believes that John's management were overprotecting their client.

'That's ridiculous,' retorts John. 'I don't think I'm overprotected at all. I know what's going on, and it's exactly the way I want it.'

Another indication of John's insecurity was his insistence that all his dance numbers in *Urban Cowboy* be videotaped. Instant video replays in his trailer reassured him that he wouldn't look ridiculous on film. The cameraman called in to tape John's dance sequences confirmed this by explaining, 'He fears that he is going to be made to look like a jerk.'

The underlying cause of the flare-ups between Robert Evans and John seems to have been John's loneliness. At one stage he got so miserable in Houston, Texas, that he flew Diana Hyland's son Zachary out for a weekend. He ended up taking Zach with him on to the set of *Cowboy*, out to restaurants and on a shopping spree to the local toy store.

John was living in a $10,000-a-month rented mansion in Houston's most fashionable area. Sometimes he even managed to wander out into the local shopping malls. The clerk at Weingarten's grocery store was astounded when John – complete with Stetson – marched in, grabbed twenty hot dogs, yoghurt and at least half a dozen cartons of Haagen-Daz ice cream. When he visited the nearby Tokyo Gardens restaurant, the manager photocopied his credit card and framed the result.

While on location in Texas, John splashed out more than $300,000 for a Cessna 414, a plush, cabin-style plane that seated six to eight people. He immediately took flight instructions in order to qualify to pilot the twin-engined plane. This included twenty-one days of training with American Airlines. He flew the Cessna most weekends.

Educationally, John was well aware that he had missed out badly by leaving school at sixteen and that was why he threw himself so wholeheartedly into his flying. When he got that commercial jet pilot's licence, it was the first time in his life that he became an 'A' student. At times, it seemed as if flying was his only real escape.

CHAPTER EIGHTEEN
EL TORO

GILLEY'S HONKY-TONK SALOON, PASADENA, TEXAS, SUMMER 1980

A mechanical bull sat defiantly in one corner of the vast bar on a three-acre site. It was a prime-for-brawling type of place nestled in the dingy heart of a busy, sun-drenched town on the edge of the Texan desert. The bull, a rock-hard hunk of bucking and swivelling hydraulic might, had been devised to toughen the timing of rodeo bull riders. But on this particular evening John Travolta was about to cool off his shit-kicking instincts by hopping aboard.

That afternoon's shooting schedule for *Urban Cowboy* concerned the movie's climactic bull-riding contest wherein Bud Davis (Travolta) challenges arch rival Wes Hightower (Scott Glenn), a sinewy ex-con with 'real cowboy' rodeo credentials, who has diverted the attentions of Bud's rambunctious bride, Sissy (Debra Winger).

The club's noisy air-conditioning system had been cut off to avoid interfering with the movie's sound technicians, and the sweltering environs had been suffused with musty artificial smoke. To make matters worse, today's ration of beer was

Gilley's own, not the far superior long-necked Lone Star variety the hundreds of extras had previously been served.

John loomed spookily on the sidelines, waiting for the sign to walk on to the set. The place was jammed right to the feed troughs with 7,000 Houstonians there for the free beer and a glimpse of John Travolta. Bodyguards stood next to the star as he made his move, parting the crowd with muscle and nasty repartee. The barrier around the stage-front VIP section protected Princess Diane Von Furstenburg and Andy Warhol and a falling-out-of-blouse bit-part actress called Jerry Hall modelling her favourite New York-to-Texas chic.

An informal posse of locals started baiting John and cracking clumsy wisecracks about the old 'Texas ways'. John ignored them, then someone in the crowd yelled out something about John being scared shitless of flying. The place was maybe thirty seconds from a serious chain-reaction punch-out. John turned and smiled gently and murmured, 'Lies, lies' at the flying accusations. No one in the crew dared say a word. Is he pissed off? Will he do an about-turn and storm off the set until it is cleared? John did nothing of the sort. He sauntered into the middle of the dance area, mounted the saddle and turned to the director. 'Let's go for it, James.'

El Toro came alive. John knew to push down whenever the bull's head was down. (Actually there was no head but an X had been painted where a rcal bull's head would be and so John concentrated on that.) The bull reared so John reared back. When the bull went into a spin -they call it 'going into the well' – John pushed his lithe body against the centrifugal force. In and over ... in and over.

John's main priority was not to let his free hand move forward over his head or he would lose his balance and go crashing to the hard sawdust floor. By this time, John was riding El Toro at full pelt. He was so adept at it that he could anticipate the bull's moves. He knew the precise half-second before each new manoeuvre.

On the dance floor, dozens of women watched his every gyration with bated breath. Their eyes seemed to follow the contours of his body as it twisted and turned astride the mechanical monster.

As one Gilley's bartender noted, 'I don't know anything about making movies but that boy has been out there working like mad all day long. The sweat just pours off him. When I first heard he was gonna play the part, I thought, Shoot, man, there's just no way he's gonna be able to play a shit-kicker. Now I'm not so sure. He seems to want to do good at this really bad.'

Shooting in Pasadena lasted more than six weeks and John was mightily relieved when it was time to return to LA. But a lot more problems were on the horizon.

TRAILER PARK, SAN GABRIEL VALLEY, NEAR LOS ANGELES, AUGUST 1980

The six men crawled over the embankment and headed towards a good vantage point overlooking the crowded film-set location in the heart of LA County. Three of them were carrying sawn-off shotguns and pistols. They were all wearing the colours of one of LA's most notorious street gangs.

Two minutes later – as the film crew hurriedly set up for another take before the sun went down – a shot rang out. The bullet ricocheted off a tin drum just twenty yards from where John Travolta was standing.

Across the trailer park, the six Hispanics – all members of the Pico Viejos – laughed hysterically as they watched the looks of fear on everyone's faces.

John went china white and dived for cover in case more shots followed. As soon as three security guards started running towards them, the gangsters retreated back over the embankment. No arrests were made and the gangsters managed to dodge six black and whites, a law-enforcement chopper and the security guards to escape into the nearby maze of low-rent housing and alleyways.

An assistant director went to help John to his feet. He pleaded, 'Let's go for it one more time before we lose the light, please, John.'

John looked appalled and started shaking his head. 'No. No. No. I cannot do this scene.'

'Come on, John,' begged the crew member.

'I cannot work under these conditions of stress and fear.'

'Get Bob on the phone now,' someone barked at an underling.

Ten minutes later, not even the persuasive powers of Hollywood player Robert Evans could get John to return to the *Urban Cowboy* set. John was convinced that the armed street gang who had gained access to the set had deliberately fired that shot at him. He walked off the set and stayed inside his trailer, refusing to talk to anyone.

After much discussion through the night, it was agreed that *Urban Cowboy* should be brought back to the security of the Paramount lot 'for the sake of John's personal safety'.

Once again, Marilu Henner – the only lady to have consistently stayed by John's side throughout his adult life – came to the rescue. She managed to persuade him to get back to work.

John had become increasingly dependent on Henner whenever a personal crisis erupted. Often, on the Paramount set of *Urban Cowboy*, he would break his self-imposed isolation by joining Henner and her colleagues from the *Taxi* comedy series for a lively lunch on the studio lot. On *Urban Cowboy*, John put his boot down and refused to allow cowboy clothes, jeans, hats and just about everything else featured on the film to be commercially endorsed. He was particularly appalled when a linen company tried to persuade him to allow his likeness to be reproduced on bed sheets.

One of the few friendships that John did make at this time was a surprising alliance with his boyhood hero James Cagney. The veteran Hollywood star and his wife visited John's ranch in Santa Barbara one weekend and ended up spending two days longer than planned. Cagney told John, 'It was four of the nicest days of my life.'

John later painted a vivid picture to close friends of how he and the eighty-year-old legend traded acolyte stories about Hollywood. They also screened each other's movies and sat up past midnight while Cagney taught his young heir how to do the gimp walk from *Love Me or Leave Me* or the walk up the wall in *Yankee Doodle Dandy.*

John even confessed to Cagney, 'Sometimes I can't cope with the pressure of the public, the studio, the press. How did you do it?'

'Let me tell you, son, vaudeville was so cut-throat that after that the films were a piece of cake.'

Then he went on, 'Start with one thing: they need you. Without you, they have an empty screen. So, when you get on there, just do what you think is right and stay with it. If you listen to all the clowns around, you're just dead.'

A few minutes later, Cagney curiously signed John's visitors' book, 'For Johnnio, Young Love.'

Some time later, John visited the Cagney farm in Stanfordville, New York, and swapped yet more anecdotes about life in Tinseltown.

And when the two actors posed for photographs for a magazine their conversation hinted at the depth of their friendship and the almost fatherly role Cagney was playing in John's life at the time.

'This way, buttercup. Now smile,' John urged the elderly Cagney. Then John turned to the photographer. 'My hair keeps getting in my eyes.'

'Then get rid of it,' snapped hard man Cagney.

The two men also discussed a script about the veteran star's early life. Cagney felt that John would be ideal to play him as a tough, streetsmart kid.

Besides the house in Santa Barbara, John also purchased a *pied à terre* in Studio City, near Hollywood. He often invited Diana Hyland's son Zachary up to that house where he adored playing pool with his adopted 'son'. He also bought him skis and took the boy up to the nearby Big Bear Mountain winter resort.

John found time to fly his new Cessna aircraft to Lake Tahoe to ski with two of his sisters and Marilu Henner. And he took great care to explain to each of his passengers how everything on board worked. 'Once I had a dentist who always prepared you for every step of the way,' recalled Marilu. 'Johnny's like that in a plane. He'll tell you gently, "Now, as I lower this thing here, you may feel your ears pop a little … As we gain altitude, there could be some turbulence." So there's no anxiety, no surprises. He's truly a great pilot. When I'm with him in the plane, a calm comes over me that I feel nowhere else.'

Also on the social front, old friends like Jerry Wurms and Kate Edwards continued to hang out with John. Kate summed up the group's Hollywood status when she said, 'We were probably the straightest group in Hollywood. In fact, we were so downright boring. None of us was into drugs or booze, and no one in our crowd even smoked cigarettes. Oh, we might drink one bottle of wine at dinner, but that was about as far as it went.'

Despite all the on-set difficulties, *Urban Cowboy* proved a good move for John and the critics hailed it as a comeback film.

'It is a powerfully dramatic performance. Travolta ingratiatingly captures the shyness, bravado, pain and compassion of his blue-collar character,' enthused *People* magazine.

John was especially delighted that the people who really mattered – his fans – also seemed pleased to have their hero back in the limelight. He certainly didn't disappoint them in *Cowboy*; he played the role to the hilt, wearing a black Stetson and a Western suit with flowered leather vest when he turned up for the movie's première in Houston, Texas. But, behind the scenes, John was as demanding as ever. He insisted that every *Urban Cowboy* poster showing his rather chunky thighs had to be retouched before being plastered around the bus-stops and railway stations of America.

Back in the real world, John decided to see if he could now move around in public without the chaotic scenes that had accompanied his every move during the peak of *Fever* mania. One Sunday at his home in Studio City he went down to his local deli to spend a quiet morning reading the papers. In no time, a mob of autograph hunters gathered and he had to flee. John then tried shopping in a nearby mall. Same result. He didn't know whether to laugh or cry. On the one hand, it reassured him that he was back in the Hollywood frame. On the other hand, he seemed doomed to this sort of harassment for the rest of his professional life.

Then the incidents started to get much more serious. Strangers would regularly pick fights. On one occasion, a reporter from *Rolling Stone* smashed the window of his car when the two men had an argument during an interview. Another ugly situation occurred when a chauffeur hit an overeager fan for trying to board John's limo as it was driving along a busy Hollywood street.

John once again started to take precautions. A burly ex-cop was hired to live in a cabin on his Studio City property after a magazine article published his full address and ten trespassers were found in the grounds of the house. One girl even got inside the property, hiding in John's bedroom closet. Fortunately, all the incidents occurred while John was filming *Urban Cowboy* in Houston.

However, John was so concerned that he took advice and began carrying a loaded .38. From that period onwards he has rarely been without the weapon and even gets special permission to carry it from state to state when travelling around the US.

But all this renewed fame did have some encouraging side-effects. Directors Francis Ford Coppola and Milos Forman both expressed a desire to make a musical with John, and John's production company was once again swamped with scripts for him to consider. During one crazy week, 300 of them were delivered to the company's Beverly Hills office. John commented at the time, 'When I get depressed, I should just look at that list of names. If I could do a movie with each one of them – what a career, no matter how the project turned out.'

John still had a few personal problems to work out, though. While he was undoubtedly happiest and healthiest when working, the insanely inflated pressure of success and failure in

Hollywood had slowed his output to a film every two years and he just couldn't cope with the lonely, insecure gaps between shooting. His performances thrived on his observation of people, but his ever-increasing isolation was cutting him off from the source of his craft.

He was also becoming increasingly eccentric. He was regularly talking to the spirits of his mother and Diana Hyland. John was convinced that when they had died they had gone on to other bodies. He told one friend at the time that he himself was also a reincarnation. 'I have a feeling of having done this before; I've been an actor before. I don't know where or when.'

Sometimes at his house, he held seances with a few chosen friends and relatives to try and contact Diana and his mother. John genuinely believed that these seances put him in touch with these loved ones.

He went on, 'I don't believe a spirit is capable of dying. It's the only thing that saves me from total disillusionment in life. It's made me want to keep going because, if I didn't believe that, I don't know how much I could deal with the set-up of business, this life. I just don't know.'

John continues to speak to his dear departed mother and lover on a regular basis to this day and he constantly dreams about them. 'A night never goes by when there isn't one of them in some part of a dream,' he says earnestly.

One night, John dreamed that the Travolta family were in Chicago and he and his sister Margaret were in the back of a car talking and having a great time and their mother was there. The dream was so vivid that when John woke the next morning he actually believed his mother had been reincarnated.

'It was such a disappointment, almost like it's all been reversed. It was as if my realities are dreams and my deepest dreams aren't yet realities.'

The reality of John's situation was that he was once again being hailed as the King of Hollywood, but his life felt completely and utterly unfulfilled.

CHAPTER NINETEEN
HIGHER GROUND

COLUMBIA UNIVERSITY, NEW YORK, OCTOBER 1980

John strode purposefully across the darkened campus virtually unnoticed by the hundreds of students leaving their classes for the day. He headed for the Arts College building and then on through the double doors and down a noisy corridor, still unnoticed. However, when he entered a room of fifteen graduate students studying to be screenwriters, a rush of astonishment swept through the place. John looked at the students and smiled, 'Good evening.'

Within minutes, he was mesmerising the men and women in his tiny audience with his views on acting and screenwriting. 'Let your imagination run wild, let your imagination go, don't be afraid to write,' he told the class. 'I'm not afraid to take the chances as an actor. I'm willing to try different parts. I want to.'

John then revealed to his class of students that he intended to try and regularly teach the art of movie writing and help encourage the students to come up with ideas they could then sell on to Hollywood. What he did not tell them was that his visit to Columbia was also a very personal tribute to his mother, who had attended the university in the thirties and told her beloved son that it had fuelled her love of the performing arts.

After that initial appearance, David Werner, the co-chairman of Columbia's film programme, explained, 'Travolta is in a position to help students, because of his superstar status and his close friendship with some of the biggest names in Hollywood. Travolta will keep in touch with the students and if he can't find the time he will get his manager or agents to read the scripts of the students.'

In 1981, John was reunited with *Carrie* director Brian de Palma and actress Nancy Allen. This time, he was playing a movie soundman who unwittingly records a murder in *Blow Out*. It was a complete departure from the traditional Travolta picture. John scuffed up his look and forewent the star-turn to play a character who was always in need of a haircut, while his clothes – jeans, a rumpled corduroy jacket and a beaten-up parka – were little more than an afterthought.

When he was filming *Blow Out*, John did not report to the set until 11 am. He insisted this was because he rarely got to sleep before 4 am. John actually feared that he had become an insomniac, 'but then I realised that it was just a question of my not getting tired until around 4 am' John's sleeping problems actually stemmed from the many nights he spent as a child waiting up late for his mother to return from her theatrical productions in local schools. Then when he was shooting *Saturday Night Fever* he rarely got more than two or three hours' sleep a night because he had to be on the set so early each morning. Because he was now a star he believed he could 'persuade' directors not to start shooting early. But some of them were not happy about this because movie shoots usually have to begin early to make maximum use of available daylight.

To calm John's nerves and provide him with a diversion at this time, he started learning the violin. He took lessons every other day and would proudly burst into his own versions of 'Sunny Side of the Street' and 'Ain't Misbehavin'' at the drop of a hat.

Although praised by some critics like Roger Ebert as 'a movie that is inhabited by real cinematic intelligence', *Blow Out* did not perform well at the box office. However, it has recently been revived, thanks to the praise showered on it by *Pulp Fiction* director Quentin Tarantino, who rates it as one of his favourite movies of all time.

But back in 1982, when the movie was privately screened at the packed Paramount Studios Theater for John, director de Palma and their cast and crew, there was some desultory applause from a few people, then an overwhelming – and long-lasting – hissing, which rapidly spread throughout the room.

Despite these depressing circumstances, John became close friends with *Blow Out* director Brian de Palma and his new wife, John's old flame Nancy Allen. John even taught Nancy the art of 'buddy breathing' while the pair were filming some very tricky underwater scenes for *Blow Out*. (Although John remained wary of the water, owing to his childhood accident when diving into a pool, he was such a consummate professional that he was able to overcome his misgivings on set.)

During this period John spent a long weekend at the beach house de Palma and Nancy rented for $30,000 a month near the Hamptons on Long Island. Most of the weekend was taken up eating lobster and ice cream, watching movies at a local theatre and having long late-night discussions about the meaning of life.

Back on the romantic front, John was now being linked with sixteen-year-old Brooke Shields. One 'friend' told the *New York Daily News* the couple had kissed and cuddled in a stretch limousine they shared to JFK Airport. The story was ruined when the newspaper claimed that John was enchanted by Brooke's movie *Endless Love*, an appalling weepy about teenage lovebirds that is only memorable because it marked the film debut of a teenager called Tom Cruise in a brief, walk-on role.

In actual fact, John and Brooke did meet briefly on a few carefully planned dates that had been requested by their respective agents. The supposed relationship reached a head when John was being interviewed by a US magazine journalist and just happened to take two lovey-dovey phone calls from Brooke during the interview. That sparked a number of personal questions about Brooke which John happily agreed to answer. He even revealed that Brooke had been to his ranch near Santa Barbara, accompanied by her mother and aunt.

But John's reaction when asked how he would 'characterise' his relationship with the sixteen-year-old Brooke was intriguing. 'At this point, well, I think I'd rather not give the details, out of respect. I would rather lean away from it. I don't mind talking about Brooke or her family but, when it comes to our relationship, it would probably be better not to tell you at this time,' came John's reply.

Close friends of John knew perfectly well there was no romance with Brooke. But the rumours certainly helped to improve John's image, which had taken quite a hammering due to the negative previews of his movies.

Following the disappointing performance of *Blow Out* in the US box office, Columbia Pictures dropped their plans to star John in a remake of the classic 1946 movie *Stairway To Heaven*. He also lost the lead in *An Officer and a Gentleman* to Richard Gere, who by this time was in real danger of overtaking John as far as sexy male roles were concerned. John even lost the second lead spot in Ron Howard's *Night Shift* to Michael Keaton. The other main role in that movie went to Henry 'The Fonz' Winkler.

John himself turned down the lead in British director Alan Parker's *Midnight Express*. The actor was worried about the graphic nature of some of the scenes in the filthy Turkish prison where the movie was set.

One problem with John's career strategy was that he did not like publicising his movies. He felt particularly vulnerable in front of television cameras and explained, 'What did it for me was the time David Frost interviewed me on my plane. He asked me a lot of personal questions, which made the interview come out grey. When the interview was seen, it disappointed a lot of people who'd liked me in my films. That was when I realised doing television interviews wasn't such a good idea.'

John's older brother Joey was faring no better with his career. After a good start – recording two albums, making appearances on various TV shows, starring in a low-budget movie and being given a $50,000 one-year exclusive contract with Paramount – things started to go downhill rapidly.

He was dropped as a recording artist by Casablanca Records. His movie entitled *Sunnyside* did absolutely no business and neither of the two albums he had recorded made the charts. There were even reports of Joey Travolta albums at Casablanca all stacked up with nowhere to go. Meanwhile, John Travolta decided he had to lighten up his Hollywood reputation. He was well aware of all the negative press going around and he knew that it was time to show another, more surprising side to his character.

THE IMPERIAL GARDENS JAPANESE STEAK HOUSE, SUNSET BOULEVARD, HOLLYWOOD, WINTER 1980

John Travolta looked up from a pair of chopsticks full of rare fillet. He had a thought, an inspiration in mid-flash. His eyes reached full dazzle mode. They were the primary energy sources on a face that tended to act as an irresistible magnet. But there was no mistake about it, the grin was impressive, too. Beneath it the shoulders twitched eagerly with their own special action. It was the shoulders that let one know that something was happening below the level of his solid neck. But it was not so easy to work out what was happening behind the face.

Just then an Amazonian black lady sauntered across the restaurant, wearing a sparkling, rhinestone-encrusted dress that clung to every contour of her body. She had been closely watching John Travolta with director Brian de Palma and his wife, actress Nancy Allen, since they arrived on the premises.

'John Travolta, you sweet thing,' she yelled as if greeting an old friend. Her voice rose even louder and purred, 'You cream puff, bring your fine self over here.'

John looked up and hesitated for a beat while he considered his options. He had made it a policy not to react to approaches by strangers, but this woman was extremely attractive. He rather liked the way she had an edge of aggression in her voice and how she said all the right things. And she wasn't finished talking to him just yet.

'I seen you in *Saturday Night Fever* ten times, honey. You better come over, bring your fine self over here.'

John smiled and muttered under his breath, 'Damn it.' He got up and walked over to her table where she was positively squirming with excitement.

When he reached her table she looked up and said, quietly this time, 'Give me some sugar, honey.'

John leaned down and kissed her firmly on the lips. They stayed attached for at least two minutes. The rest of the customers in the restaurant choked on their sushi.

The woman got up and John grabbed her hand and walked her over to his table and introduced her to de Palma and Nancy Allen. She was in no way fazed and swung her hips with glee as she shook each of their hands.

Then she turned to her new-found true love John. 'When I saw you dance for the first time, I wanted to jump right on your bones.'

John and the woman kissed passionately one more time and then she departed.

Brian de Palma and Nancy said nothing about the incident, but they were clearly taken aback. They had been discussing with John efforts to secure the rights to all The Doors' music for a biopic on the group's life and times. But a few weeks later the group's surviving members decided that John Travolta was not the right actor to play their legendary lead singer Jim Morrison and the deal collapsed in flames. It was eventually directed by Oliver Stone and starred Val Kilmer.

In New York, the hot gossip amongst showbusiness circles was that John had fallen head over heels in love with French actress Catherine Deneuve. Apparently, she had visited the Philadephia *Blow Out* location and the couple had been seen together in John's four-star trailer.

John's loyal and trusted manager Bob LeMond insisted there was no truth in the rumours. John had met Deneuve when she was in New York with French actor Gerard Depardieu and the threesome went to a French Film Office party together. But the two French stars then went off to the San Francisco Film Festival to promote their new François Truffaut movie, *The Last Metro*. It was actually John's friendship with Depardieu that was the key to the rumours because the two actors had become very good pals after being introduced when John visited Paris and dropped in on the set of a movie Depardieu was shooting. After that, whenever Depardieu visited America, he always found time to look up John and the relationship developed.

When *Blow Out* was complete, John flew his own jet to Paris to spend a week with Depardieu and his family He even decided to learn to speak fluent French. John explains, 'While I was there I suddenly realised how rude and unworldly it was not to speak French with them. They were forced to speak English, you see. So I told him, "Next time we meet I'll be speaking French." And I began my lessons.'

A few months later, John called his friend Depardieu in Mexico where the actor was making a movie and proudly asked him, '*Allo, comment ça va?*'

Depardieu replied in English, 'Who is this?'

John returned in French, 'It's me, John, calling you from California.' John explains, 'Gerard thought that was terrific.'

Another little-known friendship that John nurtured around this time was with Richard Gere. One time, John even turned up on the set of Gere's movie *The Cotton Club* with a fully laden picnic basket and the two stars headed off for a nearby grassy verge where they sat down and enjoyed a lavish lunch together. Interestingly, John recognised that Gere was his main

Hollywood rival at the time but that simply made him more intrigued by the young actor and it certainly did not stand in the way of their friendship.

Around this time, John was finally invited to place his boot and hand prints in the forecourt of Mann's Chinese Theater on Hollywood Boulevard, thus becoming the 161st name on the theatre's world-famous roster. At least someone appreciated him.

In 1983, under the direction of Sylvester Stallone, John finally reprised his Tony Manero role in the sequel to *Fever*, entitled *Staying Alive*. Before shooting he endured seven months of gymnastic training supervised by Stallone, who also co-wrote the script with the original *Fever* scribe Norman Wexler.

John literally redesigned his body at Stallone's suggestion, after the *Rocky* star showed John a small statue of a discus thrower and said, 'How would you like to look like that?'

'Terrific,' came the response.

John soon became so immersed in the keep-fit, muscle-toning regime that he opened up a business in the San Fernando Valley with his trainer.

During the making of *Staying Alive*, John became very close to Sly Stallone. The tough-guy star had much the same background as John except that he was a street scraper, a character who never took no for an answer and who had literally fought his way to the top. John often visited Stallone's home in Brentwood, near LA. One time both men were reduced to tears watching a video of *Terms of Endearment* with Jack Nicholson, Shirley MacLaine and Debra Winger. There was something fascinating about the two most macho stars in Tinseltown sobbing together on a couch in Stallone's den. John had a deep respect for Stallone and would sit and listen to him for hours as he discussed everything from politics to fashion, rarely even daring to interrupt the older actor.

On another occasion, John, Stallone and a few friends were hanging out at the Brentwood house together when John decided to test his childhood skills as a female impersonator. He borrowed some dresses from an upstairs closet and did a five-minute take on Bette Davis, followed by Barbra Streisand. Both performances earned rapturous applause from his small audience.

Not long after this, John surprised another group of friends with a superb impersonation of Mick Jagger, complete with pouting lips and mascara. Another time he dressed up as a female psychic and pretended to give a reading to his best friend Jerry Wurms.

The only time he had a disagreement with Stallone was when the *Staying Alive* director decided that he wanted to tone down the raw street language that had punctuated the original *Fever*. At first John fought this decision, but eventually Stallone won him over and by the time the film was completed John was in total agreement with his director.

With an extraordinarily well-defined torso above muscular legs, John's dancing in *Staying Alive* could not have been more superb, but the film was pulled apart by the critics because the dialogue was so lousy.

The story began five years after the end of *Saturday Night Fever*, with Tony Manero struggling to make a living as an off-Broadway dancer. Unfortunately, the movie became bogged down in anticipation of the *Rocky*-style finale. Nonetheless, it grossed $63.8 million in the United States and almost $90 million overseas, where both John and Stallone were immensely popular.

But original *Fever* scriptwriter Norman Wexler became very angry about the way Stallone and John rewrote his original screenplay. 'It's succeeding in spite of Stallone,' said a bitter Wexler, who termed the sequel a 'vacuous, impoverished, crass and crude movie. Stallone's religion is showbusiness narcissism.' Wexler claimed that John was ultimately responsible 'because it was his picture'.

John produced a book about his keep-fit training methods during the making of *Staying Alive* and he continued training two hours daily to keep up his perfect body. He also gave the designer Carushka Jarecka permission to start devising a Travolta line of workout clothes. (All this was in marked contrast to his hyper-sensitive attitude to merchandising when he was making *Urban Cowboy*. Now, influenced by Stallone and the fact that *Staying Alive* was the ultimate commercial movie, he was much happier to endorse film-related products.)

The keep-fit book, entitled *John Travolta – Staying Fit* outlined John's fitness regime for the Stallone movie and suggested various vitamin cocktails to be consumed with lunch and dinner. There was also a section on 'Hair and Skin Care' as well as the inevitable photos of the newly re-sculpted John. Many of his fans at the time actually preferred his earlier *Fever* body, which hinted at a little puppy fat on the hips and thighs but was considered by many to be a little more 'realistic'.

'John looks like he's just walked out of weightlifting class now. Yuck! He was far more dishy before, white and slightly flabby,' said one ardent female fan.

At this stage, John was completely wrapped up in the muscle toning and sunbed-tanned look. But, like most things in his life, it would prove to be a passing fad and eventually be completely forgotten.

John's follow-up to *Staying Alive* turned out to be an even more unfortunate choice. He selected *Two Of A Kind* with Olivia Newton-John, whose own brief movie career was fading fast. The two stars had kept in touch after the success of *Grease*, and John later claimed he chose the script mainly because he felt it was perfect for Olivia. He also felt a tad guilty about turning down an opportunity to star opposite her in *Xanadu* which actually flopped badly at the box office.

The following description from *Halliwell's Film Guide* sums up the movie's plot and most people's opinion of it:

'Four angels propose that Earth be spared from a second flood if two arbitrarily chosen human beings can be seen to perform a great sacrifice for each other.

'Curious reversion to angelic comedies of the thirties and forties. Lacking the right measure of wit and whimsy, it is totally unsuccessful.'

Two Of A Kind was a disaster. John constantly interfered with the script, written and directed by first-timer John Herzfeld, who tactfully agreed with every one of John's changes when he should have been fighting his star more strongly.

John later insisted, 'I'll never understand writers being reluctant to let an actor change a line if it doesn't sound right. I've seen writers doing new lines for shows on the road before they get to New York. If they can improve a line, why can't an actor?'

Significantly, John had not changed a line in the earlier Stallone-directed *Staying Alive, and* that still got destroyed by the critics.

In fact, John was nursing an ambition to direct movies himself and he even persuaded two major studios to help develop a couple of scripts, with a view to him taking over at the helm.

But the Hollywood trade papers were more interested in the movies he'd been passed over for, rather than film projects he was involved with. Besides Richard Gere – whose career undoubtedly got a kick-start thanks to John's problems at the time – Tom Hanks got a big break when he landed the lead role in *Splash*, a movie that John had at one time been considered for. John then turned down a $4 million offer to dance in a movie version of *A Chorus Line* because he believed the part was too small.

But at least *Blow Out* director Brian de Palma was pushing for John to agree to play the lead in *Scarface*. Unfortunately, John found it difficult to cope with the idea of playing a cocaine-crazed mobster and turned it down. The film was eventually made in 1986 as a highly acclaimed vehicle for Al Pacino.

After the death of his mother and Diana Hyland, John often sought out the friendship of families as opposed to individuals. He spent a lot of time with James Taylor and Carly Simon, as well as Gerard Depardieu and his family in France.

Back at the ranch in Santa Barbara, John's daily regime seemed strangely detached from the real world. He usually did not get up until eleven, had a jazz-dance lesson at one, a light breakfast, a ninety-minute 'brush-up' French lesson, then dinner, a violin lesson at eight, followed by a movie. One of John's few friends in the neighbourhood was Robin Williams. The two stars met up fairly regularly and one Saturday they even gatecrashed a local wedding, much to the surprise of the guests. However, most of the time John continued to lead a solitary existence at the ranch. Meanwhile, Scientology still prevailed as the dominant force in John's life outside work and he often found himself having to explain his religious preferences to outsiders.

'People misunderstand. You can be a Catholic, a Jew, a Protestant – and a Scientologist. It doesn't interfere with your beliefs at all. That's a category left up to you. They talk about everything else, but the God aspect, the religious aspect is left up to you. It's good to feel you've got some answers to some of these things that we think there are no answers to.'

But in Los Angeles, John was wondering if his career was on a permanent downward spiral. No one in moviedom had ever recovered after being written off twice.

The threat of success underlies every action and reaction in Hollywood. John liked to compare Hollywood to flying one of his beloved planes. Most trips were routine. But sometimes a thunderstorm would whip up on a sweltering summer's night and John the pilot would find himself hanging on for dear life. Leaning back, he would try to pull the plane back on course as it dipped and weaved through the storm. In such circumstances, the pilot simply flew on, virtually blinded in the blackness. And then it would happen, that strange feeling when pure elation and sheer terror joined. Some called it pushing yourself to the edge, riding the lip of the envelope.

CHAPTER TWENTY
IMPERFECT

JOHN'S PIED À TERRE, STUDIO CITY, 17 FEBRUARY 1984

John was pacing up and down the wooden floor of his sparsely furnished living room. He was in a complete quandary. The following day was his thirtieth birthday and he couldn't decide whether to be traumatised or delighted.

He had originally planned to make it a momentous occasion with a Hugh Hefner-style celebration, complete with champagne, bikini girls and lots of cigars. After all, John Travolta was just about to enter his thirties so what better way than as a jet-setting playboy?

He planned to take his latest plane down to LAX, pick up his closest friends and fly them all over the country on a non-stop airborne party, stopping wherever took their fancy.

But the day before his actual birthday, John found himself panicking. He was no longer looking forward to the big day. He dreaded it. He actually didn't want to see anyone. He decided to stay at the house on his own and not answer the phone all day. No one would know he was there.

Just then the phone rang. John didn't reach for it at first, then he heard his father's voice on the answering machine and picked up. When John said he was planning to do nothing on his birthday, Sam Travolta was outraged. He immediately called up his other children and they started swamping John with calls that evening. Eventually, John caved in and agreed to hold a small party. He flew them all to LA and a low-key affair was held at the house in Studio City. Afterwards, John acknowledged that his worries about turning thirty were ludicrous.

In fact, John's real fears concerned his career. After turning down *An Officer and a Gentleman* (which became such a big hit for Richard Gere), he started to wonder about his ability to pick roles.

One day he ran into Warren Beatty in a Beverly Hills restaurant and decided to test the water.

'Do you think I should have done *Officer and a Gentleman*?' he asked Beatty.

'Why would you want to have done it?'

John replied, 'Because it's a big commercial hit.'

Beatty scratched his chin and then responded, 'You've starred in two of the biggest movies in movie history. Why do you need another one? Just do good movies, John.'

All John wanted was a little reassurance.

In the July 1985 issue of *Playgirl*, John held forth on how he was 'freed by the realisation' that he was a spirit and not just a body. And when he was feeling especially good – like at an awards ceremony – he sometimes travelled outside his 'exterior'. Apparently, John's decision to discuss his spiritual self was prompted by reading Beatty's sister Shirley MacLaine's book *Out on a Limb*, in which she wrote about similar experiences.

In 1985, John starred in *Perfect* opposite fast-rising star Jamie Lee Curtis. John played a reporter for *Rolling Stone* magazine who was investigating health clubs and the possibility of their becoming the disco clubs of the 1980s. What follows is a typical scene:

The photographer's task is a demanding one, but she's not about to flinch.

'All right,' barks Frankie, entering the men's locker room for shots to illustrate a magazine story on the fitness craze. 'Let's see some ass. Come on. Hurt me. Make me suffer.'

The three strapping men, in varying stages of undress, look at one another with amusement. Paul Barresi, a striking Burt Reynolds lookalike, begins to peel, feigns hesitation, and says, 'Wait a minute. Are we going to get paid for this?' More mock embarrassment then, 'What's my mother going to say?'

He considers the matter for, say, a nano-second and, undeterred, accommodates the request.

Cut to the next scene.

Perfect was filled with these sort of scenes. It was an attempt to dissect the health-spa phenomenon that had swept the nation in recent years. Just like *Fever* and *Urban Cowboy*, *Perfect* actually stemmed from a magazine article. Journalist Aaron Latham hung around a Los Angeles spa called the Sports Connection and then wrote a *Rolling Stone* cover story comparing the health clubs to the singles bars of the seventies. Once again, John found himself teamed up with *Urban Cowboy* director James Bridges.

In many people's eyes, *Perfect* was John's last chance. He took the part of Adam Lawrence, a bright, dishonest reporter who, oddly, discovers idealism after spending hours in the gym staring at Jamie Lee Curtis's obscenely thrusting pelvis. It was a movie full of neat ideas about journalism and the early-eighties fitness culture which just did not work for a mainstream audience.

At least *Perfect* gave John a chance to work with close friend Marilu Henner. One day they were riding in a limo to the studio when they heard a KIIS-FM disc jockey pose a trivia question asking listeners to name three sitcoms with numbers in the title and offering a pair of tickets to the Jacksons' concert for the first correct answer.

The DJ in question – Rick Dees – actually used to spice up his show by regularly doing impersonations of John's *Kotter* Sweathog character whom he called John Revolting. But John wasn't bothered. He wanted the Jackson tickets so badly that he grabbed the limo's mobile phone and got through to the station. He gave the correct answer and screamed like a teenager when told he had won.

When *Perfect* was released in the early summer of 1985 it was considered an enormous disappointment. Director Bridges was criticised for choosing John as his leading man and accused of turning the movie into 'a vulgar, voyeuristic movie that cruelly exploits both sexes' according to the *New York Daily News*.

The well respected *Variety* showbusiness newspaper scoffed, 'Set in the world of journalism, this pic is guilty of the sins it condemns – superficiality, manipulation and smugness ... As an actor, Travolta never really gets a hold of the character and is unconvincing as a reporter or a man of feeling.'

AUSTIN STRAUBEL AIRFIELD, GREEN BAY, WISCONSIN, FEBRUARY 1984

The ancient four-engined Lockheed Constellation rumbled over the military air strip on the edge of Lake Michigan. The ground crew looked up as the great metal bird in the sky swooped low above the tiny watchtower, before circling around the bay to attempt a landing on the icy blacktop.

The plane itself had transported General Douglas MacArthur throughout much of the Second World War and he nicknamed it the 'American Caesar'.

In the cockpit, a super-cool John Travolta was having the time of his life. The thirty-year-old actor and his personal pilot were ferrying the classic aircraft, which he had just bought in Canada for a bargain $200,000, to his ranch in California.

John eventually landed at just after two in the morning to refuel. He jumped out of the aircraft and headed straight for a local motel for the night; he could hardly sleep with the excitement of having flown that plane. He took off for Santa Barbara the following afternoon.

But in Hollywood things were not going so well. John was being linked with fewer and fewer projects. Steven Spielberg almost offered him *Raiders of the Lost Ark*, but decided against even speaking to John's agent because he presumed the star would want too much money. By the time John found out about the project, it was too late and Harrison Ford had been cast.

Then John was offered *Top Gun*, but that fell through, partly through his wage demands and also because the producers were unsure if John was hot enough at the box office. That was a particular blow for John, as it would have been a dream come true to star as a fighter pilot. *Top Gun* eventually became the movie that launched Tom Cruise as a major Hollywood star.

On the clothes front, John had developed a penchant for designer labels after being fitted out for his ill-fated role in *American Gigolo* before pulling out of the movie. Milan's Giorgio Armani outfitted John with sports coats and suits he adored because 'they're very comfortable, very baggy and very cushy'. After that, he started wearing styles by Valentino, Yves St Laurent and, occasionally, Calvin Klein.

John was as aware as ever of his appearance, explaining in complete earnest to one writer, 'I go for what looks best on me. If I misdress, I can look heavier and less wellproportioned than I am.'

The actor was feeling completely burned out following the release of *Perfect*. He had done almost 700 press interviews and he couldn't face any more work in terms of movie roles. He needed to do something completely different, to stimulate his enthusiasm for the business.

Once again, he headed for his beloved planes and tried to forget his troubles by spending more and more time flying. It was the only escape he knew.

CHAPTER TWENTY ONE
BEWITCHED

THE WHITE HOUSE, WASHINGTON DC, NOVEMBER 1985

'Would you care to dance?'

John's request to the pretty young blonde brought a flush of red to her cheeks. Then a discreet smile erupted and she murmured quietly, 'Yes, I'd love to.'

All around them, the floor cleared of other dancers as John spun his beautiful partner around the marbled entrance-hall area of the home of the President of the United States. Other celebrities present that evening included Neil Diamond, Tom Selleck and Clint Eastwood.

The jive was to the beat of John's own hit single 'You're The One That I Want'. The crowd looked on in disbelief.

John and his partner – wearing a low-cut ball gown of midnight blue – continued spinning and turning as every pair of eyes in the room watched. When Neil Diamond burst into 'Sweet Caroline' and 'You Don't Bring Me Flowers', the couple continued dancing.

After it was finally time to part, John held Princess Diana's hand for a few beats and said simply, 'Thank you.'

The Princess looked down demurely. She was embarrassed and thrilled. Her husband Prince Charles forced a smile to his face and immediately took his wife's hand and started to dance with her. But it all seemed very stiff and formal and the Princess's mind clearly wasn't on the task in hand.

John had been invited to the White House gala after the Princess asked President Reagan's wife Nancy if she could persuade John to attend. The glittering party for eighty-eight of America's top people was billed as one of the most spectacular events ever seen at the White House.

First Lady Nancy even took John aside just before the dancing started and said the Princess was hoping he would ask her to dance. Afterwards, a breathless John declared, 'She's good. She's got style and good rhythm. She knew how to follow me and we did quite a few spins and turns. She did real well. I'd give her ten out of ten.'

And even Prince Charles admitted, 'I am not a glove puppet so I can't answer for my wife but she would be an idiot if she did not enjoy dancing with John Travolta.'

Actor Peter Ustinov was refreshingly candid when he commented, 'My impression was that she was very impressed with seeing people in the flesh that she had seen on the screen. She seemed euphoric.'

The dazzling dance display with the Princess was a very significant event for John because it came at a time when his career was on yet another downward spiral. The publicity which accompanied that dance did a lot to help lift his sagging spirits. John cherishes to this day the memory of that evening. 'When Princess Di wanted to dance with me I thought, Even when things are bad for me, they're pretty damn good.'

That Christmas, John sent Princess Diana a gift of a diamond brooch and he has secretly sent her a present every year since. She in turn always sends him a Christmas card, followed by a thank-you letter each January.

Twice in the past five years, the Princess and John have met at private functions; once in New York and then in Los Angeles.

'Diana is quite a flirt when she wants to be and what John did on that night was make a dream come true for her and she still talks about it to this day. It was of particular significance to her because she was so unhappily married at the time,' says one Travolta confidant who should know. 'It is a truly genuine friendship and they seem destined to stay in touch for life.'

John even asked Diana and her two sons to stay at one of his country homes, but she was been unable to take up his offer. He told friends he was shocked and saddened by the Princess's separation from Prince Charles in 1992, but made it clear that he fully intended to keep in contact with Diana.

John sat down nervously at the table at the Russian Tea Rooms, in New York City, just as the grey-haired middle-aged man arrived.

'Good evening,' said John in an accent that sounded more like Michael Caine than Tony Manero.

He was meeting director Robert Altman to discuss a role as a cockney in a Harold Pinter play called *The Dumb Waiter*. As the two men ate, John launched into some dialogue from the play. John proudly explains, 'He really loved the idea that I would just do that for fun.'

The Dumb Waiter centres around two hitmen panicked into hiding out in a secluded house. Gradually they start to lose their cool as a number of mysterious events occur in front of their very eyes.

John co-starred in *The Dumb Waiter* with British actor Tom Conti and it was shown on ABC TV in America in the summer of 1987. It was supposed to mark a turning point in John's career, but it came and went with little interest from anyone.

While the sparse, repetitious but often slyly humorous dialogue was undoubtedly an influence on people like Quentin Tarantino when he was penning *Pulp Fiction* years later, *The Dumb Waiter* just wasn't the right vehicle for John. The two-character play dramatises the tensions between the hired killers as they await further orders from an unseen figure upstairs in the house where they are stranded. But John Travolta just wasn't accepted as a cor blimey cockney.

Nevertheless, he enjoyed doing *The Dumb Waiter* and insisted that the play was a welcome break from the high-pressure Hollywood productions he was used to. Although he knew that Tinseltown would interpret the move as a career comedown and a clear sign of his own desperation, he saw it differently. 'When they mentioned Altman and Pinter, how could I refuse?' he explained.

The quality of movie offers for John at this time was going from bad to worse. Cannon Films had plans for Whoopi Goldberg and John to play rookie cops in *Public Enemies*. The word in Hollywood was that John might just make a success of the role if he could fly in on the coat-tails of Goldberg, fresh from her critically acclaimed lead in *The Color Purple*. In the end, the deal fizzled out.

In 1986, John took his own steps to try and restart his movie career by signing up with a new manager called Jonathan Krane, who was married to *MASH* actress Sally Kellerman.

A former-lawyer-turned-manager, Krane had already produced more than twenty movies and was a co-founder of Blake Edwards Entertainment. He believed that the key to reviving John's career was to keep him working in movies he was excited about in order to shed 'the baggage of his past'.

John admitted that his rather spoiled upbringing meant he needed the kind of management that would spoil him, too. In recent years, he had been just one of a vast number of clients at the CAA Talent Agency which was getting so big and powerful in the eighties that clients like John did not necessarily get their undivided attention.

John had never forgotten how he had been encouraged to do a movie he did not much care for called *Running Scared* and dissuaded from doing *Splash* because of a rumour that Warren Beatty was about to do a mermaid movie.

John's former co-manager Lois Zetter was less than optimistic about John's chances of mounting a serious movie comeback in the late eighties. She surmised, 'He'll have to have a moderate hit so he can be viable for the big picture, and compete with the Kevin Costners. I don't think it can be done. Showbusiness has no memory.'

The first big offer under his new management came from the producers of a smash-hit musical in the West End of London called *Time*. They were keen to hire John for $100,000 a week. After much soul searching, he decided to turn down the offer, as he feared that he'd end up being forgotten in Hollywood if he relocated to London.

One of his first new movie roles was *The Experts* with Deborah Foreman and Arye Gross. The movie had a ludicrous plot in which John was captured by Russian spies and made to live in a town full of other Russian spies all posing as Americans. In some ways, it was an apt description of the way his career was going at that time. There was even a scene in which John did a typically pelvic thrusting dance with a beautiful girl.

When the film makers came to do some additional shots before the final edit of the movie could be released, they found that John had put on approximately forty pounds in weight following the original wrap of the shoot. Release of the movie was seriously delayed.

When *The Experts* finally made it to the big screen, it opened briefly in January 1989, and was rapidly relegated to home video by the midsummer of that year. *Video Review* magazine warned of the preposterous plot, 'you'll have to see for yourself (although you'll wish you hadn't)'.

In November 1986, John put his ranch near Santa Barbara up for sale for $3.9 million, over $2 million more than he paid for it six years earlier. He had added considerably to the property so that it now had twenty rooms, including five baths, a library, a wine room and seven original antique fireplaces. John wanted to start afresh. The ranch had some good memories, but it was time to move on.

In Japan, John earned a cool $1 million for appearing in a TV commercial for Sake coolers. He was certainly proving adept at earning an impressive income from sources outside the movie industry.

Inside Hollywood, he let it be known that he was interested in any projects connected with his beloved hobby of flying. In a two-picture pact with Columbia, he agreed to star as the young Howard Hughes and then keep his flying togs on for air-combat flick *Jet Star*. Once again both projects eventually foundered in development hell and were never actually made.

As if to prove that he was far from broke and washed up, John proudly purchased yet another aircraft in 1986. This time he picked up a Lockheed Jetstar 731 mini-airliner, complete with all the comforts of a Hollywood mansion. It seated ten, had its own crew, including a steward, and allowed John to travel anywhere in the world at any time he wished. Within weeks of buying the plane, he'd jetted off to England, Greece, Switzerland, France and Egypt, where 2,000 fans turned up to greet him at the airport.

During this period, John also decided he would pen his own version of a second sequel to *Saturday Night Fever*. In many ways his decision was incited by the poor response to his recent movies. He actually felt he could do a better job than anyone else. John's storyline took Tony Manero to Hollywood and put him in MTV rock videos and in movies. When that didn't work out, he brought him back to Brooklyn, broke and unsuccessful because he'd lost his values, though John ensured that the story had the requisite happy ending. The project never saw the light of day, but it definitely had similarities with John's own life.

In Hollywood, many key players – including Sly Stallone – were saying that John's career would never have dipped if he'd continued playing the Tony Manero-type roles.

Throughout those difficult days of 1986–89, John increasingly found himself considering the ultimate exit from Hollywood – becoming a commercial airline pilot. 'I thought, Wouldn't it be wild to give up this career and then be going, "Hello, this is your captain, John Travolta ..."'

In 1987, still angry about the failure of *Perfect* and the lengthy delays in releasing *The Experts*, John agreed to star in *The Tender*, which was immediately projected in the media as yet another comeback vehicle for him.

The Tender teamed John with a ten-year-old actress and a Doberman Pinscher. The movie revolved around the story of a Chicago street dog, wounded and left for dead, that's befriended by a young girl. The dog then becomes the protector of a father and daughter struggling to survive in the big city.

This film marked a turning point for John when he decided to take softer roles because he actually believed that his fans preferred to see him in such parts. In 1988, he agreed to appear alongside *Cheers* star Kirstie Alley in a relatively low-budget movie called *Daddy's Home*. It was another soft role, another easy option.

John intended to continue turning over such movies in order to finance the jet- liner lifestyle. He was also convinced that it was impossible to find classy projects.

Daddy's Home director/writer Amy Heckerling's initial movie pitch of a baby that talks left Hollywood studios unimpressed. When she managed to get Bruce Willis to be the voice of the baby and John to play one of the two lead roles, they could see some earning potential in the project. But it was actually not until Kirstie Alley came on board that the movie got the green light.

It was then retitled *Look Who's Talking* and took an enormous amount at the US box office. It should have relaunched John's Hollywood career, but the best any reviewers could say about the movie was that it was 'cute'. The fact that it was deemed to be a meaningless family-orientated film didn't help. But John did get some well-deserved credit for his engaging performance as a big-hearted cabbie who woos and wins single mom Kirstie Alley and her talking baby.

Hollywood observers insisted that *Look Who's Talking* was a success because it had followed the immensely popular *Three Men and a Baby* and *Parenthood* films of earlier that year. Also, they pointed out that there were virtually no big movies released at the same time as *Look Who's Talking*.

At thirty-five years old, John took the success of the movie completely in his stride. It didn't even particularly bother him when some reviewers pointed out that he looked to be a little on the plump side. He admitted, 'I was called some names when I was overweight this year. People would say things to me like "Man, you're fat" and "Why d'you gain so much weight?"'

The John Travolta of the late seventies and early eighties would have retreated to his ranch and got incredibly depressed about such comments. But now he took them on board and immediately lost thirty pounds by working out extra hard with his personal trainer.

He also had high hopes for a small-budget film he had agreed to star in for a peppercorn fee. It was called *Chains of Gold* and featured John playing a social worker who infiltrates the gritty world of street gangs and crack dealers in order to save a young boy.

'I play a reluctant hero. A regular Joe caught up in a situation. He loves someone so much that he wants to save their life,' he said excitedly at the time.

Old flame Marilu Henner co-starred with John as a woman from his past who helps him in his quest. But the problem with *Chains of Gold* was that – despite the apparently tough subject matter – it was another soft option.

Neither *Chains* nor *The Tender* were produced by major studios and John's basic fee was only in the early hundreds of thousands as opposed to the multi-million-dollar contracts of yesteryear. *Chains of Gold* was eventually considered unreleasable on the main movie-theatre circuit and was aired on cable TV in the fall of 1991, more than two years after it had been made. *Tender* never even got that far in the US.

John also made two other movies just after this – *Shout* and *Boris and Natasha* – which both sank without trace and are never even mentioned by him.

By the late eighties, John had moved to Spruce Creek, Daytona Beach, Florida, after selling the Santa Barbara ranch for a profit of more than $2 million. On his new property was a landing strip for his jet liner and he proudly told friends, 'It's so cool. When I look out of my bedroom window, I can see my plane in its hangar.'

He also liked the new house because 'there's no full-time household staff which is nice because now I can walk naked into the kitchen if I feel like it'.

John was certainly feeling less obsessed with his career. In Spruce Creek, he led a very low-key lifestyle in what was really a country-club community. One neighbour said he was 'such a nice person … he fits right in'.

He started to spend an increasing amount of time at the four-bedroomed, four-bath, grey-and-white French-provincial style home in Florida. The house, with its own swimming pool, only cost him in the region of $500,000. It was a clever move on John's part because he had consolidated his financial status without having to make another lousy movie to finance his luxurious lifestyle.

By all accounts, John spent his days in Spruce Creek sometimes jogging, doing eighteen holes on the Spruce Creek golf course and playing tennis on some of the community's eight courts. The only visitors to his house were a houseboy, his trainer and the occasional scriptwriter. John even popped into nearby Disney World three times during his first year in residence.

The only slight hiccup with the house in Florida occurred when John discovered there was a ban on aircraft as heavy as his latest purchase, a Gulfstream G-2, landing on the Spruce Creek strip. But that was lifted after residents voted to allow the weight limit to be increased.

John bought the aircraft – the size of a small commercial airliner and weighing 62,000 pounds fully loaded – just after moving into Spruce Creek. Before that, he had been happily landing his other 22,000-pound jet on the airstrip.

One time, John dropped in to his local Daytona Beach video store and spent several thousand dollars on tapes to be watched between stops on his aircraft. There were movie classics, workout tapes, comedies, dramas and cartoons. 'About the only movie he didn't get was *Saturday Night Fever*,' revealed the bemused video-store clerk.

John tried very hard to get out to see movies at real movie theatres, but it wasn't easy. In the end, he came to an arrangement with his local cinema in Daytona Beach whereby they allowed him to come in after ten or midnight to see a particular film.

After such late-night outings, the insomniac actor headed for the nearest fast-food restaurant, like Bennigan's or Denny's. John's appetite was still a big problem.

During an interview in a London hotel as part of the promotional trip for *Look Who's Talking* in early 1990, John surprised one British reporter by eating a range of puddings which included: three scoops of ice cream; chocolate truffle cake in raspberry sauce; and a large bowl of chocolate mousse-cum-trifle piped with white cream.

By the late eighties he admitted he was liable to gain two stone in any month-long rest period. He even hired Brad Bigelow – a friend of the fitness fanatic who taught him to stay fit in *Staying Alive* – to keep him trim.

At this time, John started dating an attractive actress called Kelly Preston, who'd come out of a messy broken engagement with Hollywood brat-pack member, Charlie Sheen.

Kelly's biggest claim to fame had been playing the love interest to Danny De Vito and Arnold Schwarzenegger in *Twins*. And, besides her highly publicised brush with Sheen, she had been through one failed marriage and another engagement over the previous three years.

The first time John and Kelly met was back in 1986, in Canada, when they were both shooting *The Experts*.

Kelly was married at the time to her *SpaceCamp* co-star Kevin Gage, and she turned to John for advice about her troubled marriage. He helped her by using some of his Scientology techniques. John was impressed that Kelly was so open-minded about the Church's teachings. Kelly went on to live with George Clooney, now the star of TV's *E.R.* and Quentin Tarantino's blockbuster *From Dusk Till Dawn*. Maybe it was George's notion of romance – for her twenty-sixth birthday, he gave her a black pig named Max – but within a year Kelly had declared that relationship over as well.

In place of Max the pig – which George kept custody of – Kelly found herself the recipient of an engagement ring from Charlie Sheen in April 1989.

Then John and Kelly ran into each other at a party at Kirstie Alley's home. Kelly was by this time dating Charlie Sheen, but Alley clearly thought it was a mismatch and even said to John, 'Why don't you two get together?'

John laughed off the idea until he ran into Kelly a few months later. John had heard that Kelly had split with Charlie Sheen and asked if she had got over it.

'Yes,' came the instant response. They went to dinner that night, then dancing, and then for a romantic stroll through the city streets. Within a few weeks John even persuaded Kelly to join the mile-high club with him, while his jet was on automatic pilot and the couple were thousands of feet above the Rockies en route to LA. Kelly found it one of the most erotic moments of her life. It was also extremely risky, although it has to be pointed out that John did have a co-pilot on board at the time.

Years later John admitted to friends that he had actually fallen in love with Kelly the first time they had met in Vancouver. At a wrap party at the end of shooting on *The Experts*, Kelly and John spent the entire evening together and John believed from that moment onwards that they would eventually marry.

John was concerned about not having settled down yet. He even admitted, 'I want kids too much. I'll be like Jimmy Stewart (who married at forty-one) – I'll do it at forty or something.' He wasn't worried about being an older parent because his own mother had been closer to fifty when all the other moms around her were in their late twenties. He never forgot how Helen Travolta would come to his school to pick him up and people would say, 'Was that your mother, or your grandmother?'

Meanwhile, Hollywood was still speculating as to why John's career was turning into such a roller-coaster ride of ups and downs. One studio executive said, 'When John first became a star, the image he projected was sincere, appealing and open. He was the kid from the wrong side of the tracks who'd made good. But the image changed. John stayed nice – but the image changed. He was always posing with cars and airplanes and at his estate … To some extent he lost the appeal of the underdog.'

John didn't exactly help his cause when he turned down a chance to present (with Olivia Newton-John) an Oscar for the Best Musical Score at the 1989 Academy Awards Ceremony. He told the show's producers that he'd rather present a major award – in keeping with his own Oscar history. After all, reasoned John, I was once a nominee. He had also earlier presented the 1978 Best Supporting Actress Award to Vanessa Redgrave, the honorary 1981 Oscar to Barbara Stanwyck and the 1982 Best Actor statuette to Ben Kingsley. The Academy was not amused by his refusal.

Look Who's Talking was largely ignored before it hit the movie theatres in America because no one would take it seriously. Even when it took a whopping $12 million in its first weekend at the box office, there wasn't much more than a ripple of real interest from Hollywood itself. The film had only been budgeted at $8 million, including a modest $600,000 fee for John plus a share of the eventual profits. It was to prove a goldmine for him.

Time magazine called it 'the baby-faced sleeper hit' of the autumn 1989 season, while *Variety* criticised it as 'Yuppie-targeted' and 'destined for a short life in theatres'. Although the movie definitely had its faults, it was a pleasurable excursion with a winning gimmick.

Look Who's Talking went on to gross over $133 million in the US and turned into John's first big hit in years. It was definitely a comeback of sorts. His fee for the sequel, called *Look Who's Talking Too,* the following year was $2 million. Even so, John noticed that not many of the meatier roles were coming his way.

One of the most intriguing aspects of the phenomenal success of *Look Who's Talking* was that the film's backers, TriStar, admitted they had been unsure whether John's association with the movie would help or hinder its success. Jeff Sagansky, TriStar's president, explains, 'I didn't worry that John's name would keep people away, but I didn't know if he would be a huge draw'

No one was prepared to sell *Look Who's Talking* as a John Travolta film and that proved a very clever move on the part of the distributors. Even the print ad campaign featured a hipper-than-hip baby, complete with shades and a Walkman, with no sign of John.

But *Talking* director Amy Heckerling insisted that this did not mean John was box-office poison. 'John has proved he's a wonderful actor with good comic timing, and he's sexy. What else do you need from a guy?'

Look Who's Talking's success simply had the knock-on effect of encouraging producers and directors of every sickly sweet project in Tinseltown to come rushing to John's front door with a bucketful of screenplays, which was exactly what John did *not* want.

CHAPTER TWENTY-TWO

FEELING HIGH

PALACE HOTEL RESTAURANT, GSTAAD, SWITZERLAND, 31 DECEMBER 1990, 11.59 PM

They seemed like any other loving couple, blissfully unaware of the freezing temperatures outside. As the last few seconds of the old year slipped away, John suddenly seized the moment. Undaunted by the presence of nearby revellers, he went down on one knee and pulled out a six-carat diamond ring and asked, 'Kelly, will you marry me?'

The first stroke of midnight was about to chime.

Kelly screamed with delight and surprise. John took that to mean yes.

The next moment, he eased the ring on to Kelly's finger. It was a square-cut yellow diamond supported by a white diamond on each side end cost $700,000. They kissed passionately.

Though an engagement had been rumoured for months, even the couple's closest friends hadn't seen it coming.

'I had no idea he would propose,' insisted John's manager Jonathan Krane who, with wife actress Sally Kellerman, was sharing a table with the couple that evening.

John had finally made the big decision earlier that day when he'd passed a jewellery store and seen the diamond-studded ring. You're going to propose in six months anyway, he'd thought to himself. Why not just get the ring now?

Kelly's highly publicised relationship difficulties over the previous five years came as a complete contrast to John, who had effectively shut down all public information about his own love life in the late eighties.

'I wanted someone who would never leave my side. I wanted that kind of commitment and I knew she was the one for me. But I couldn't tell her that, not then. Her marriage was a precarious thing, but we were very clean in our interplay with each other. We were above board. That was when I first loved her.'

Another thing about Kelly, which made her even more attractive to John, was that she reminded him of Diana Hyland. 'There was something different about Kelly, a quality that reminded me of Diana in many ways,' he admits. Sometimes, he would take her out shopping for new dresses and find himself homing in on the sort of outfit Diana would have chosen.

John's family were delighted that he seemed to have settled in a relationship. His sister Ellen pronounced, 'She's a doll. Everyone in the family is thrilled.'

However, some months later, stories started circulating in Hollywood that John and Kelly's engagement was off. The couple were still discussing a pre-nuptial agreement. It was a very sensitive issue because John did not want to consider that the marriage might not last for life, but his advisers were most insistent that he had to finalise the agreement before going up the aisle.

In the middle of all this speculation, the couple jetted off together in John's airliner to Italy where John was being awarded the 1991 François Truffaut Award at the 21st annual Giffoni Film Festival. Past recipients included Robert De Niro, Jeremy Irons and Peter Ustinov. John and Kelly also attended a special screening of *The Tender*, which only got a release outside the States.

Then, completely out of the blue, John announced that he and Kelly were expecting a child the following April. Children out of wedlock were hardly a scandalous event in 1990s Hollywood, but John felt strongly that he and Kelly needed to sort out their relationship and head for the altar sooner rather than later.

The couple then went house-hunting on the isolated island of Dark Harbor, Maine, which John had fallen in love with after visiting close friends Kirstie Alley and her husband Parker Stevenson at their home there. It had a year-round population of just 700. The area was so quiet that the only bar closed down because it generated too much noise and one local shop opened for just two months a year. The ferry to the island stopped running at 5 pm and most planes found it impossible to navigate the dense fog that frequently shrouded the area.

John eventually paid $995,000 for a fifteen-bedroomed mansion that sat on thirty-five acres of land and boasted more than 1,000 feet of private beach, as well as stacks of antiques left behind by the previous occupants. The house had actually been on the market for more than a year at $1.7 million.

In September 1991, John and Kelly married in a midnight ceremony at the Hotel De Crillon, in Paris. Kelly, twenty-eight, wore a strapless pearl-beaded gown purchased from Renée Strauss in Beverly Hills. The couple were married by a French Scientologist minister and, after tying the knot, they were serenaded on the historic Place de la Concorde, where King Louis XVI and Marie-Antoinette were guillotined during the French Revolution. Following the nuptials, onlookers showered John and Kelly with rose petals and he told the crowd, '*Je suis tres heureux*' (I am feeling high). The new Mr and Mrs Travolta stopped briefly at the famous nightclub Regine's to celebrate. They rose late the next day and dined out on a terrace, to the cheers of fans below.

The cake had not been ordered until 4 pm that afternoon which suggests that the wedding was very much a spur-of-the moment decision. The marriage was not even registered with the French authorities. But, at a press conference after the ceremony, John insisted that the pair would wed again in a US civil ceremony 'when we get over our jet lag'. However, there is apparently no record of the couple ever marrying in the United States.

Whatever the truth of the matter, there is no doubt that John and Kelly are deeply in love. One close friend pointed out, 'No one wants to even suggest that the marriage might not be for life, but in Hollywood the odds are not in favour of long-lasting marriages. John has to protect his interests in relation to the pre-nuptial situation.'

In a remarkably honest admission to a French writer, John conceded that he probably would not have got married if it had not been for the impending birth of the couple's first child. 'Marriage is complicated and you can do without it. But a baby has to have a real father and a real mother.'

The afternoon of the wedding, John and Kelly drove for two hours to Deauville to attend the town's film festival. Two days after the marriage, the couple boarded John's Gulfstream and headed back to the States.

In California, Sam Travolta – now seventy-eight – was busting his buttons with excitement about his youngest son's marriage. 'Johnny is the baby, so it's fitting that he would be the last one in the family to marry and have a child.' And he added, 'We love Kelly. She's a very nice lady.'

When John was asked about honeymoon plans he replied, 'We're not planning a honeymoon. We go on a honeymoon every other week.'

Afterwards *People* magazine ran a vast spread about the marriage and Kelly's previous love life, including her highly publicised affair with Charlie Sheen. The article made John and Kelly's blood boil and she immediately sent off an outraged letter to the magazine in which she said:

People *ran a lovely story of my recent wedding to John Travolta. However, there were several inaccuracies: 1. That*

Charlie Sheen gave me a 25-carat ring. The ring was 2.5 carat. 2. That I kept the ring against Charlie's wishes. In fact, Charlie and I sold the ring and split the money between us. 3. The story mentioned that my mother, Linda, and stepfather, Lee Carlson, were contacted. For the record, my mother and stepfather are proud of my marriage to John. Their decision not to comment stems from their experiences of the last six months, in which the press have called them at home and then distorted or made up inaccurate quotes. My mother and stepfather have since decided that 'no comment' was a much better position to take rather than run the risk of being misquoted again. Thank you for helping to set the record straight.

    KELLY PRESTON-TRAVOLTA, *Beverly Hills*

Kelly's response reflected a certain sensitivity about the way some sections of the press had behaved throughout her romance with John. The fact that she felt obliged to point out that her engagement ring was 2.5 carat rather than 25 carat, and that she and her former fiancé had sold it and shared the profits, suggests that she had no idea how that might make her look to the public.

John was just as sensitive about certain press reports and was infuriated by an article in one LA-based magazine that seemed very negative towards Scientology. So he blasted off a letter, in which he wrote:

I've seen many media reports on Scientology, and they have not once gotten it right. It stands for integrity and honesty. And all the Scientologists I know live fulfilling lives – without drugs or other vices.

Since 1975, my experiences with Scientology have been well documented, and I've always credited it with my success. L. Ron Hubband stated it very well when he said, 'A man is as well off as his goals and dreams are intact.'

Through Scientology, my dreams and goals have only been strengthened.

Scientologists are tired of having their religion misrepresented in the media, and I think it's time to set the record straight.

John signed the letter simply 'John Travolta, Actor', and it came amidst dozens of similar letters received by *Los Angeles Magazine* following their so-called exposé of the Church of Scientology.

DAYTONA BEACH MEDICAL CENTER, FLORIDA, 13 APRIL 1992

John – whose weight had ballooned to 230 pounds during his wife's pregnancy – watched in stony silence as Kelly strained to give birth to their baby. A doctor and two nurses tried to help but had been warned not to utter a word. 'It made it kinda awkward,' explained one of them afterwards. Eventually little Jett weighed in at 8 pounds 12 ounces.

In a rather stuffy joint statement announcing the birth, the couple said, 'We took an active part in preparing for the smooth birth following the method recommended in *Dianetics*, which stresses complete silence during delivery.' It had been a fully fledged Scientology birth.

John later explained, 'There's a lot of pain going on so the idea is you don't want to contribute to that pain by adding verbal statements, because they're recorded in the mind of the baby.'

He also admitted the reason why he had put on so much weight during Kelly's pregnancy. 'When Kelly ate, I ate with her.'

Minutes after Jett's birth, John picked him up and held him. He didn't let go for hours while Kelly slept peacefully. When the doctor and nurses came to take Jett away for various standard tests, John wouldn't let them.

'No, you can't see him today. You'll have to do it another day,' he told the astonished medical team.

John had actually gone, by his own admission, 'a little nuts'. He was *that* happy at becoming a father.

The name of the baby and the birth method raised a few eyebrows, but John and Kelly didn't care. As one observer quipped, 'He likes his planes so much he's even named his son after them.'

John's old friend Charlie Baum, manager of the Rainbow Room Club, in New York, even wired the couple with his congratulations. 'Looking forward to Jett's first dance here. Reservations are made for him and date for year 2010.'

Just nine months after his birth, John astonished customers at the Rainbow Room Club when he was spotted on the dance floor waltzing with his baby son.

John agreed to do a third *Look Who's Talking* movie in 1992. This time it was called *Look Who's Talking Now* and did moderate business at the box office. Instead of the voice of Bruce Willis, the director made do with Danny De Vito. The general opinion amongst the critics was that 'Kids'll probably eat it up'. John's performance was described as that of 'a nice schlamp, and self-deprecatingly endearing and all'.

But new challenges lay ahead.

CHAPTER TWENTY-THREE

GETTING INTO CHARACTER

THANKSGIVING EVE, NOVEMBER 1992, SKIES ABOVE WASHINGTON DC

The bolt of lightning cracked across the fuselage of the Gulfstream and the entire instrument panel snapped into darkness. John felt the plane lose at least 2,000 feet.

'MAYDAY! MAYDAY! MAYDAY!'

The jet continued plunging in a steep dive. All the power in the aircraft remained shut off. The engines were still working perfectly well, but it was virtually impossible for John to pilot effectively because he couldn't see the instruments. He just managed to pull the plane out of its steep dive and levelled it out at 5,000 feet, skimming the low cloud cover.

'MAYDAY! MAYDAY! MAYDAY!'

Just then John made out the shape of a Boeing only a short distance away and heading straight towards him. He swung the Gulfstream to his left and avoided the airliner by no more than 100 feet. It later emerged that the Boeing had been carrying 180 passengers.

Remaining remarkably calm, John informed his passengers, Kelly, baby Jett and four friends. 'It looks like we're in trouble.'

This was real. The plane was in danger of crashing unless he could land it virtually blind. John knew from his training that the nearest airport would have to guide him down and then he would need to accurately guess the speed as the craft hit the tarmac. If he was going too fast, the plane would break up on impact with the ground. But the biggest danger was going to be that he could not control his wing flaps because the electrics were out.

Five minutes later, the Gulfstream landed at an airstrip in Washington, as half a dozen emergency vehicles stood by, lights flashing and sirens blazing.

John was going 20 mph too fast. But fortunately it was just slow enough for the plane to stay in one piece, although all his tyres burst on impact and the craft veered to an angle as John and his co-pilot fought to keep control before the Gulfstream came to a halt in a muddy bank on the edge of the blacktop.

First on the scene were a pilot and some stewards from a nearby commuter airliner that was being cleaned out before picking up a fresh load of passengers. Inside the plane they found John, his co-pilot and passengers sitting quietly and calmly in the pitch dark. Not even Jett was crying. John unstrapped his belt and walked through to the main area of the plane and they all walked out of the Gulfstream.

The plane itself took six hours to be removed from the runway and it emerged that John had been piloting it from Florida to his new home in Maine at the time. He was by this time regularly flying three planes – a Lear jet, a British Vampire and his greatest pride and joy the Gulfstream G-2, eighty feet long, leather-upholstered throughout, with a galley kitchen, a movie screen and room to sleep ten.

Afterwards, John tried to play the whole incident down by saying, 'The plane landed safely and everyone was fine.'

Despite the success of the *Look Who's Talking* films, by the end of 1992 decent movie offers had all but dried up for John. He seemed to attract only soft-centred, weak scripts – basically poor men's versions of *Talking*.

John then tried to create his own project about his great passion for flying. For almost two months he toiled on a book called *Propeller One-Way Night Coach*, the tale of a nine-year-old boy who flies to California with his mother. In some ways it was very autobiographical, but John was reluctant to concede this to anyone but his closest friends.

The story was an unashamed love poem to flying. It began like this:

> *The excitement ran through my body like nothing I had ever felt before. Knowing that within minutes I would be airborne for the first time was comparable to nothing, including playing doctor with the kids on the block, and that was saying a lot for a nine year-old.*

The image of John Travolta rose up from within the pages of that short book, published privately so that he could hand copies of it to his closest friends. There was a gentleness, a defensiveness, a seductiveness; the embracer and the evader; the husband and the father, the teen idol, the mature actor, the man entranced by 'the seduction of dangerous charm' as John put it in his book. He went on:

> *I did feel a loss of some sort. I started to cry. Mom asked, 'What's wrong, honey?' I just couldn't explain it all to her, so something really stupid came out of my mouth like, 'You, the only woman on an all-men's flight!' She didn't say anything, and I felt really bad as we climbed the ramp to this absolutely perfect specimen of an aircraft. It was Art, believe me.*

Around this time, John got word that Robert Altman – who had directed him in the TV play *The Dumb Waiter* – wanted him for one of the leads in *The Player*. John was delighted and went along for a meeting with Altman presuming it would be a mere formality The movie's backers New Line also wanted John because of the success of the *Look Who's Talking* films. But then Altman changed his mind and cast Tim Robbins instead. John began to wonder if he would ever be offered strong roles again.

His favourite movie of that year had been Quentin Tarantino's highly publicised debut *Reservoir Dogs*. John wished he'd had a chance to be in such a hard-edged project.

If only he had known that Quentin Tarantino had been a John Travolta fan since the age of thirteen, when he'd fallen in love with the horror classic *Carrie* and had spent several weeks wearing a red flannel shirt just like the one worn by John in the movie. As an adult, Tarantino's interest in John also frequently got him embroiled in colourful arguments with his friends when discussing *Blow Out* because it was one of his all-time favourite movies even though no one else remotely rated it.

By 1992, with the buzz on Tarantino's talents already reaching epic proportions, the young director persuaded his agents at the powerful William Morris company to arrange for a meeting with his hero John Travolta. There was no particular reason for the get-together. Tarantino told them he just wanted to bounce a few ideas off John.

Tarantino had just finished writing *Pulp Fiction* and was planning to cast Mike Madsen (Mr Blonde in *Reservoir Dogs*) as hitman Vincent Vega. However, he did have John in mind for a role as one of the bank robbers in a horror flick he had been playing around with for years called *From Dusk Till Dawn*.

John and Tarantino shared a lunch at the Four Seasons Hotel in Beverly Hills after John's manager Jonathan Krane urged him to meet the director. John was flattered by Tarantino's enthusiasm.

The Four Seasons lunch was a complete gusher as Tarantino heaped praise on his movie idol John Travolta. At one stage, Emma Thompson, who had won Best Actress Oscar for the previous year's *Howard's End*, approached them from a nearby table. She had been a Travolta fan ever since her uncle had taken her to see *Saturday Night Fever* nearly twenty years earlier. She told John this and then turned to Tarantino, admonishing him, 'Put this man in one of your movies, he needs a good movie.'

John and Tarantino looked a little embarrassed at this remark and immediately switched subjects, as Emma Thompson moved back to her own table. At the end of lunch the young director invited John to drop by his West Hollywood apartment and play some board games he had which were based on the *Welcome Back Kotter* show, *Grease* and *Saturday Night Fever*.

When John rolled up at Tarantino's apartment on Crescent Heights he was shaken to discover that it was the same place where he'd lived after arriving in LA in 1974. Tarantino had added some characteristic touches to the gothic-French-style 1920s apartment. The main feature of the living room was an outsize Panasonic TV on which friends and journalists alike have watched various flicks and moments of flicks ever since.

With the coincidence firmly established moments after meeting, the two men reconnected very rapidly. They sat down in Quentin's movie memorabilia-infested living room and talked, drank a glass of Californian Chardonnay, which John accepted even though he rarely drank, and then headed off for dinner. Later, they returned to the apartment and played some of Quentin's movie-buff board games. In the *Grease* game, each person had to play a disc jockey collecting hit records. Tarantino explains, 'When we started, John said, "This is a really lame game," but every time a song title came up, we'd both start singing. You're not supposed to, but we did. It was great.'

If Tarantino's neighbours were wondering why two grown men were belting out the lyrics to 'You're The One That I Want' that night, what they were doing was sowing the seeds of John's bravest and most successful career move ever.

That evening John (naturally) won all the board-game contests before the pair headed out for a late-night coffee at Canter's Deli, on nearby Fairfax Avenue.

When they returned to the apartment once again, Tarantino let John have it. 'What did you used to do, John?'

'What?' replied a bemused John.

'Don't you remember what Pauline Kael said about you? What Truffaut said about you? What Bertolucci said about you? Don't you know what you *mean* to the American cinema? John, what did you do?'

John was stunned and extremely hurt by this stinging attack. But he also felt moved. Tarantino was actually telling him he'd had promise like no one else's. John left Tarantino's apartment in the early hours of the morning with his tail firmly between his legs. He was upset, even devastated. He kept thinking to himself, Jesus Christ, I must have been a fucking good actor. Here he was, an actor who had once been compared to Brando, with a career that had completely run out of steam and challenges.

A few months later, Mike Madsen pulled out of the Vincent Vega part in *Pulp Fiction* because he was already committed to three back-to-back movies. Tarantino sent a copy of the screenplay to John with a note scribbled on the first page, 'Look at Vincent.'

Tarantino had actually already decided that Travolta would make an even better Vincent than Madsen. But he seemed to be the only person who was actually thinking that way. *Pulp Fiction* backers Miramax were horrified when they first heard Travolta's name being bandied around. They wanted an actor with a higher profile. When the director called John to see if he would consider the role, John said, 'This is one of the best scripts I've ever read, one of the best roles I could ever have, but good luck 'cos I don't think you'll get me in it.'

But Tarantino stuck to his guns and made it clear that he would only shoot *Pulp Fiction* if Miramax agreed to John. As Tarantino later explained, 'In some ways it would have been easier casting an unknown than casting Travolta because John had a lot of baggage with him. When I mentioned his name to people. I was working with they were like, *"What!"* And then they had to live with people going, "You cast who?"'

There was also another problem; John was very concerned about what kind of role model *Pulp Fiction*'s Vincent could possibly be, armed with his hypodermic and machine gun. He explains, 'I tried to measure it up against other violent films, then I thought about it this way: in *Pulp Fiction* the drug addicts either die or almost die; the murderers die; the guy that has a revelation quits; and the one guy who is a lot of the reason for the evil gets his due in a sexually humiliating way. People get back the evil they put out.'

Significantly, John ended up signing on to do *Pulp Fiction* for a fee that barely covered his expenses – $140,000.

He recalls, 'I just had to look at it as an investment, and it worked out pretty well.' (He later calculated that he probably lost money by taking the role of Vincent in *Pulp Fiction* because it cost him half that fee just to ensure Kelly and Jett were with him throughout the shooting.)

John immediately offered to tone his body up for the role of Vincent Vega, but Tarantino felt that a middle-aged hitman addicted to heroin and French fries wouldn't spend much time in the gym.

John's only specific problem with the *Pulp Fiction* script was the way in which his character shot a man in the head, creating a bloody mess in the back of their car that takes Vincent and Jules almost twenty minutes of screen time to clean up.

In the original script, John's character shot the man once in the throat and he didn't die instantly so he shot him in the head to put him out of his misery. John was convinced that this scene was not very funny. He suggested a few subtle changes, including only shooting the man once. The alterations actually softened Vincent's cruelty and took the entire sequence into a black-comedy mode.

Tarantino deliberately chose both John and Bruce Willis for *Pulp Fiction* because he wanted them to play out of character. John had never been seen as a villain since *Carrie* and even then he ended up as the hero, and screen hard man Willis was going to play the most gentle and sensitive of lovers.

John researched the controversial drug-taking scenes in *Pulp Fiction* with as much thoroughness as he had done the discos of Brooklyn for *Saturday Night Fever* seventeen years earlier. He insisted on meeting Tarantino's so-called drug adviser and former acting-school friend Craig Hamann.

Hamann was introduced to John at a Beverly Hills hair salon where John was having those long rear hair extensions fitted for his role in *Pulp Fiction*. The two actors hit it off immediately and, while a hairdresser delicately and painstakingly attached the extensions, they talked drugs. John was particularly concerned with how he should plunge a needle into his own arm as well as that infamous scene where he did the same to Uma Thurman's chest.

Hamann visited John in his trailer on the set of *Pulp Fiction* five times to coach him on how to use heroin. One time, he was prevented from leaving the trailer to go on the set by a huge bodyguard because Bruce Willis was shooting his motel love scenes with girlfriend Fabienne (Maria de Medeiros). Willis was paranoid about the tabloids getting a snap of him making out with anyone other than his then real-life love Demi Moore.

Hamann says that John 'treated me real well. Every time I'd show up on the set he'd give me a big hug.'

Tarantino came up with all sorts of trickery to avoid John and co-star Uma Thurman actually having to inject themselves in front of the camera. John had a phoney syringe filled with liquid which was specially designed so that when the plunger was pushed down it looked as if it was emptying. In fact, it was all going into a tube.

With the infamous adrenaline scene after Mia's accidental overdose, the huge hypodermic never actually went into Uma Thurman. She had a fake chest piece strapped to the front of her body, and the shot was reversed so that the needle was pulled out rather than plunged in. It was a sequence that had *everyone* talking.

John deliberately pushed his performance in that scene to the edge because he felt it was not only highly dramatic, but also very funny. As Tarantino explains in his inimitable fashion, 'The comedy is coming from the real-life situation of "Whadda-we-gonna-do? Whadda-we-gonna-do? Get the book. Hold the book. I'm not going to do it. You are. No, *you* are." The kicking and screaming of real life.'

Meanwhile, the woman is on the brink of death and the needle looks about thirteen inches long, and drug dealer Lance and hitman Vincent are arguing about how to save her.

All this shooting from the hip was pretty alien to John, but he was relishing every moment on the set. He found Tarantino unlike any film maker he had ever worked with before. Certainly, chaos ruled, but it was fun, the sort of fun John thought he'd never actually have while making a movie. He had a good feeling about Vincent in *Pulp Fiction*. He knew he was giving a superb performance each time he did a take. It was the same feeling he had when he became Tony Manero from *Saturday Night Fever*.

CHAPTER TWENTY-FOUR
CRUISE CONTROL

CANNES FILM FESTIVAL, FRANCE, MAY 1994

The palm-lined Croisette was jammed with gawking tourists, film hacks, journalists, producers, directors, would-bes and has-beens, hustlers of every conceivable stripe, exhibitors and exhibitionists, starlets seeking ever more outrageous ways to strip off for the gangs of paparazzi. John fought his way through and headed inside the hotel entrance. The crowds were even denser in the lobby but all eyes were by now firmly on Travolta.

He blew past the reception area of the Majestic Hotel and headed straight for the restaurant. When he reached the restaurant, John nodded quickly at the other guests at the table who included *Pulp Fiction* co-star Bruce Willis and movie critic Jami Bernard of the *New York Daily News*. He was just settling down at a table when a beautiful woman holding a baby walked over shyly, leaned down and whispered in John's ear.

'I'm a great fan and I hope you'll have time to let me get a photo of you and me together later,' she told him.

John looked bemused. It was clear he had no idea who this

woman was. Willis and movie critic Bernard held their breath in the hope that he wouldn't dismiss this 'fan' as an irritating intrusion. John could sense the trepidation amongst his fellow diners and retained his charm. He told the woman, 'I'd love to do that later. It's great to see you.'

She then spun round and headed off to the other corner of the vast restaurant looking like the cat who'd just got the cream.

John looked up and smiled, 'Who the hell was that? Should I know her?'

A beat of silence followed as his fellow diners waited to see who would speak first.

'That was Greta Scaachi.'

'Oh,' replied John, obviously completely unaware of who she was.

'She's an actress.'

'Right …'

A few minutes later, John finished his salmon appetiser and left the table to move from one to another in a media ritual known as the round-robin interview that ensured maximum adulation and minimal in-depth interviewing. The critics and journalists on hand all said they loved *Pulp Fiction* and many of them made a point of saying they particularly loved John's performance.

John revelled in the back-slapping. 'Thank you.'

'Brilliant movie, man.'

'Great. Glad you liked it.'

'You gotta get an Oscar for that one, John.'

'Thank you very much – I'll be right back.'

The actor moved swiftly behind a huge room divider, found an empty corner and quietly sobbed with joy. For the first time in his life he was actually being acknowledged as a movie star of some magnitude. Not even during the dizzy years of *Fever* had that ever happened.

Many critics were blown away by *Pulp Fiction*.

Jack Day in the *New York Newsday* wrote from Cannes, 'Tarantino's perversely inventive humour, his randy dialogue, and some sensational tongue-in-cheek performances give you little chance to regret your laughter.'

The respected Janet Maslin in the *New York Times* was low-key, but complimentary. 'Mr Tarantino has devised a graceful circular structure that sustains his film's bold ambitions and two-and-a-half-hours running time. The storytelling is solid and the time flies.'

Literally overnight, Pulp became the hot ticket at Cannes. It was the movie everyone was talking about.

Anthony Lane, in the *New Yorker*, wrote, 'The architecture of *Pulp Fiction* may look skewed and strained, but the decoration is a lot of fun. I loved the little curls of suspense that kept us waiting for fresh characters.'

Peter Travers in *Rolling Stone* pointed out, 'Tarantino refuses to patronise, glamorise or judge his band of outsiders. Instead, he lets us see the glimmers of humanity that emerge when they drop their masks of control.'

A small number of commentators were actually angry that overcomplimentary write-ups for *Pulp Fiction* appeared to sanction the violence and moral depravity highlighted in the movie, and they lashed out at irresponsible executives for financing the film in the first place.

USA Today columnist Joe Urschel complained, 'Like contemporary tobacco chiefs who deny any link between cigarettes and cancer, Hollywood executives will be sitting before congressional committees ten years from now in adamant denial. They will continue to callously brush off the connection between their product and the violence in society – despite an avalanche of scientific studies showing the connection.'

But one thing everyone agreed on was that *Pulp Fiction* marked the return of John Travolta, even if he had gone soft – literally. In the movie, his gut, breasts like a junior-prom queen and skin as pale as a Norwegian vacationing in Greenland gave him a look reminiscent of late-period Elvis. But John's flab was only skin-deep – with his Prince Valiant haircut, he was clearly willing to be jeered at in order to bring a certain truth to the screen.

John's appearance in Cannes for the première of *Pulp Fiction* gave many who knew him well their first clue that he was on the edge of regaining superstardom. A blurry newspaper photo showing John penned in by flashbulbs and hordes of journalists, but smiling gamely, seemed to say it all. Plump and shaggy, anonymously dressed, he did not resemble Tony Manero at all. But John Travolta was back.

Nik Cohn – the man who wrote the article upon which *Saturday Night Fever* was based – had not seen John for almost twenty years when he was sent by *Vogue* magazine to interview him following the release of *Pulp Fiction*. His article brilliantly captured the reborn John Travolta, and helped to explain his rediscovery as a major force in Hollywood. Cohn commented, 'John Travolta is quite superb. He shambles through the action in a narcotic glaze. And yet, insanely, he does not end up unlikable. The lumbering bear's gait, the shit-eating grin and hopeless shrug, even the ravaged leftovers from his youthful prettiness combine to suck one in, positioned to forgive. Somehow Vincent seems more unlucky than evil. It is, by any standards, a dazzling seduction. Travolta does not visibly perform; he simply *becomes* the person he plays. In *Pulp Fiction*, the result is one of cinema's great anti-heroes, simultaneously monstrous and irresistible.'

During his interview with Cohn, John opened up to a remarkable degree, especially when talking about one of *Pulp Fiction*'s pivotal scenes – the dance sequence in Jack Rabbit Slims. John explained to his old friend, 'In the twist contest there's Vincent, barely able to stand up; but there's also the memory of Tony Manero, and the audience thinking, John Travolta, I wonder can he still make the moves?'

Afterwards Cohn gave an impartial appraisal that seemed to sum up John perfectly: 'What struck me was how much he liked to give, and how little he liked to be asked to give. Left to his own devices, he seemed extraordinarily generous, considerate and gentle to a degree. He also seemed, by movie-star standards, surprisingly candid. But the moment that a tape recorder was switched on, defences went up, and he switched to cruise control. As a result, I wound up learning exactly what he wanted me to, not one word more or less.'

Jury president Clint Eastwood finally announced *Pulp Fiction*'s Palme d'Or victory on the last Monday evening of the festival. A few moments later, an elated John joined Quentin Tarantino on the podium with Samuel L. Jackson and Bruce Willis. Most of the black-tie crowd cheered the choice, but from the back of the hall an angry dissenter shouted her disgust at the decision.

The film's distributors Miramax pumped up their marketing efforts just before the US theatrical release of the movie in the fall of 1994. The launch of what was essentially perceived as an arthouse movie into the mainstream market on more than 1,300 screens across America was an expensive roll of the dice that Miramax chiefs feared could seriously backfire if *Pulp Fiction* did not get off to an outstanding opening. In the event, it opened with a whopping $9.3 million, putting it firmly at the top of the US box-office charts, ahead of the Stallone/Stone action flick *The Specialist*.

Another risky aspect of *Pulp Fiction* was the violent content. The film's distributors deliberately concentrated on the humour of the film and the posters featured John Travolta doing the twist. The marketing department at Miramax coped with the potential violence problem by using the shout line, 'You won't know the facts till you see the fiction.'

But one aspect of the opening few weeks of *Pulp* that Miramax had no control over was the response of audiences actually in the movie theatres. One man in New York passed out as he watched John's character Vincent Vega plunging the hypodermic into Mia. 'Is there a doctor in the house?' someone actually asked. The movie was stopped for nine anxious minutes before the announcement came: 'The victim is just fine.'

John announced that he wanted to pilot his Gulfstream to Tokyo for the Japanese première of *Pulp Fiction* but the movie's backers Miramax refused to splash out the $100,000 in fuel that the trip would have cost. An offer was made to fly John first class, but he declined. Officially, John announced he would not be attending that première because it came the day after the New York one. He may have just appeared in a movie for a knock-down fee, but he still expected to be treated like a star.

In the middle of all the hype and excitement over *Pulp Fiction*, John's baby son, Jett, had a brush with death when he was rushed to hospital having inhaled toxic fumes from a carpet detergent. Years later, Kelly, choking back tears, talked about the incident for the first time. 'We've never spoken about it before but when Jett was two he was poisoned by the chemicals in the carpet. We cleaned the carpets religiously because we did not want to have bacteria in them. But because he had breathed in the fumes, his immune system just shut down and he had to be rushed to intensive care.' The couple spent a week of anguish at Jett's bedside before he made a complete recovery. Real-life dramas seemed to follow John wherever he went.

CHAPTER TWENTY-FIVE
THE LOOK

HOLLYWOOD, FALL 1994

John and Uma Thurman entered the trendy diner Jack Rabbit Slims. The hired help were still dead ringers for Marilyn Monroe, Buddy Holly and the young Elvis. John was startled to see them there; he put up his hand as if in self-defence, as if warding off ghosts. Then, he gathered himself, deciding to be amused instead. Lazily he ran his pinned gaze across the room filled with icons, noting who was present, who was missing. He was looking for Tony Manero.

Uma, a blanched witch in a shiny black wig, began to tease and ride him. Gradually, he roused himself from his nodding stupor, and they embarked on that famous *Pulp Fiction* ritual flirtation. Uma ordered him to partner her in a twist contest; they stumbled blindly on to the dance floor. For a beat, before the music started, John hung motionless, his heavy shoulders bowed, staring at the battleground below. His stoned face, all sag, had a half-drowned look. Then the record blared, and his feet began to move him.

John started having this recurring nightmare after making

Pulp Fiction. In it, Uma Thurman would depart from Jack Rabbit Slims, leaving him with Marilyn Monroe and James Dean and Buddy Holly and all those other stars who'd died. It seemed as if Tarantino had only written the movie so that he had some place to go.

Before *Pulp Fiction* was even on general release, John signed for two new movies, including one – an MGM adaptation of Elmore Leonard's bestseller *Get Shorty* – that provided him with $5 million, the highest up-front fee of his career, plus a $750,000 bonus if he received an Oscar nomination for *Pulp Fiction*, plus another $750,000 if he won.

Yet John almost didn't take on the role and it wasn't until a well-timed call from *Pulp Fiction* director Quentin Tarantino that he made his final decision. Tarantino told John, 'This isn't the one you pass on, this is the one you say yes to.'

But John still wasn't completely convinced. 'Well, why?' he asked Tarantino.

'Did you ever read the book?'

'No.'

'Well, *read the book*, now!'

A few minutes later, Danny De Vito – whose company Jersey Films was planning to make *Get Shorty* – called.

'Please read the book, and you'll see why.'

That was it. John immediately signed *before* he'd read the book!

John was to play Chili Palmer – a two-bit hoodlum who is sent to Hollywood to collect gambling debts and finds himself entangled in the movie business. Everyone in real-life Tinseltown agreed that John was born to play Chili.

What no one told him at the time was that Warren Beatty had turned down the role months earlier when he told *Get Shorty* director Barry Sonnenfeld that he couldn't accept that a guy as handsome as him would only be a lowly ranked Mafia hood.

However, before signing the contract, John insisted that much of author Elmore Leonard's dialogue from his original novel be restored to the screenplay. The actor gave a classic example of what he meant: 'In the original script it said something like, "Where's my coat? You better find it. It cost $400." But in the book it was, "You see a black leather jacket, fingertip length, has lapels like a suitcoat? You don't, you owe me three seventy-nine … You get the coat back or you give me the three seventy-nine my wife paid for it at Alexander's." It was the detail that it needed.'

While *Get Shorty* was getting a rewrite, John started work on *White Man's Burden*, a low-budget independent feature being produced by Quentin Tarantino's movie company and directed by Tarantino's friend Desmond Nakano. John adored the story, a dramatic fable about a society in which the roles of whites and blacks are reversed. And he'd agreed to work with first-time director Nakano out of loyalty to Tarantino and his producer/partner Lawrence Bender.

While shooting *White Man's Burden*, John met up with the real Chili Palmer, the mobster upon whom writer Elmore Leonard based the character in his book *Get Shorty*. John was not accustomed to taking acting lessons from a complete unknown. But in this case his 'coach' was a man with a decidedly violent past who had once made his living collecting loan repayments for the Mafia.

Although there were a lot of sinister aspects to the real Chili Palmer, John found him a magnetic, appealing man and especially adored his menacing gravelly voice. He studied and copied the way Chili chomped melodramatically on his Havana cigar, memorised the anecdotes and, above all, perfected the look that says, 'You're mine. I own you.' That look was the piercing stare Chili used to give anyone unfortunate enough to fall behind with the monthly payments (often including extortionate interest).

The real Chili admitted openly that he had shot people and been shot at. His association with the Mob began when he ran nightclubs in New York with money reputed to be from the infamous Colombo crime family. His trademark look was the key to his success and survival and John had to get that right if he was going to portray him accurately on the big screen. As Chili explains, 'I told Mr Travolta, I really didn't want to hurt anyone. I found that if I could give 'em a look and make 'em think that I'm really serious it worked. And that's the way the look came about. I learned that, when you have a hard time getting your money, your best asset is fear. Fear does wonderful things.'

Other projects concerning Travolta at this point included the development of a novella written by Scientology founder L. Ron Hubband. 'Fear' was a horror story about a man who loses four hours of his life and tries to account for them: an evil spirit warns him that, if he solves the mystery, he'll die.

John once again got the writing bug around this time and began playing around with a movie idea that he wanted to direct. It was to be a very sixties-style film from the perspective of people who were on what he considered the other side of the Vietnam experience. John was fascinated by the world inhabited by Andy Warhol, *Vogue* magazine, sex and drugs and music and 'all that great superficial stuff that was juxtaposed to the significance and heaviness of the Vietnam war'.

From 1994 onwards, John and Kelly began spending more and more time at their house in Maine and a recently acquired property in the mid-Californian seaside town of Carmel.

In Maine, the adoring parents put together an extraordinary playland for son Jett. His bedroom was designed in the shape of the hull of a plane, a replica of his father's beloved DC-3 aircraft; a floor-to-ceiling papier-mâché beanstalk wound up a beam; and an ice-cream parlour, a seesaw, a pretend school and a Peter Pan-themed room with glow-in-the-dark stars on the ceilings were all at Jett's disposal. He also had the run of two other rooms painted with Wild West murals. John and Kelly appointed the relative of a senior Scientologist as Jett's nanny.

Jett certainly loves to play-act. One Travolta family friend even disclosed that Jett likes to dress up in his mom's clothes and

Above: His dancing even wooed Princess Diana. The pair are seen here dancing in the White House in front of Ronald and Nancy Reagan.

Below: It was Kelly Preston who captured John's heart, though. The pair married in 1991 in Paris.

Travolta starred as the cuddly father figure in the popular comedy film trilogy, *Look Who's Talking*, alongside Kirstie Alley.

John played the ultra-cool hitman Vincent Vega in Quentin Tarantino's cult classic *Pulp Fiction*. The film had an impressive cast with Samuel L. Jackson, Uma Thurman, Tim Roth and Bruce Willis all starring.

Above: Flying high with Christian Slater in *Broken Arrow*.

Below left: John has never lost his penchant for rich desserts.

Below right: As John's acting profile reached the dizzy Hollywood heights, he moved to this luxurious house in the hills above Sunset Boulevard.

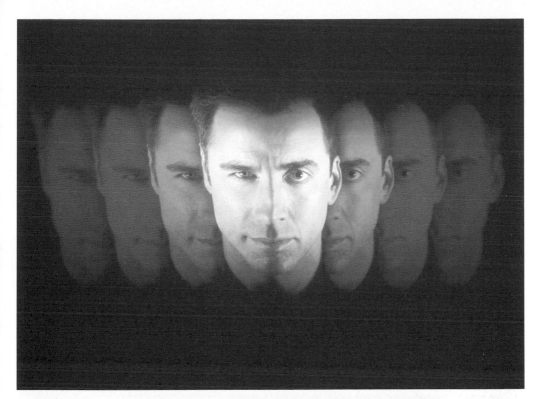

With a succession of lead roles under his belt already, John starred in *Face/Off* alongside Nicolas Cage, *above*, and in *Swordfish* with Halle Berry and the Welsh ex-footballer, Vinnie Jones, *below*.

A licensed jet pilot, John has a passion for flying. He has several planes including a Boeing 707.

Above: Adopting a more rugged look for the 2004 film, *A Love Song for Bobby Long*. He starred alongside Scarlett Johansson and Gabriel Macht.

Below: Uma Thurman teamed up with Travolta for the first time since *Pulp Fiction* in *Be Cool*.

The family man. John and his wife, Kelly with their daughter, Ella. The couple also have a son, Jett, named after Travolta's hobby of flying.

give impromptu performances on a specially constructed stage. It seems that John Travolta's son is clearly following in his father's footsteps.

The Christmas celebrations in 1994 were almost as spectacularly over-the-top as Jett's bedroom. John made lavish preparations for a party to which he had invited his sisters, brothers, father and a few close buddies. Every bedroom in the fifteen-berth property had its own Christmas tree and all John and Kelly's household staff were expected to dress up in red and white throughout the Christmas season. Then on the day itself a Father Christmas arrived by sledge to distribute gifts to all the children. Jett got his own toy car complete with a real engine. John was disappointed that he couldn't find an aeroplane. None of the guests missed out, as videos of some of Hollywood's finest movies hung from each bedroom tree like tinsel. And there was John, perched back on top of his own tree.

CHAPTER TWENTY-SIX

MAKING THE IMPOSSIBLE POSSIBLE

TUDOR-STYLE HOUSE, HOLLYWOOD HILLS, WINTER 1994 – 95

John, Kelly and Jett leased a plush home on the hills above Sunset Strip just before he began shooting *White Man's Burden*. The rent was $25,000 a month and the property had been on sale for $4 million until the Travoltas decided to make it their temporary home.

John took the house on for a total of nine months so that he could go straight on to *Get Shorty*. The property had four bedrooms, seven bathrooms, an office and maid's quarters. It was built in 1926 and the owners had recently spent $1.5 million having it remodelled.

John had the time of his life working on *Get Shorty*. The real Chili Palmer was on the set for much of the time coaching him on getting the look just right. John also had great fun working with co-stars Danny De Vito and Gene Hackman. But it was the continuing friendship with Chili Palmer that gave him the most satisfaction. Those on set watched the pair at work and play and witnessed a remarkable rapport growing between the two men.

After one particularly menacing take, John turned to him and said, 'How was that, Chili? Was that like you would have done it?'

The one-time hood even got a small role in the movie as one of the mobsters in the opening scenes. And the movie's producers agreed to have the end-of-shoot wrap party at the Scientologists' Celebrity Center on Hollywood Boulevard. Some crew members mumbled about the lack of alcohol on offer but John was happy.

Meanwhile, rumours were abounding in Hollywood that John's $5 million fee for *Get Shorty* would be more than doubled for a John Woo-directed action adventure yarn called *Broken Arrow*, with Christian Slater.

John was to play a 'total psychotic' mentor pilot in a movie that has been described as being like '*Speed* on a stealth bomber.' But, best of all, John actually got to fly most of the planes himself. It was also his first real baddie role since *Carrie* back in 1975.

There were also rumours that a fee of even more than $10 million was being offered for John to star in another project entitled *Michael*. The movie is a comedy about two reporters sent to find an angel rumoured to be living in Iowa. John took that one on board after Steven Spielberg called him and told him to do it. 'I think I have the best guardian angels that the planet has to offer,' mused John.

In the middle of 1995, John signed up to star in Rysher Entertainment's *Lady Takes an Ace* from a script by *Cheers* co-creators Glen and Les Charles. His fee was a reported $8 million. Rumours that Sharon Stone would co-star with John faded out towards the end of the year.

There was also another project called *Phenomenon*, about an ordinary man in a small town who becomes a genius after being struck by lightning or, perhaps, hit by an alien force, which was shot in the middle of 1996.

There was no doubt that the movie's title summed up the rebirth of John Travolta.

Meanwhile, as if to prove that *Saturday Night Fever* would

never die, the white three-piece polyester suit worn by John in that movie fetched an extraordinary $145,500 when it was auctioned at Christie's in New York in June 1995. That price smashed the previous record of $46,000 for Marilyn Monroe's dress from *There's No Business Like Showbusiness*. The suit had been owned by movie critic Gene Siskel who'd outbid Jane Fonda when he bought it for just $2,000 two years after *Fever* was made.

John's father Sam died of a heart ailment at a nursing home in Santa Barbara at the age of eighty-four on 29 May 1995. John was comforted in his loss by the presence of his own son Jett and Kelly. He also once again used Scientology as a means of 'handling' his grief, just as he had done all those years earlier when he lost both Diana Hyland and his mother in the space of eighteen months.

BEVERLY HILLS HOTEL LOBBY, SPRING 1995

The movement of his toes passed into his hips, and the movement of his hands passed into his shoulders and arms and his body became a medium of graceful connections as he walked through the most famous hotel lobby in the world. He didn't seem to be heading any particular place, but his arms kept swinging; he stepped on some imaginary beat as though he had just stepped off the streets of Brooklyn.

John presented himself at the entrance to the Polo Lounge inside the freshly refurbished hotel, wearing a houndstooth jacket, khaki slacks, a black band-collared shirt, a pair of black Adidas Sambas and sunglasses with small oval lenses. He was unrecognisable to every man in the bar that afternoon but female eyes were locked on to him. They knew immediately. Just then the piano player broke into 'More Than a Woman' and everyone became aware of the presence of an icon.

Yet on that day John hardly looked like an icon at all. His face wore a coat of grey stubble, he was grey at the temples and he looked like an older man whose face had been stamped with John Travolta's features. He had a large face and a large head. He had short, spiky hair, with the shine of his scalp showing through. He stood very still. Then, spotting the producer he had come to meet, he walked towards a corner at the far end of the bar.

By this time the walk had become much more contained, clenched and careful than before and he seemed to be pulled along by the tips of his toes. The producer got up and greeted John warmly. John whispered something and a waiter was called. He led them to a table on the verandah which was sprinkled with some pollen from the overhanging trees littered with coral pink blossom.

John removed his sunglasses and revealed his eyes. He folded his finely manicured fingers into a stand for the cleft of his famous chin, sniffed the air and looked across the table at his friend. 'Right. What you got for me?'

His voice was slow, soft and sounded much younger than he looked. The producer unlocked his briefcase, pulled out a script and began his pitch ...

It must have been the fiftieth such meeting that year. Ever since *Pulp Fiction* John had once more become the hottest movie star in Hollywood. Every day more than a dozen screenplays were landing on his manager's desk. He was positively overwhelmed and loving every minute of it. John reckoned this had to be his sixth or seventh comeback, but there was something about it this time that convinced him he was here to stay.

Every time he went to the Polo Lounge he would order a hamburger which the staff always appreciated had to be made from ground *filet mignon*. When he ordered dessert, he expected to have at least three choices on the table at any one time. He even demanded a certain brand of iced tea and was renowned at the Polo Lounge for sending it back to the kitchen three or four times: for being too strongly flavoured, for being too weak, for insufficient clarity.

But John didn't bully people to do what he wanted. Instead, he used a quiet voice with a wincing smile and then would try to enlist whoever he was angry with as his collaborator in the task of achieving something worthwhile, be it iced tea or a new movie role. Now that he was a major Hollywood player, every public appearance became a performance worthy of a brilliant – and sometimes eccentric – actor.

At the Polo Lounge that day, John glanced over at the waiter in a white jacket and speculated to his associate, 'I see him standing there, in his nice white jacket and it occurs to me that this man may be a doorway of some kind – a doorway to something to eat.'

The waiter approached the table. John addressed him more like a lord: 'Am I correct in my assumption that you, standing before us in your fine white jacket, will be our doorway to some food?'

The waiter looked bemused. He handed menus out but, before John had even opened his, he ordered fish for both of them. 'Two souls who want sole,' he said, with a chuckle.

Then John stood up and announced to his associate, 'I have to get up now and go' – he scrunched up his rubbery face and gave his voice a high, whimsical fillip '- pee-pee.'

In 1995, John was still driving the same black Rolls-Royce he had bought more than fifteen years previously. It wasn't one of those trim-types, either, the kind that Hollywood wives tend to favour. No, this Rolls was one of those cavernous coupés, tall and formal and anachronistic – a supper club of a car, its interior a parlour of wood and leather, only made contemporary by the baby's car seat perched on the big back benchseat.

By now John was, at just over six feet, nearer to his fighting fit weight of the late seventies than he had been in many years.

One of the main topics of conversation amongst the Hollywood elite at this time was how John had managed to make himself so much money and still hang on to it.

John heard about this when he met Tom Hanks at the Oscars in March 1995, and the actor told him that he'd recently had dinner with Steven Spielberg and some other Hollywood bigwigs and they were saying out loud, 'Where does Travolta get all his money? How much did he make on *Look Who's Talking*? Did he get a percentage on *Saturday Night Fever*? And how did he keep it?'

John was actually rather proud of what he heard. When *Entertainment Weekly* magazine called him a millionaire who lived like a billionaire, he not only accepted the tag but wore it like a tattoo.

'Oh, I love that, because that's just taste – that has nothing to do with dollars. I drive a '78 Rolls-Royce instead of a '95 Rolls. One's $300,000, and the other you can get for 30 grand. But they have the same effect, don't you see? I have a mansion in Maine. Well, you can get a mansion in Maine for X amount of dollars, and you can spend all you want on lifestyle. But if you're going to buy a mansion in Beverly Hills, you're going to spend five times the amount. So I rent a mansion in Beverly Hills and own one where I can afford it. You see? Logic. I could have a G-II Gulfstream or I could buy a brand-new GIV for $30 million. Well, why the hell do I need a GIV when for many millions less I can buy a G-II? The G-II has the same style. It gets you to Hawaii in the same five hours the GIV does. It serves you dinner. You recline in the big seat … You see? It's all a matter of perspective and style. It has nothing to do with anything else. You've seen people in certain areas of the country – how they decorate their homes. They have billions of dollars. Well, you go into their homes, and they have velvet paintings on the wall? You see? Lifestyle is lifestyle. You can wake up, and you can have a gourmet cup of coffee, or you can have … Sanka. You can have it in fine china or you can have it in a Styrofoam cup. You can go to a French movie, or you can see *Die Hard 3*. It's your choice. It's what you want … All it is, you observe how people have done it and, if you like how they've done it, you become the chameleon that you are and live your life like, well, like you're a blue blood or something.'

OSCAR NIGHT, DOROTHY CHANDLER PAVILION, LOS ANGELES 27 MARCH 1995

As Sir Anthony Hopkins ripped open the envelope to announce the winner of the Best Original Screenplay Award, there was a buzz of expectation in the audience.

'Quentin Tarantino and Roger Avary for *Pulp Fiction* ...'

While the opening track from *Pulp* played, Tarantino and his writing buddy Avary met just on the lip of the podium and hugged. In the audience, John applauded. It was his first visit to the Oscars in five years. His wife Kelly – wearing a 'museum piece' Oscar de la Renta gown on loan for the evening – smiled but there was a certain weariness to their reaction. John was happy for his friend Tarantino but he felt he should have been up there, too. Kelly had persuaded him to lift his self-imposed ban on going to the Oscars. But in many ways; he wished he hadn't gone there that evening.

Tarantino was also incensed by the way the Academy ignored John's performance in *Pulp Fiction*. Some said John should have been grateful for at least being nominated for the first time since *Saturday Night Fever*. But John wanted to win. However no one could have countered the enormous success of Tom Hanks and *Forrest Gump*, which took Best Picture, Best Actor and Best Director prizes, besides four other lesser categories.

There was a genuine feeling amongst some of the Academy members that John had been overlooked simply because *Pulp Fiction* was not considered good-quality art by some of the old guard. It had been virtually the same seventeen years earlier with *Saturday Night Fever*.

It was a puzzle that both John and Samuel L.Jackson only managed Oscar nominations for *Pulp Fiction* – and a further riddle that the white man was nominated for Best Actor and the black for Best Supporting Actor. As one respected critic later pointed out, 'They are a pair, not just an intricate study in friendship ... The more you see *Pulp Fiction*, the more ghostly and angelic Travolta becomes, and the bolder and more prophetic Jackson seems. They are like brothers out of Dostoevsky.'

CHAPTER TWENTY-SEVEN

TRUE ROMANCE

SEEDY MOTEL, SUNSET STRIP, HOLLYWOOD, NOVEMBER 1995

John undid the shabby door of the room and crept in quietly. There, waiting on the water bed for him was a beautiful blonde dressed in a black silk basque, seamed stockings and black stilettos.

'Hi,' he whispered.

'Hi, baby.'

'How d'you feel?'

'Hot.'

'How hot?'

'Hot enough for you.'

'Come here.'

'Why?'

'Cos I say so.'

'What happens if I don't?'

'Just do it ...'

She smiled, licked her lips seductively, clearly enjoying his pushy response, and then got up and approached him. They began kissing passionately In the background, a soft-porn movie flickered on the TV screen.

Then John began to slowly strip off his $1,000 Donna Karan suit. His companion looked on in feverish anticipation as, item by item, he peeled off the remainder of his clothes. She took a deep breath and sighed, clearly unable to believe her eyes, then turned towards the bed before beckoning him to follow her.

Stripped naked, John crossed the room and slid between the tacky silk sheets with ... his wife Kelly.

John first got into the habit of slipping away from movie sets for afternoons of sex with his wife during the shooting of *Get Shorty*. He believed that it would spice up his three-year-old marriage – and help him to keep trim.

The couple deliberately picked 'adult' motels with mirrors on the ceiling, soft pink lights and blue movies on the TV. The seedier the better.

The key to all this daring behaviour was John's obsession with never wanting to do anything predictable. Before each love-making session, he would call up Kelly, give her the name of the place and the room number and bark at her to 'Be there'. For Kelly, her husband's domineering attitude was even more of a turn-on.

John particularly loved acting out the role of an adulterous husband meeting a lover by sneaking into the room. Anyone seeing him for real at the motel assumed he was committing adultery.

The couple frequently tried out new love games and sexual positions. They called their romantic sex sessions 'afternoon delight'. And John sincerely believes it has helped keep their love for one another alive.

Sometimes, John acted out the part of Vincent Vega from *Pulp Fiction* or Tony Manero from *Fever*. He'd even introduced Chili Palmer from *Get Shorty*. All the characters he'd played had become a part of John's psyche – he was the ultimate chameleon.

In Hollywood the word was that John's action adventure debut in director John Woo's *Broken Arrow* was going to be packed with excitement. Some of the viewing rushes, particularly those dealing with the cinematic conflict on and around a moving train, looked spectacular. And the swirling camerawork during a gunplay sequence inside a mineshaft was outstanding.

The title *Broken Arrow* referred to a military codeword used to indicate a missing or stolen nuclear weapon. From page one on, *Broken Arrow*'s script hit the ground running and rarely slowed down.

Director Woo – a legend in Hong Kong for his fast-paced action movies – and John hit it off from the moment they first met. They soon built up such a rapport that they did not even feel it necessary to sit around and talk about John's character. Woo explains, 'We just come to the set, talk about the scene and the camera movement and that's it. We don't need a rehearsal because we have great communication.'

The release of *Get Shorty* in America in the fall of 1995 marked yet another turning point in John's career. The movie received very encouraging reviews and went straight to the top of the US box office in its first weekend.

Henry Sheehan in the *Orange County Register*, in California, summed up the movie's appeal. '*Get Shorty* did more than just knock *Seven* off the top of the box-office perch last weekend. The widely praised and obviously popular gangster comedy also confirmed what *Pulp Fiction* had suggested: John Travolta is a star once more.'

Also in November 1995, John signed up to star in *Dark Horse* with respected Hollywood producer Brian Grazer, who'd snapped up the rights to the book of the same title written by Doug Richardson after he'd heard it was one of John's favourites. The movie was expected to shoot in Texas in late 1996.

And John's comeback was further confirmed when it was announced that US cable TV was planning to re-run *Welcome Back Kotter*. Only a couple of years earlier, rumours of a planned movie version of the show were scotched when John refused to sign up as the star.

By the end of 1995, it was reported that John's asking price for movies had rocketed to $21 million and some Hollywood observers predicted it could climb to $30 million by the end of 1996 if his movies continued to do such good business at the box office.

It then emerged that John's $21 million price tag had been deliberately arrived at to ensure he was paid more than any other star in Hollywood where the ceiling on such salaries had reached the $20-million mark.

John even had one extraordinary day when he received seventeen firm movie offers from studios for a total in excess of $200 million. Many of the movies were not worth even considering but it certainly didn't do his self-confidence any harm.

Meanwhile, John's adoration for his young son Jett continued unabated. He was seriously considering giving the child a tutor when he grew older rather than sending him to school. John could not forget how much he had hated school and wanted to ensure that his son would never experience the same trials and tribulations.

As far as more children were concerned, John and Kelly discussed the subject at great length during 1995, but Kelly wanted to reignite her career first.

Yet, throughout all this elation, the ghost of Diana Hyland continued to haunt John. He still missed her terribly despite his newfound happiness with Kelly. One day in the summer of 1995, he was even reduced to tears when a driver who picked him up at his rented home in LA revealed that he was an actor whom Diana had taught back in the mid-seventies. It was so typical of Diana to have helped others just like she'd influenced John. At moments like these John realised she could never be entirely replaced. Then it hit him that he was forty-one years old, the same age as she had been when she died. She had experienced as much as he had now. He just prayed that heaven was as good a place as he thought.

John's Gulfstream came to the rescue of his celebrity friend

Lisa Marie Presley when her marriage to Michael Jackson broke up in January 1996. John lent her his plane to flee LA for New York following the shock news. John knew Lisa Marie through her involvement in Scientology.

John also became close friends with Tom Hanks and, in late 1995, the two actors met with Quentin Tarantino to talk about a possible collaboration. No concrete project has yet emerged, but the three Hollywood stars are convinced that something will come along in the near future.

In the spring of 1996, John managed to squeeze in yet another movie project when he agreed to work with director Roman Polanski in Paris on a film called *The Double*. John explains, 'I am this boring accountant who's in love, from a distance, with Isabelle Adjani, and he has a double in his mind who is suave and sophisticated: the side of his personality he'd like to be. So I've got to be cool and then uncool.'

Get Shorty continued to do great business and hit the $100 million mark in the United States in January 1996. Hollywood remained convinced that John's performance as Chili Palmer had ensured its success.

In the middle of January, at the prestigious Golden Globe awards – considered the first hurdle for the Oscars – John won the Best Actor in a Comedy Award for his starring role in *Get Shorty*. Hollywood started to talk in deadly serious terms about John getting all the way to the Oscar podium, which would be the ultimate confirmation, if any were needed, that he had achieved the most remarkable comeback in movie history.

But when the Oscar nominations were announced in February 1996, John's name was not among them. He was clearly upset, and he admitted, 'Everyone seemed to assume that I would get one, and when it didn't happen it hit me like a tidal wave. Then I had to get over it and get on with my life. I've put my personal hurt aside and, really, I'm pleased for the people who did get chosen.'

The last word was left to John's diminutive *Get Shorty* co-star,

Danny De Vito. He quipped, 'Next year John is going to be nominated for playing a farmer who has a pig ... I play the pig. It's going to be called *Yo, Babe!*'

One quiet Sunday morning in the late 1990s, John decided to take his latest acquisition – a beautiful red 1964 Jaguar – out for a spin near his rented home in Beverly Hills. He put the top down, dressed in his favourite Donna Karan suit and designer sunglasses and headed for Sunset Boulevard.

On a hairpin bend, the car spluttered to a stop. 'My face goes as red as the car,' he explains. 'I hear honk, honk, honk. I'm thinking, Why did I try to be cool? People are screaming, "Fuck you." Then suddenly the drivers recognise me and it's "Need any help?" I'm like "No, I'm fine." A guy finally comes down from one of the mansions and helps me push the car in his driveway.'

Travolta asked the man, 'Do you want a picture for your kids, anything?'

'No, but I'd love a dance lesson.'

The memories of Tony Manero will never fade.

CHAPTER TWENTY-EIGHT
ON A ROLL

HOLLYWOOD, 1996

In Tinseltown, they say that the definition of a star is when an actor's presence can turn even the biggest load of nonsense into a piece of high-octane entertainment. Many were saying that *Broken Arrow* was a classic example. As the respected Baz Bamigboye wrote in the *Daily Mail*, 'Really, it should be called "*Speed* Goes Ballistic" because it reminds me of the Keanu Reeves – Sandra Bullock movie *Speed* – only, in this, Travolta plays an ace aviator gone bad who steals two thermo-nuclear missiles and is tracked by former buddy Christian Slater and park ranger Samantha Mathis.'

John was already starting to feel he'd been re-processed more times than corned beef, the confetti of compliments had long since fallen away and he was feeling very wary about his apparent 're-birth'. On the surface he hid his insecurities well by being friendly and shaking everyone's hand – even the most sleazy of hacks. But, despite all the latest praise being heaped upon him, John didn't want to be seduced by it. He'd even lost the stone in weight he'd put on to play Tarantino's smack-addicted hitman in *Pulp Fiction*.

251

But then John had never lost the will or ability to work hard and now all that was at last once again paying dividends, although he privately confessed to some friends that he thought he'd had his twenty years of fame and was about to completely fade out when Quentin Tarantino popped up on the horizon.

Now John was, once again, up and running as a major Hollywood star and seemed to be loving every minute of it. No wonder he'd jumped into the part of Chili Palmer in *Get Shorty* after Warren Beatty passed up on that golden opportunity. John's performance in that movie summed up his attitude towards life at the time: he wore cool, dark clothes despite the onset of a paunch and delivered a few knockout lines as if he was adding fudge sauce to a sundae. He stayed effortlessly in command. It was a set of tried and trusted routines summed up by that warning line in *Pulp*: 'Just because you're a character doesn't mean you have a character.'

Many believed by now that John deserved an Oscar and some even speculated (rather wildly) that it might come thanks to *Broken Arrow*, which had shot to the top of the US box office immediately after its release in February 1996. But John's role as an evil Stealth-bomber pilot who plans to hijack his own nuclear weapons and sell them back to the US Government was hardly the type of movie that demanded Oscar attention.

John's great evil gesture in that film was to brush the underside of his chin with the backs of his fingers. In many ways it was a ten-year-old's idea of evil but in John it looked like a twisted combination of smart and attractive. At forty-two, he was holding the camera like few others, and his confidence continued to grow by the second. John Travolta was on a roll and he had no intention of getting off.

Projects were lined up years in advance. In *Phenomenon*, released at Christmas 1996, he played a man possessed of extraordinary intelligence. There was also talk about him going to Paris to star in Roman Polanski's version of Dostoevsky – *The Double* – about a cool dude who wakes up one day to find the world contains his mirror image. John was intrigued by the Polanski project if only because he always seemed to carry his own intellectual and spiritual mirror with him. These days John might have been bigger, wiser and even more assured than before but he still retained a sense of being a kid whose ultimate dream had come true.

However, within weeks of agreeing to do *The Double* with Polanski, John was facing a $40-million lawsuit for allegedly walking out on the diminutive Polish director. The film company, Mandalay, was also reportedly threatening to hold John's personal $130,000 trailer hostage to get him to pay the costs that had been run up to date. One French magazine claimed Travolta had fallen out with Polanski when he was asked to do a nude scene. The actor told *Paris Match* magazine, 'I've never acted naked in my entire career and I'm not going to start now that I'm fat.'

Polanski, who had already started rehearsals in Paris, replaced John with comic Steve Martin. And highly respected Hollywood newspaper, *Daily Variety*, also reported that John had walked off the set after a row with Polanski. John even told the American magazine *Entertainment Weekly* that about thirty pages of the original screenplay were dropped and confirmed that a new scene had been added – in which he was to appear naked.

In the middle of all this, details of John's extraordinary perks on the film were leaked to the press. According to newspaper reports, he'd demanded more than a dozen assistants, including personal trainers and massage therapists, on location. John had even insisted on having his own chef flown in to satisfy his delicate palate. The movie's producers continued to insist in public that John had quit the set because of a medical crisis with his son Jett. Later reports claimed that John eventually settled his differences with the producers of *The Double* by agreeing to make a movie for nothing and pay compensation for the delays caused by his earlier walkout. The full story as to why John did not make the film may never be known.

Some in Hollywood were concerned that John was not utilizing his obvious talent to the full and might make a series of *Broken Arrow*-style action movies that barely exercised his acting muscles. As Peter Bart added, 'It's crunch time for Travolta. He should think it over. There might not be a third chance.'

John himself considered he had been carefully building, movie by movie, a protective wall around his professional life. He wanted to be in control, to dictate and be the master of his future. Walking out on the Polanski project, *The Double*, had been, in his eyes, a classic example of his new determination. He'd even shrugged off that threat of a lawsuit.

But, no matter how bright the future looked, John could never completely escape his traumatic past. Even filming a moving scene in another new film, *Michael*, brought painful memories flooding back thanks to a deathbed scene that had uncanny parallels with the tragedy of Diana Hyland's death more than twenty years earlier.

John admitted, 'The movie wasn't dissimilar to what happened before. The way I die in the movie was not unlike how Diana died in my arms. You've got to understand that the whole script is riddled with emotion. You couldn't get on set without laughing or crying ... the movie was so beautifully written.

'In the bed, in every take, it was easy to contact that real emotion. Throughout the movie it was like that. There was a sense of déjà vu. I had experienced death in my life – my parents, girlfriend, loved ones, friends. I've witnessed that, so I was kind of able to identify with the loss. I've learned that death is part of life and I'd experienced the reality in playing that aspect of the character. I think I've worked around those tragic moments like everyone has to. As you get older you lose people, but I think that I had a source of experience to identify with. I don't like losing people. It's painful, frustrating to feel that you can't keep Mom and Dad. When I read the script I cried very hard. I threw it across the room because I was so moved by it.'

In the middle of all this, stories began appearing in British newspapers claiming that John was 'ballooning into a tub of lard' because he was eating *eight* meals a day. One source told a newspaper that filming on *Michael* had become farcical because he was stopping constantly for meal breaks. Director Nora Ephron was even quoted as saying, 'We'll be on set when his caterer will materialise, carrying a little silver tray with a club sandwich for John. That's the meal between the 10.00 snack and the 11.30 snack.'

As one newspaper cruelly pointed out, 'Travolta is playing a middle-aged angel in the movie but looks more like a chubby cherub. He gobbles cakes, chocolate, steak, chips and any other fattening food he can get his hands on.'

Actress friend and co-star Kyra Sedgewick told one paper, 'I was with John recently and they bought him a big plate of chocolate cake, vanilla cake, fruit tart and a large brownie. I said, "Are you going to eat all that?" and he replied, "Probably." I thought, Oh my God!'

In the middle of all this, there were rumours that John was set to take the lead role in the movie of Andrew Lloyd-Webber's *Phantom of the Opera*. As one of his associates pointed out, 'I dunno about a phantom. In John's current state he might prove a little too large for such a role.'

In the middle of 1996, John was rumoured to be about to clinch a $12 million deal to star in *Primary Colors* for veteran Hollywood director Mike Nichols. It might help make up for the disappointment of never actually buttoning down a deal on Andrew Lloyd-Webber's *Phantom of the Opera*, for which many still believed John was tailor-made. Not even a personal appeal by Lloyd-Webber to John could help settle the deal and eventually the project floated away only to be finally made into a feature film with a less well-known actor called Gerald Butler in the lead role in late 2004.

In early 1997, John and Kelly splashed out $2.3 million on the six-bedroom, Spanish-style house they'd been renting in the LA suburb of Brentwood. But the outlay on the property, which included a tennis court, gym, library-study and bar set in nearly 2.5 acres, would have little impact on John's healthy finances. He'd just copped a $12 million fee for the movie *Michael* and had at least three similar-priced deals in the works for the following eighteen months.

In June 1997, the Hollywood trade press suggested that John was being lined up to play a *Batman* villain alongside Madonna for the fifth instalment of the blockbuster movie series. John and Madonna were even said to have been offered more than $12 million between them and director Joel Schumacher had even informed John he'd like him to play the Scarecrow while Madonna was to play the avenging wife of The Joker, played by Jack Nicholson in the first *Batman* film.

In the summer of 1997, Kelly gave one of her most revealing interviews about life with husband John to the *Mail on Sunday* magazine in London. In it, she even admitted that John got very jealous of her love scenes on film sets. Said Kelly, 'He hates them. When it comes to the scene, he closes his eyes and puts his hands over his ears.'

She said that her love scene with Tom Cruise in the hit movie *Jerry Maguire* was 'not easy'. Kelly explained, 'It was supposed to be easier because Tom is a close friend of us both. But it was not easier for any of us, to be honest. I knew it was going to be a wild scene and I tried to convince the director that we could do it with our clothes on. But he didn't go for that at all.' Not even a few harmless words from Cruise made the sex scene any easier. As Kelly explained, 'Tom asked me if I'd had a nice weekend and what I'd had for breakfast. A few seconds later, the director called "action" and I had my legs wrapped around him.'

Equally sexy scenes in another of Kelly's movies called *Addicted to Love* proved just as difficult for the couple to handle. Kelly admitted, 'They were no easier for me or John. It is always hardest on the one you love. Even when he knows how technical these things are, once he is caught up in the movie, watching the love scenes is no fun at all.'

Kelly happily explained the depth of her love for John to any enquiring journalists and said she wanted to have six children by him. But she did admit to one reporter that John considered his own worst fault to be his big appetite. However, she qualified this by saying, 'He would say that he eats too much and puts on weight. As for me, I like to see a man enjoying his food.' Kelly summed up her feelings when she was asked, 'What is your idea of heaven?' and she answered, 'I think I'm already in it.'

Also in the summer of 1997, John and Kelly were voted 'Showbusiness Couple of the Year' in a ceremony at New York's Friar's Club. John even piloted Kelly in one of his planes from their summer home in Maine. John, looking fitter and trimmer than a few months earlier, told club members that he attributed the stability of their eight-year marriage to the fact that 'We never appear in the same film. Being together twenty-four hours a day wouldn't be good for either of us.'

At another ceremony in New York a few weeks later, John buddied up to old playmate Sylvester Stallone at Manhattan's Waldorf Astoria, sidelining their womenfolk in the process. Stallone paid his dues with some friendly looking respect, including direct eye contact and constantly seeming to appreciate John's every word. John looked less impressed with his Hollywood rival.

Around the same time, a bizarre request was made to John when he was offered $1.5 million to escort an Arab billionaire's daughter around Paris. Part of the deal was that he would collect the spoiled seventeen-year-old in his private jet from Riyadh, in Saudi Arabia, and whisk her off to the French capital. But John – then getting around $20 millon a movie – said, 'I don't need the money. And I'm married.'

In June 1997, the blue silk and velvet gown that Princess Diana wore when she danced with John at that White House dinner back in 1985 was sold for £134,000, a record price for a costume, in a charity auction held at Christie's in New York.

In the middle of his busy shooting schedules on several multi-million-dollar movies, John found time to make two days of appearances on Capitol Hill, in Washington, to speak about the 'frightening level' of intolerance in Germany towards Scientologists such as himself and Tom Cruise. John even suggested, 'Are the Thought Police far behind?'

His appearance, along with two other Scientology celebrities, musicians Isaac Hayes and Chick Corea, was part of a vitriolic feud between the group and German authorities. Germany had voiced alarm over the Scientologists and called it a dangerous cult that brainwashed its members. Scientologists were already barred from the main political parties and Bavaria was screening applicants for civil service jobs to see if they were members of the group.

John urged US legislators to complain about the Germans, especially since the country's two leading political parties had called for the boycott of Cruise's movie *Mission: Impossible*. John said, 'The mere attempt by politicians to censor art because of the artist's religious affiliation sends chills down my spine.'

CHAPTER TWENTY-NINE
TEARS FOR DIANA

MAINE, SEPTEMBER 1997

John was reduced to tears by the news of the tragic death of Princess Diana in a car crash in a Paris underpass. He'd always been immensely proud of dancing with the Princess at the White House all those years earlier and found it hard to accept that the controversial young British royal was gone forever.

A few weeks after Diana's death, John even went so far as to pledge that if he and Kelly had a baby daughter they would call her Diana. He'd already renamed one of his fleet of planes 'The English Rose'. John explained, 'I just thought, Well, I don't know what I can do but I'd like to reach out to her husband and children. I gotta do something. It was more for them than it was for me.'

Around this time, John was so outraged by a British TV documentary about his beloved Church of Scientology that he wrote to Channel 4 in protest. In his letter to Michael Jackson, then head of Channel 4, he even accused the programme makers of slander. Alan Hayling, deputy commissioning editor, insisted the documentary was portraying church founder L. Ron

Hubbard as 'charming but flawed'. He also pointed out that John hadn't even seen the film. 'He didn't give us a fax number so we had to reply by airmail. We told him the programme would be fair.'

But, in his letter, John implored television executives to let so-called 'true' friends of Mr Hubbard, who died in 1986, be interviewed for the fifty-minute programme. He also claimed the makers were inciting hatred of the Scientologists, who had a flourishing UK base in East Grinstead, Sussex.

Also in the autumn of 1997, John's latest movie *Face/Off* was completed and released. John, naturally, wanted the world to believe it was the best action film ever made. Driven by the star power of John and Nicholas Cage there seemed little doubt that it would make hundreds of millions of pounds worldwide. But the film was criticised on a number of fronts with many reviewers criticising the motivation for Travolta's supposedly heroic character.

In November 1997, John's wife Kelly sought a legal ban on a supposedly sex-mad writer who she claimed was stalking her. Kelly said that Joseph Cheffo had a fixation about being her husband and he'd written to her about his sexual hang-ups – and his lifetime of love for Kelly. Then in a bizarre development, Cheffo, thirty, also claimed he'd been mirroring himself on movie idol John for the previous fifteen years. The court application was sparked after Cheffo managed to get on to the set of a movie Kelly was making with Eddie Murphy in Florida. The part-time waiter with Hollywood ambitions then handed a typed letter addressed to Kelly to one of the film crew. Kelly later described the letter as 'extremely offensive' and 'sexually disturbing'. Cheffo's father later insisted to reporters that his son meant no harm to Kelly and had apologised to her.

When in January 1998, US President Bill Clinton endured a week of humiliation facing sensational allegations of sexual infidelity starring Miss Monica Lewinsky, John Travolta was limbering up for the most topical role of his career. For, while Clinton starred on TV denying an affair with his intern, John was acting his socks off in *Primary Colors*, a $40 million movie based on political writer Joe Klein's bestselling novel that was a thinly disguised account of the rise of Bill and Hillary Clinton.

Director Mike Nichols – who also made *The Graduate* and *Who's Afraid of Virginia Woolf?* – bought the book rights with £1 million of his own money, beating all the Hollywood studios, so he would have the freedom to make the film the way he wanted to. He first offered the Presidential part to Tom Hanks who turned it down. John was more than happy to step in. As Nichols explained, 'The story deals with honour, a subject that the movies love. Whatever dirty deeds the candidate and his staff engaged in, they're reaching for the high ground. We haven't changed any central events of the story in any way ... That's the beauty of it. It's not small or mean, it's much larger than that.'

The producers of the movie eventually cut out a scene involving the governor's wife called Susan Stanton (British actress Emma Thompson) and the couple's communications strategist, played by black British actor Adrian Lester, whom she seduces in a one-night stand. Veteran Hollywood director Mike Nichols insisted the cut was for 'artistic reasons'. Sex scenes involving the would-be President (John Travolta), including one where he bedded the teenage daughter of the owner of his favourite restaurant back home in the south, were present in the film.

Primary Colors was later described by one critic as being 'a coruscating, savage indictment not just of the bankrupt morality, ruthlessness and manipulative talents of the presidency, but of the corrupt machinery they used to get in the White House'. The President and his wife were depicted as vacuous and indecisive, eager to jump into bed with any campaign helper willing to oblige them. Their marriage isn't about fidelity, it's about power.

Given the 'Monicagate' scandal then engulfing Clinton, the film was set to become an event movie. John played 'President Stanton' as a podgy, sexually amoral Southern governor while his wife (played by Thompson) was an ambitious, scheming bully. The movie centred on the couple's extraordinary journey to the White House.

John went to enormous lengths to take on the persona and style of Clinton. He copied the President's hair colour, gestures and honey-dipped Arkansas accent. He even adopted Clinton's mannerisms from the hands draped limply over the lectern in mid-speech, to the chin resting on a fist while listening.

There was one extraordinary scene in which John patted his blow-dried hair and allowed himself a self-congratulatory smile – body language that was as much Clinton's trademark as his rasping Southern drawl. John, who studied hours of video tapes of Clinton, even admitted to one journalist, 'I'm really playing him.'

John was believed to be getting $12 million for appearing in *Primary Colors* but, he later told friends, the fee was irrelevant. 'I thought this was a challenging part and I wanted it real bad.' Playing the most powerful man in the world was a role that John Travolta had always hankered after. And for that reason, *Colors* could be seen as not just an insight into the Clintons but also an epitaph to John, the man who genuinely believed he should be king of Hollywood.

It was said that John had even met with national security adviser Sandy Berger to research his role although suggestions that President Clinton had tried to influence his performance were strongly denied, with John insisting, 'You have to be dead not to see that this film favours Clinton. I've always said that I think he'll be pleased with it because, more than anything, it promotes what a decent fellow he is.'

But makers Universal had bigger worries on their mind. They feared that the avalanche of advance publicity around the film threatened to drive audiences away because they were sick of hearing about the Clinton scandal. Director Mike Nichols commented in the run-up to the film's release, 'Clinton's a great man. He's great with people. Unfortunately, he can't keep his pants zipped.' Nichols always strongly denied removing any damaging scenes in the film in order to be nice to the Clintons. Many believed that the first man in the queue when the film opened would be Bill Clinton himself yet most believed that the President would not suffer any lasting harm by the portrayal of him by John up on the big screen.

Just before the film's release, Clinton even invited John to re-enact his role in *Primary Colors* during a White House party. John explained, 'I declined because I decided that it was best to leave the character on the screen and not go and do parties. However, it was a very funny and interesting invitation. I think it was to show his sense of humour about the whole thing. I understand the President is anxious to see the film and would like to see it, but in private.'

In May 1998, *Primary Colors* opened the Cannes Film Festival, four months after its disappointing showing at the US box office. John relished the glamour and attention he received in France and openly admitted that *Pulp Fiction* four years earlier had given him what he called his 'second act'.

John stood in front of a table groaning under the weight of sticky buns and doughnuts. Picking up one of the calorie-packed delights, the often chubby star greedily wolfed it down in just two bites as he delivered a line of dialogue. As the director shouted 'Cut' cast and crew members broke into applause. But John was totally oblivious to the attention and simply carried on eating ... and eating. One member of the crew later explained, 'I watched him demolish six doughnuts by himself. We filmed that scene at around 11 am. An hour later, John was hungry again. I couldn't believe it when he sat down to a three-course meal.'

Friends were starting to fear that John was becoming the Hollywood heavy of all time in every sense of the word. He might have been grabbing $12 million a movie but it was his ability to grab every bit of food on a movie set that was really getting tongues wagging. John even boasted to one journalist that putting on an extra stone to play the presidential candidate in *Primary Colors* was 'the easiest thing in the world to do'.

John was fond of recalling his days as the svelte star of *Saturday Night Fever*: 'I often look back at those days with fondness. But I don't think I'd dare even try to wear that outfit now. I love my food.' Back in 1978, John had been eleven stone of carefully toned muscle. But, since those heady days, he'd fought a virtually nonstop battle with the bulge. He even insisted, 'I do try and eat healthily and stay fit by exercising. But life's too short to diet constantly. Food is one of the greatest pleasures in life.'

By 1998, John was tipping the scales at a whopping fifteen stone and he had three full-time chefs travelling with him everywhere, taking it in turns to prepare his favourite food. On movie sets, the chefs prepared three different breakfasts and three lunches each day. One later explained, 'He loves having a choice. But very often, he'll ask for all three meals to be made and then he'll demolish most of each. He's a larger-than-life character with a larger-than-life appetite.'

Many of John's closest friends and associates say that food is the actor's only vice. One explained, 'John is a loyal, wonderful family man. He doesn't drink, smoke or play around. Food is his only weakness. When he's not away filming, he pays close interest to that day's meals. His private chefs prepared a selection of printed menus and John gets very involved in choosing the dishes of the day, based on the fruits, meats and vegetables of the season.'

John's typical day at this time began with a lavish breakfast of calorie-packed fruit milkshake, eggs benedict, ham or sausage on the side, topped off with a large pot of coffee and fresh cream, toast and buttery croissants. Lunch was a choice between his favourite garlic-mashed potatoes with meat loaf and gravy, deep-fried scampi and chips, or an entire prime rib steak with baked potato and cauliflower cheese. One associate said, 'John is also very particular in taking his lunch and dinner breaks with fine bone china, crystal glasses, white napkins and fresh flowers on the table.'

A close friend added, 'John rarely drinks alcohol but, if he does, it's a single glass of fine wine. Between meals, John is constantly snacking. He loves cakes and chocolates. There's always enough food to feed an army in his trailer.'

At dinner, John pushed the boat even further out! He had his favourite meal – fresh lobsters tails in hot butter – at least once a week. He also adored pasta smothered in cream, sauces and high-calorie Chinese food. John even managed to make a joke about his weight when appearing on a US TV chat show in which he talked glowingly about his *Grease* co-star Olivia Newton-John. 'She's still the same perfect size six she has always been. Lucky her! But hey, I'm having fun and life's good – and so is the food!'

Wife Kelly insisted she didn't care how fat John got and the actor himself admitted, 'I know I have a love handle or two, but I'm lucky that, at this stage in my career, it's not hurting the work I do. And my wife loves the extra meat on me!'

So perhaps it was rather apt when John was rumoured to be interested in a role in a new movie called *It Ain't About The Food* in which he would be playing the part of restaurant owner Bobby Ochs. New Yorker Ochs even told one reporter, 'You cannot believe how much John Travolta eats. When we ate together, he ordered three servings of every dessert on the menu – for tasting purposes, he claimed. There were just the two of us, and he polished off every one of them – even the ones he said he didn't especially like.' Ochs, evidently impressed with John's stamina, continued, 'I've owned restaurants for forty years and I have never seen anyone eat that much bulk at one sitting, to say nothing of the calories. He ate so many desserts.'

And then there was John the mystic healer. In the middle of 1998, he bumped into rock star Sting during a trip to Canada and offered to help cure him of a sore throat and flu symptoms. John explained, 'I did two or three different types of assists, and he felt better.'

John's ability to 'cure' Sting provoked headlines across the world, especially as an 'assist' was a term used by Scientologists to describe 'tuning into the sick body' to cure it. John also claimed to reporters that Sting was just one of many people cured by his healing powers. 'They just help the person heal quicker ... by getting in communications with the body ... I use them if someone's not been feeling well, or if there's been an injury,' explained John. Even when patients were not miraculously healed, John claimed, 'I have never failed helping a person feel better, at least.'

And John continued to take fatherhood very seriously. Jett was already a miniature version of his dad with soft blue eyes, dark hair and the famed dimpled chin. 'Everyone who knows Jett falls in love with him,' explained John to one reporter. 'He affects people in a way I've never seen before. When we're out he'll be in my arms, like a koala bear with his arms wrapped tightly around my neck. We're inseparable.'

In the summer of 1998, John was taken to hospital after getting a marble stuck up his nose while showing Jett some magic tricks. One of his Hollywood spokesmen explained, 'John always fancied himself as a bit of a magician. But now he's sticking to card tricks.'

In June 1998, John revealed for the first time how he had bought the 'Connie', one of a handful of Lockheed Constellations still flying. Back in 1984, John had taken over the controls of the aircraft with a view to restoring her to her former glory. But he soon discovered she was one of the most expensive planes in the world to run, with four 56-litre Wright Cyclone engines burning 1,250 gallons an hour on take-off, and John eventually sold her in 1987, having failed to do any restoration work on her. The buyers were a restoration group and the airliner eventually flew again in 1992.

By this time, John's extraordinary collection of planes included, his Gulfstream II, which slept ten and had a full kitchen and a cinema, and his less ostentatious LearJet, which he used to travel between his mansions across the United States including the property in Florida, where his home in Spruce Creek was part of a development built around an airport. His third aircraft at this time was a 1947 single-engine Vampire fighter plane, used for fun not transport. As he had earned more and more money, he'd flown bigger and more complex aircraft. By now he had seven different jet 'ratings' and more than 4,000 hours in the air. His only close accident was that incident over Washington. In 1997, John even wrote a children's book entitled *Propeller One-Way Night Coach* as 'a homage to the great aviation experiences I had growing up'.

In late 1998, John surprised even his closest Hollywood friends and associates by making a brief cameo appearance in the movie *The Thin Red Line*, playing a US Admiral in veteran director Terence Malick's Second World War drama. He explained, 'I took the part because twenty years ago Terence had really wanted me to star in his film *Days of Heaven* but I couldn't get out of my contract with the TV sitcom *Welcome Back Kotter*. He was heartbroken about that and says he didn't make another movie for two decades because of it. This is his first movie since and, although there's no main part in it for me, he wanted me anyway so wrote in a cameo. I'm only in the first few minutes so don't be late.'

John's next big role in *A Civil Action*, featured him playing a real-life personal-injury lawyer called Jan Schlichtmann, who was famous in America for being a renowned legal crusader. His turning point came when he fought and won a labyrinthine lawsuit for a group of Massachusetts families whose children died from leukaemia after drinking water contaminated by two of the USA's largest corporations.

The film caused ripples on the corporate pond, shooting to the top of the US box office and winning John an award for his commitment to social and political issues. John even admitted, 'I chose *A Civil Action* because the subject matter – toxic-waste poisoning – is one that needs attention and I'm thrilled that this movie has raised people's awareness. I'm convinced that we all have to pay attention to things we use, we eat, we handle.'

John then went on to talk about the appalling chemical incident involving his baby son Jett back in 1994. 'His body swelled up and his temperature hit 105. Apparently, 11,000 people have had similar reactions to the same brand of cleaner. Now I'm on several boards concerned about pesticides, the rain forest, pollution of the ocean and toxic-waste issues. Casa Travolta has become a totally natural house.'

John really was back at the top of the showbusiness tree this time; he was the highest-paid star in Hollywood and he had a young family to go home to every night. As he admitted to one reporter, 'I live a blessed life.' However, John still never missed an opportunity to thank his mother for his first break in life. 'My mother told me that when she was pregnant with me I danced in her womb. I've always used the dance thing as a metaphor for my life. You can't dance without legs, so during the bad years I simply continued to work with the best that was offered, which wasn't always great.'

John also didn't hesitate at this time to once again publicly credit the Scientologists with keeping him afloat during the bad times. 'It's always been a safe haven for me in Hollywood. The reason I didn't end up like Marilyn or Elvis is that I had Scientology to go to. Gosh, it's helped me.'

Now forty-five years old, John's lustrous black hair might have been thinning and turning salt-and-pepper and his gut seemed omnipresent, but there remained a quality about his eyes and a physical presence that made him still grab the screen in every scene. He even admitted, 'I'm OK with getting older. I don't even care about the weight business. When I'm not working I put on a few pounds but I'm good at getting into shape. I don't want a trainer prodding me all the time. For my epitaph they could write, "He only wanted to be comfortable."' Then he added, 'And if I go bald I could have someone colour the bald spots or I could wear a hat. Who cares?'

But then John seemed to have everything so why should he care? He owned at least half a dozen properties, which kept him more than occupied. He was immensely proud of getting his First Officer's rating with American Airways. He was regularly flying himself to movie sets and on publicity tours in one of his favourite new toys.

John admitted to friends at this time that he also had other, more important priorities. 'It's time to do some family stuff. Hang from monkey bars with Jett and go swimming in the creek or do another boat trip and take him flying, sitting on my lap. Having a kid has changed my life more than anyone ever told me. I thought it would be like having a nephew or loving your best friend's child. But it's this other universe of affection and care that compares to nothing.

'We're planning another child. We're "in talks" right now – but Kelly's arrived at a point in her career, which is crucial. [She'd just completed *Daddy and Them* with Billy Bob Thornton and *For The Love Of The Game* with Kevin Costner]. But I'd put my money on Kelly being pregnant by the end of next month!'

After *A Civil Action*, John's latest roles included *The General's Daughter*, co-starring Madeleine Stowe, *Battlefield Earth*, taken from one of L. Ron Hubbard's Scientology-inspired books, and *The Shipping News*, rumoured to be alongside wife Kelly. She also was due to co-star in a film being made by John called *Standing Room Only*, about a nightclub singer called Jimmy Roselli, who never got out from under the shadow of Frank Sinatra and Tony Bennett and who refused to use Mob connections. John explained, 'I sing in the film, so I'm back in singing lessons. I should have brought my little cassette with me. I've already recorded sixteen songs.'

John added, 'Y'know, we joke about dancing now being written into my contract! Well, I wanna return to my roots and do a musical with Barbra Streisand. Barbra and I are turning out to be the last dinosaurs of the musical. We could dance up a storm and at least now I won't have to wear white polyester.'

Meanwhile, back at home in Hollywood, John was still regaling a small, select band of friends with camp impersonations of Bette Davis and his good pal Barbra Steisand. One friend explained, 'John's still adores mimicking people and is very proud of being able to do any voices, any accent and any pose but he particularly loves taking off women performers.'

John even hired a well-known Hollywood wardrobe designer to supply special big-size dresses so he could entertain his pals. 'His private shows are sensational,' commented one friend. 'He once performed a superb version of Barbra Streisand's "The Way We Were". It was incredible and everyone gave him a standing ovation.'

Also, on the home front, Kelly was pregnant once more. John was delighted and told anyone who would listen that he was desperate for a girl to complete the perfect family unit.

CHAPTER THIRTY

WELCOME TO BATTLEFIELD EARTH

THE SKIES ABOVE THIS PLANET, 31 December 1999

Plane-crazy John decided on the ultimate special treat for wife Kelly to celebrate the millennium together. John spent the entire evening racing the time zones around the world aboard one of his collection of aeroplanes just so he could say 'Happy New Year' to Kelly 'more than once'. John had even put in some extra pilot training during the autumn months of 1999 and, although he avoided champagne on the big night, he did have his personal chef on board to whip up some gourmet food.

In February 2000, John and Kelly were preparing for the impending birth of their second child and, once again, Kelly would be expected to do so without the aid of painkillers, breathing techniques or even a scream. The actress had, once more, taken a self-imposed vow of silence to follow the teachings of their shared religion, Scientology. John explained, 'It's called quiet birth.' That vow was intended to avoid having the baby hear words because, 'as she grows up and hears these same words, it will stimulate memories of the pain of birth'.

John steadfastly refused to leave Kelly and their home near

Santa Barbara, California, because of the impending birth so the producers of his latest movie, *Numbers*, had to provide fake snow for a toboggan chase costing the production an extra $500,000 because it had to be filmed in Calfornia rather then Alaska. His loyalty to wife and new child was rewarded when a beautiful little girl called Ella was born.

Soon afterwards, John began devoting his time to a Scientology-inspired $50 million film called *Battlefield Earth*. The project came under fire even before filming had started. John was to play an evil nine-foot alien, but critics were soon accusing the project of being a huge advert for the Church of Scientology founder L. Ron Hubbard – who wrote the book on which the movie was based on. Rumours were flying around Hollywood that John had taken virtually no upfront fee for the role, although he insisted to journalists that the film had no sinister meanings, pointing out that Hubbard wrote science-fiction books before founding Scientology.

John had secretly struggled for many years to get the movie made and defended his decision by saying, 'This is the pinnacle of using my power to do something I like to do.' He added, 'In the film, it is my face but I put on this whole apparatus. I'll have four-foot stilts so I'll be walking and then the camera crew will shoot certain angles that will capture more difference between the heights. I also have a big tall head with hair and these strange things. I have amber eyes and talons for hands. It is a quite remarkable and detailed production.'

John had originally intended to direct the movie himself but then stepped aside for science-fiction expert Brit Roger Christian to go behind the camera. John explained, 'You have to have someone who knows what they are doing and Roger did every *Star Wars* film with George Lucas.'

Godzilla creator Patrick Tatapoulos provided the special effects and, with heavy use of computerised digital effects, the film's costs sky rocketed. In a cinema trailer shown on big screens across the world, John's character tells the audience, 'When we came to Earth, all your soldiers with all their technology could only put up a measly nine-minute fight. That is why man has become an endangered species.'

Battlefield Earth undoubtedly alarmed many in Hollywood who saw it as John trying to use his power at the box office to promote the teachings of Scientology. But John still continued to insist, 'I'm doing it because it's a great piece of science fiction. This is not about Hubbard. I'm very interested in Scientology, but that's personal. This is different.'

In the early summer of 2000, *Battlefield Earth* was released to a less than enthusiastic Hollywood reaction. Many of John's Tinseltown associates admitted they were 'underwhelmed' by the new movie. The fact that John now admitted he'd campaigned tirelessly for ten years to get the movie made seemed to make the whole project even more embarrassing for him. Many critics were calling it the 'worst movie in history' so it was no surprise that it proved such a flop at the box office. It was even rumoured that audiences and critics in the US were so appalled by the film that some cinemas even resorted to giving away tickets.

Set in the year 3000, the movie described a world enslaved by Psychlos, a race of aliens in platform boots. John had originally wanted to play the leader of a 'man animal' resistance that fought the aliens. But he felt he was too old and instead settled for the role of the villain, Teri, who was described in one newspaper as 'midway between a *Star Trek* Klingon and a reject from the glam rock band Kiss, plunged into an Edwardian melodrama'.

Critics called *Battlefield Earth*'s plot implausible and its dialogue clichéd. 'A million monkeys with a million crayons would be hard pressed in a million years to create anything as cretinous as this,' said the respected *Washington Post*. 'This is a contender for worst film of the century.'

Classic examples of the crass dialogue included: 'the grass is greener on the other side', 'a good woman is hard to find' and 'I will do it for the children.' The *New York Times* described it as 'like watching the most expensive school play of all time'.

With John optimistically talking about a sequel in the days following the movie's release, distributors had quietly reduced the number of cinemas across the US screening the film from 3,000 to just a few hundred. At the film's Hollywood première, hundreds of Scientologists were bussed in after being given free tickets at local cinemas. As *Newsweek* magazine put it, 'Contrary to cult-hater reports, nothing about *Battlefield Earth* will draw vulnerable movie-goers into the open arms of the Church of Scientology. That would be like saying that *Showgirls* was a recruitment film for strip clubs.'

Worse still, the film was trounced at the box office by *Gladiator*, starring Russell Crowe. The roman epic made more than twice the amount that *Battlefield Earth* achieved. As CNN TV critic Paul Clinton pointed out, 'Let's get one thing straight. *Battlefield Earth* was only made because John Travolta wanted it made. It's been his baby from start to finish. It's not a pretty baby.' *People* magazine declared it 'Travolta's travesty' while *Entertainment Weekly* labelled it 'dismal'. The *Los Angeles Daily News* branded the film 'a hollow and unintelligible movie' and the *LA Times* questioned John's 'embarrassing performance'.

In the middle of all this, John was given a controversial profile in the *Sunday Telegraph*, which was headlined 'Ron's Man On Earth: Devotion to Scientology led the star to make "the worst film of the century".' The article perfectly summed up the damage John had done to himself by making *Battlefield Earth*: 'The good news is that in the year 3000 you'll still be able to find a British accent on the planet. The bad news is it's coming out of John Travolta's mouth and, in his new film *Battlefield Earth*, Travolta's mouth is not a pretty sight. He plays Teri, an evil alien from the planet Psychlo, and, aside from talking like some moustache-twirling villain complete with maniacal cackle, he's also decked out in bad teeth, metallic green eyes, flapping brows, nostril tubes, oversized claws, lank dreadlocks hanging down the front and half a Martha-and-the-Vandellas beehive stuck on the back. Presumably we were supposed to look at him and think,

How about that John Travolta? Just when you think you're got him pegged, he takes on a challenging role that really stretches him as an actor. Instead, you look at him and think, What high-school production of *Cats* has he wandered out of?

In *Battlefield Earth*, Travolta spends two hours as a talking moggie with the worst bad hair day in cinematic history. You'd think a major motion-picture star like that would want to kill the producer responsible for making him look such an idiot but, unfortunately, in this case the producer is John Travolta.'

The article finished by concluding, '*Battlefield Earth* is more than just a flop. Travolta's been a highly successful pitchman for his church, schmoozing Bill Clinton to get Scientology into American schools. When this film was first mooted, critics were worried that the Scientologists would use it to impress movie-goers. Instead, the sound you hear from the dwindling number of customers in America's multiplexes is that of coast-to-coast derision. *Battlefield Earth* is so bad it must surely be testing the faith of even the most loyal Scientologists like Cruise and Kidman. Despite the assurances of L. Ron, Travolta's engrams have apparently been re-stimulated to throw out the correctness of computation. No doubt he'll recover, but will his church?'

In the winter of 2000, John was hit with a $400,000 tax bill following a five-year battle with the notorious US Internal Revenue Service. The scrap had begun when John was accused of 'improperly' trimming his taxable earnings by the IRS. They demanded nearly £750,000 in back tax for the years 1993–95. The two sides later settled for $400,000. The tax officials had accused John of incorrectly stating his income was $1.5 million 1993 and '94 and $3 million in '95.

A few months later, doting dad John revealed to the world that he'd given his baby daughter Ella Blue one million dollars for her first birthday. He also planned to give her a million bucks for each year of her life, which meant that the following year she would get two million and so on until she was eleven, making a total of $68 million, or £47 million. John intended to put the money in a trust fund that Ella would be able to access later in life. One of his closest aides explained, 'John's family means more to him than anything and he wants to make sure they have a secure future. So he's going to give his daughter and his son millions each year so they'll never go short.'

In June 2001, John was offered half a million pounds to appear at a British convention celebrating his turkey of a movie, *Battlefield Earth*. The offer was made by a millionaire fan who belonged to a group that adored the movie because it was so bad. A spokesman for the devotees explained, 'We've spoken to John's manager and we're awaiting a response. It would be great if he came. I know the movie had bad press, but it really has become a cult piece of cinema in a few people's eyes.' In the end, John's management politely declined the offer.

By the summer of 2001, John was once again facing Hollywood criticism that he was still the 'king of the comebacks' thanks to the disastrous Scientology-inspired *Battlefield Earth*, which made back just $14 million of its $54 million budget. He even admitted to reporters, 'Every movie to me is a comeback. I've always invested a lot in each film I do and you can't obsess about the ones that go wrong.'

CHAPTER THIRTY-ONE

THE ULTIMATE ACCOLADE

VENTURA COUNTY, NORTH OF LA, MIDDAY, 10 JUNE 2001

A thick cloud of black smoke hovered beneath the midday sun as bullet-riddled cop cars lay smouldering on the glass-strewn pavement. SWAT team members with gaping head wounds and third-degree burns rolled around in agony. Suddenly, one of them jumped up as if nothing had happened, pulled out his mobile and called his agent. Welcome to the set of John's latest action adventure flick *Swordfish*.

It was the final week of shooting and the $80 million movie was keenly anticipated by many Tinseltown insiders who believed it would help take John back to the top of the Hollywood heap following the *Battlefield Earth* fiasco. Two hundred yards away from the orchestrated mayhem on the streets of this LA suburb, John and co-star, *X-Men*'s Hugh Jackman, could be found making some music of their own. The two men were locked arm-in-arm, grinning ear-to-ear, performing an old-fashioned dance routine before switching back to killer mode and stepping back on to the set. 'It's our version of a Holiday Inn nightclub act,' explained John to one slightly surprised showbiz hack assigned the task of writing an on-location piece for his magazine. 'You do these stupid things to keep your spirits going between takes.'

As usual, John was philosophical about the ups and downs of his career. 'You get disappointed. You get sad. And then you move on because you have to,' he told one reporter on the set of *Swordfish*. 'Because there are other things, other new responsibilities … You can't get hooked up on all that.' But then John – the self-acclaimed 'Living Legend' now commanding in excess of $20 million a movie – knew only too well that it could all crash down around him once more if he wasn't careful.

In *Swordfish*, John was playing Gabriel Shear, a spy and criminal who wants to do a computer-hacking bank job to finance his operation to wipe out terrorism against America. John even offered an unusual perspective on the popular retired soccer player and his co-star in the movie Vinnie Jones. 'I get approval on the cast of the films I do and I saw Vinnie's tape and thought, He's just so cute. He's real street smart but also good to be around. He adds a lot to the set and even has a British flag flying all the time outside his trailer.'

John's other co-star in *Swordfish*, Hugh Jackman, was impressed by the sound advice he picked up from John during filming. Handsome Jackman later recalled, 'John explained that fame amplifies whatever you already have. So if, for instance, you are a complete butthead before you become successful, then, once fame arrives, you become a bigger butthead. But, if you're a good performer and charitable, like Paul Newman, then you become more charitable and an all-round good guy.'

Australian Jackman admitted he was under no illusions about the quality of Swordfish. 'Listen, it's a roller coaster summer movie – nothing more, nothing less. What I would really love to do is a movie musical. I said to Travolta, "Have you still got your falsetto?" He said, "Try me." And that why we found ourselves doing a little rendition of "Summer Nights" from *Grease*, and one of the crew threw in the "wella, wellas" on deep bass.'

Swordfish was well received in America where some cinema audiences even gave it standing ovations after the first twelve minutes. John explained, 'I've always been treated more like an athlete than an actor. Each film – or race – can be taken on its own success.'

In the middle of John's tour of the US promoting *Swordfish*, a super-rich Hollywood wife offered him $1 million for his sperm. The mystery millionairess from Beverly Hills wanted the star's baby so badly that she even rang his lawyer to make the offer. She even tried to make it easier for John to say 'yes' by insisting he didn't even have to sleep with her! His sperm in a test-tube would be enough.

John turned down the extraordinary offer but later joked that he might have seriously considered it if she'd offered him $20 million! John told top US talk show *Tonight with Jay Leno*, 'The lady said she didn't want to have sex. She just wanted the goods. She explained she wanted the genetics. This Beverly Hills woman wanted my sperm to make a baby. I was flattered but not interested.'

Chat-show host Leno even joked, 'Come on, how long would it take for a million bucks? Per minute that has to be a good deal.' John was on the programme promoting his latest movie, *Swordfish*, and even proudly bared his flat belly after telling how he had shed four stone for the action role. John explained, 'I haven't had a six-pack of abdominal muscle since 1983. But the studio said to me, "You are playing a spy, and you can't be fat and be a spy!" I love to have that kind of motivation. It gets me going.'

John ignored all the latest gossip about his supposedly fading career and let his fans do the talking when *Swordfish* took £14 million in his first week of release in the US – trumping animated blockbuster *Shrek* and *Pearl Harbor*. When John arrived at New York's Bryant Hotel to promote *Swordfish* he promptly ordered the entire room service menu – plus that of the rival Four Seasons hotel – because he was unable to decide what to eat.

It seemed that some bad habits never died.

BRENTWOOD, LOS ANGELES, 11 SEPTEMBER 2001

John watched the TV screen with morbid fascination as the machines he adored most in the world were used to destroy buildings in New York and Washington during the most lethal terrorist attack in history. As John later recalled, 'When September 11 happened the thing I loved most was used as a destructive tool.' But nothing would deter him from his quest to spread the good word about flying. He told one friend that his biggest fear about 9/11 was that the US Government might make amateur flying even more restricted.

In October 2001, John celebrated his tenth wedding anniversary with wife Kelly at New York's Rainbow Room. But, uncharacteristically, he tried to avoid dancing because 'everybody was so good on the floor. When it was really crowded I sneaked out with Kelly and hid between couples to dance.' John later explained, 'I was embarrassed. I said, "Something's up, I've never in my life seen so many people dance ballroom so perfectly like that." Kelly said, "But honey, you're great, you're John Travolta, you can dance ballroom." I said, "Not that good. It's like the Arthur Murray [dance school] out there." Later I found out it was the Arthur Murray School!'

Inside the eccentric mind of superstar John lurked a man with a penchant for the unpredictable. He told one reporter he'd unearthed a cure for road rage – listening to Spanish radio. He admitted he didn't understand a word of Spanish but found the language's cadences relaxed him. These days John apparently has his car permanently programmed into the top Spanish-speaking stations in the US. 'There's something about not knowing what anyone is saying that relaxes me,' he explained. 'I turn it up enough just so I can hear and it chills me out. I don't identify with anything and it helps me clear my head.'

And John's sensitivity about his membership of the Church of Scientology continued to bubble to the surface. When he travelled to France to help promote one new release in early

2002 and heard that local journalists intended to ask him some questions about the church, he cancelled all interviews and cut short his visit to Europe before flying home to LA to begin work on yet another new film project.

In March 2002, John splashed out $30 million on a Boeing 707 jet airliner. He planned to use the massive passenger plane to fly to movie premières around the world. He also let slip to one friend that he was looking forward to rejoining the mile-high club with wife Kelly! John snapped up the plane – with a range of 8,000 miles – from Qantas Airlines, in Australia. As one of his publicists explained, 'By flying himself and all his passengers John cuts out time wasted at airports for regular flying on normal commercial flights. He believes this investment will save him loads of time over the next few years and, of course, he gets to choose who travels on board with him.'

Wife Kelly even made a point of letting slip to one reporter how she and John had already enjoyed sex in one of his other aircraft: 'I played a naked stewardess. My husband sure loved it.'

One newspaper calculated that each time John's airline crossed the Atlantic it would cost him more than $200,000 in fuel. He also needed at least three other commercially trained pilots to fly alongside him at the helm of the big beast. That would cost him a salary of $100,000 each per year. John's 707 performed at 180 mph on the ground and then usually settled into a cruising speed of 565 mph before landing at 160 mph. He would also have to set aside a fortune on maintenance costs. The Boeing had six million parts, 171 miles of wiring and was as high as a six-storey building.

John's penchant for aeroplanes certainly knew no limits. When a paparazzi photographer flew over John's latest family home near Ocola, north of Orlando, Florida, he snapped an aerial shot that showed that John was able to park his 707 airliner outside his house – thanks to the personalised runway that was connected to the estate where the property was built. John even also had room for one of his Gulfstream executive jets. The 1.4-mile-long runway was more than long enough for his 707 to land on and take off. His plane was then able to taxi right up to his home where there were two docking stations. The house was even built to resemble an airport terminal complete with an imitation control tower, eight bedrooms and special quarters for his flight crew, plus a pool and two aircraft hangars. Thanks to two spur walkways on either side of the house that lead to where the aircraft were parked, John and his family could stroll from his living room direct to his cockpit without stepping outside.

Over in Los Angeles, California, however, John's obsession with aircraft was not so warmly received. Families living in the San Fernando Valley close to his local Van Nuys Airport were so fed up with the deafening jets landing and taking off near their homes they complained to the city council. One angry resident told journalists, 'John Travolta is the worse offender. Apparently he is oblivious to the thousands of children, elderly and working people whose lives he is disrupting.'

Another local added, 'It's disgraceful that these stars are still allowed to fly out of Van Nuys. It just goes to prove that being famous gets you preferential treatment while we have to suffer.'

In June 2002, John announced plans to fly his family on a 35,000-mile round-the-world trip on his private 707. He planned to visit thirteen cities, including London, Tokyo, Hong Kong, Sydney and New York. A beaming John announced his plans at a press conference in Los Angeles, which he entered wearing full Qantas pilot's uniform and singing 'Come Fly With Me'.

His 707 had undergone a multi-million-pound overhaul with its passenger seats replaced by a double bedroom, private cabins and a kitchen, but retaining the Qantas markings on the outside. The Aussie airline was also providing back-up crew and stewardesses, although officials refused to say if John was being paid for the trip. He told journalists, 'It's going to be great. I'm really looking forward to taking to the skies with my whole family.' John even admitted, 'I guess you could call me an airline geek. Flying puts your attention outside yourself. You are responsible for a machine that's going through the air at 600 mph. The sensation is thrilling and there is a beauty and an art form to it.'

But any suggestion that John might give up acting following a few questionable choices in recent years provoked this response, 'I can't give up acting. The movie business is what gives me the kind of money to do this type of thing.' And he dashed rumours that he was about to buy a Boeing 747 Jumbo jet by adding, 'I'm not going to buy a 747. The 707 I have is big enough. There are limits to these things.'

One of John's first stops on his so-called 'world tour' was a five-day golfing break at the world-famous Gleneagles Hotel in Scotland. The actor hired twenty hotel rooms to accomodate an entourage of seventeen, including 100 suitcases, two chefs, two nannies, a fitness trainer, one stylist, a personal aide and two bodyguards.

After playing golf each day, John took long walks in the picturesque grounds of Gleneagles with Kelly and a couple of bodyguards. The party also enjoyed the hotel's shooting, fishing and riding facilities. John then proudly announced plans to build a replica nine-hole course at his Hollywood home. Other guests reckoned he still had a lot to learn about golf after watching him hack his away around the course dressed in an £800 Dunhill tweed shooting suit.

As one eye witness pointed out, 'Travolta really stood out in the suit but it was obvious he had never played golf before. His swing was awkward and he was lucky to hit the ball.'

One Travolta aide said, 'John is really keen to get better at golf – that's why he wants to build a course in his back yard.'

When John later flew into the Far East as part of the same world tour, local journalists made fun of him after he intimated that he'd piloted into Hong Kong's 'very beautiful' airport when in fact he'd been forced to land in nearby Macau. Asked about his supposed landing at HK's Chek Pal Kok Airport, John said, 'It's new and modern and very beautiful and I enjoyed my landing – it was very smooth. I'm very happy with that.' But later explaining away newspaper headlines reporting his fib as 'a flight of fancy', his spokeswoman Leslie Llewellyn said, 'It could be that he was confused.'

By the time, John piloted his 707 into London in August 2002, he was being billed as a 'friendship ambassador' trying to persuade Britons to fly again in the run-up to the anniversary of the 11 September terrorist attacks. And no amount of similar threats would put John off flying. 'The pleasure of flying can never change for me. It's always there. The sad thing is the level that recent events have hurt the airline industry. I've always looked at the industry as a heartbeat for the planet. I've joined Qantas, to inspire air travel again. My joy hasn't gone.'

Meanwhile, John the prima donna still occasionally raised his head. While shooting a new army-training movie called *Basic*, the actor demanded, and got, eight new Armani T-shirts per day at a daily cost of $200. 'His contract stipulated that he would not wear the same shirt twice,' explained one source on the set of *Basic*. 'And dry cleaning is impossible because the chemicals used in the process are regarded with suspicion by the Church of Scientology.'

Back at John's Santa Barbara mansion, north of Los Angeles, he ensured that, whenever he was in residence, disco would always be 'Stayin' Alive', by hiring a dance instructor to teach any guests moves from *Saturday Night Fever*.

In September 2002, John and *Grease* co-star Olivia Newton-John reunited to belt out a few songs from the smash-hit movie at a Hollywood party to celebrate the ninetieth anniversary of Paramount Studios. John, now forty-nine, and Olivia, fifty-four, both admitted that the previous twenty-five years had seen them have their fair share of ups and downs. But undoubtedly the scene of them back together brought back happy memories for millions of thirty- and forty-somethings who saw *Grease* on its release in 1978 and for whom John and Olivia are Danny and Sandy. The gathering also coincided with the release on DVD of *Grease*, which meant a new generation of kids could get down to the movie's many hit songs.

And, despite his immense wealth, John worked hard at trying to convince the world he was really very careful with money. He even told one reporter, 'I drive a Rolls-Royce but it's not a brand-new one. And I have my own jets but not the latest most expensive models. I've always been conservative with money. Lifestyle is all a matter of perspective.'

Just a few weeks later, British tabloids were reporting that John was showing 'a keen interest' in buying 700-year-old Castle Lee, near Braidwood, South Lanarkshire, Scotland. He even paid a secret visit to the property, expected to fetch £8 million. There were rumours that he might be planning to turn it into a centre for the Church of Scientology. The sale to John never went through in the end, but his alleged interest implied that he would find a suitable property eventually.

John had in his own words 'calmed down considerably' since those heady, early days of *Saturday Night Fever* and *Grease* but he continued to enjoy being a world-famous celebrity. 'I wouldn't trade it for anything. I appreciate what I get in return for the celebrity status, like doors opening and four-star restaurants that are closed serving you what you want to eat at 4 am. The perks are amazing.'

By early 2003, John had been on yet another crash diet and looked trim and fit. He explained, 'I'm not a big fan of hard stuff like dieting and getting in shape, but I knew I had to do it for my kids. I started to think that maybe it might be better for me to behave a little bit, so I can stick around longer.'

John claimed his secret to dieting was simple; 'If I eat something fattening, I recognise how many calories are in it and then I work them off. If I've eaten 600 calories too many, then I work out an extra half an hour on the treadmill with my trainer.'

But in one slight, uncharacteristic slip-up, John summed up his attitude towards life when he admitted, 'There are two areas where you can't stop people misbehaving: eating and sex. Seriously, if you want to hurt me, take away food or sex. I need them to survive. I will never stop eating what I want and, because of that, I know I have to exercise. It's not fun, but you have to do it and I've lost nearly two stone in the last year.' He'd had to get super fit for a movie role and even spent time training with US troops before they departed for Iraq.

However, John insisted Kelly loved him thin or fat. He added, 'If you're attracted to the person's personality, you love them regardless of how their shape and size changes. That's the key. And Kelly and I have never made sex an issue. It's always been natural and organic for us. The longer you are with your partner, the easier I think it is to explore sex and intimacy – it has nothing to do with how the other one looks at a particular time. If you break up because of an unhappy sex life, then it was really about something else.'

John was mightily proud that, after eleven years of marriage, he was still capable of immensely romantic gestures towards Kelly. 'When I first met her, she loved flowers but I didn't pick up on it. One day she started crying and said, "Flowers are really important to me." Now she gets flowers all the time.'

Undoubtedly, John's life at this time particularly revolved around his children. 'Despite being only three, my daughter Ella is the most amazing little girl – she has the personality of an engaging fifteen-year-old. She will talk in-depth about anything you want and is really funny. I just can't get enough of her. My son, Jett, who turns eleven today, is a wonderful boy, too.'

John saw himself as a 'pretty lenient' father although he qualified this by adding, 'Unless my children are in danger, I don't interfere with what they want to do. I also make them and Kelly a priority. I'd rather be late for a meeting than cut short a conversation with one of them.'

But always in the back of John's mind remained *Saturday Night Fever*, looming as a reminder of the good old days when he was footloose and fancy free. His most vivid memory remained the famous bridge scene. John explained, 'This was where Stephanie asks about my future and I kind of inadvertently start to cry. And the solo scene of dancing, which was such a kind of freak of nature that day. We put the cameras in the right place and I let loose – I had a whole prepared dance. No one expected what I did – the people in the club watching had never seen anything like it.'

John remained convinced that without 'Fever', disco dancing would have died without trace. And he still loved dancing. 'Oh yeah, I always feel it's brave of people to ask me to show them a few steps because I'm associated with it,' he told one journalist. 'So I always do if they dare. I show people those locking steps where I move my arms, and people get so excited. I still like to sing, too. The actress Connie Nielsen likes classic tunes so one day on the set of my latest film, *Basic*, Harry Connick Jr and I serenaded her with "Spring is Here".'

Secretly, John still harboured a strong urge to make a musical, although he admitted, 'But Hollywood has a tendency to give up on musicals and westerns quickly. I've been waiting 25 years to do another one … I know a studio has been talking about *Guys and Dolls* recently. They talked about *Grease 3*, but I have no idea what that would be like. Little kids think *Grease* was made yesterday, so why bother with a sequel?'

John still looked back fondly on films like *Yankee Doodle Dandy*, starring James Cagney, as being one of the most important influences on his career. 'I think I've inherited the joy of performing. You can't kill it in me. I'm just a ham. I have been from the time I was twelve, or eight even. They say "Action" and it's like "Gentlemen, start your engines!" That's what it's like – click, and you're off and running. A friend of my dad's recently gave me his high-school yearbook, and the caption under Dad's picture said, "I crave action!" We're the same.'

The *Sunday Mirror Magazine* put John's stardom status to the test by asking him to answer a 'Reality Test'. His responses are intriguing. They went as follows:

Q. Do you ever wear your sunglasses inside?
JT: Only if I forget to take them off on a sunny day.
Q. Do you ever fly economy?
JT: No. Because I'm a pilot I tend to fly my own plane.

Q. Do you ever refuse to sign autographs?

JT: I try not to. I've been up and I've been down, and I owe a great deal to the fans who've stayed by my side.

Q. Have you ever said, 'Don't you know who I am?'

JT: No, my parents taught my siblings and I not to be full of ourselves, so that's just not something that would come to mind.

Q. Do you do your own housework?

JT: It's not my favourite thing, but I will help the kids put away their toys and other house stuff. It's not a big deal.

In early 2003, John was asked to give a tribute speech to movie legend Elizabeth Taylor at the Kennedy Center, in Washington, where she was being honoured for her contribution to American culture. In the middle of his speech, John remarked that he used to dream about Miss Taylor when he was a young man, adding, 'I dreamed you were naked.' As the audience, including President Bush and his First Lady, laughed, 70-year-old Liz, famous for her earthy sense of humour, shouted, 'I don't have any panties on tonight!' Huge laughter ensued, although the comment was edited out of the televised highlights of the ceremony by US TV executives.

Around this time, John told one journalist that he was having the best sex of his life after that recent crash diet. 'When I was overweight I was not as good a lover because my wife had to do most of the work,' explained John. 'Now she loves the new stamina. That's also why she loves my personal trainer so much, because getting fit makes you so much better in that area. You have to move the bits so you can get everything flowing again. And I mean everything!'

And Kelly herself even told chat-show queen Oprah Winfrey, whose programme they were both appearing on, 'It's the stamina that's so good. His body is amazing! But I love him whether he has a big body or this tight body. He is sexy!'

John even admitted to Winfrey, 'I started off by just walking to get my pizza, walking to get my ice cream.'

CHAPTER THIRTY-TWO

LIFE BEGINS AT 50

BRENTWOOD, LA, WINTER/SPRING 2003

Kelly lay in bed watching her about-to-turn-fifty husband standing naked in front of the full-length mirror in the bedroom of their Hollywood home. Suddenly she started making gagging noises. John turned and looked at his wife in fury, then he started laughing and laughing. As he later explained, 'There is no excuse not to admit you are not a young guy any more. I am middle-aged.' Within weeks, John had begun yet another punishing get-fit routine.

In February 2003, John's sister Ellen contributed to a TV documentary on his life and revealed a lot of new material about the actor. She even spoke about the influence of their mother Helen. 'She gave up acting when her family disapproved and she wanted us to do what she had wanted to do.'

The documentary – which aired on the Biography Channel – highlighted the influence that strong women had had on John's entire life. He was even quoted as saying of his tragic older lover Diana Hyland, 'I had more fun with Diana than I ever had in my life and the odd thing is, just before we met, I thought I would never have a successful relationship.'

The programme pointed out how John had handed over responsibility for his career to Kelly Preston when they met in 1989 on the set of *The Experts*. Kelly was even quoted on the documentary talking about how hurt John was by the state of his career at that time. 'Johnny had been hurt by rejection more than he admitted to anyone. Here was a great actor with shattered confidence. I like to think that I helped him restore his self-belief by reading every script he was sent and encouraging him to change some of his choices.'

John himself even admitted on the programme that Quentin Tarantino 'gave people permission to like me again'. The documentary also highlighted John's immense wealth and how, despite the film flops, he still managed to become 'as rich as Croesus' from his early twenties. This included a staggering alleged $150 million from the *Look Who's Talking* series thanks to a profit-sharing clause in his contract. John even explained, 'Twenty years ago I was fortunate enough to run into some blueblood people, meaning people who had money they'd inherited through the generations. They taught me some rules of thumb, such as you must always strive to live off the interest on your money. These are things that the nouveaux riches, whom I would soon join, don't always know.'

By this time John had properties in Maine, Santa Barbara, a new one in Hawaii, plus the sprawling Spanish villa in Brentwood, LA. Cars included a Chevrolet Tahoe, a Rolls-Royce, Mercedes 560SEL and that Mercedes 280SL, plus the aircraft, including the Learjet, Gulfstream and Boeing 707. John also owned a Canadair Tebuan CL-41 two-seater jet fighter trainer and his 'airport garage' in Florida also housed a tiny microlight plane and another trainer fighter similar to the type used by the Red Arrows. He'd also just bought a hotel in the Bahamas.

In that TV documentary, John also talked candidly about his

membership of the Scientologists and how they had filled a gap when nothing else could. He'd stopped heavy boozing after he joined but admitted it could do nothing to curb his appetite. 'I amaze people with my capacity to eat. I can put away a chocolate cake, vanilla cake, fruit tart and a brownie in one sitting,' he said almost proudly.

Although not referred to directly, there was little doubt that the Travolta marriage was solid and destined to last, although it did come over as more of a partnership rather than a passion. John had even mentioned that, 'by nature, I don't think man is monogamous even though by agreement he tries to be. But who knows?'

As one of John's oldest friends pointed out, 'John's childlike. He has moments of doubt and at other times he's the confident superstar. He's happier today than he has ever been and a lot of that is to do with the security he feels living in his own, perfectly ordered world. I once said, "John, you must be careful not to get cut off from reality there in your castle," and he replied, "Oh no, I go out all the time. Last night Kelly and I went to dinner and took in a movie."

It only later emerged that John had flown his wife in one of his private planes down to Florida and then arranged for a cinema to open specially for a private movie screening.

In April 2003, John had to be rescued from a blazing building while training as a firefighter for his latest film, *Ladder 49*. He and co-star Joaquin Phoenix got lost in thick smoke when the building was set on fire with them in it. 'We had to locate a door and get out while dealing with real smoke and fire,' said Travolta, 'but we got lost.'

A few weeks later, John entertained one lucky journalist with a gourmet dinner on board his 707 airliner. She described it as 'a living room that flies. An elegant dining table. Mushroom-coloured velvet sofas and even a double bed with a fake fur wrap thrown around it.'

In the same article, Kelly was quoted as describing her

husband as 'such a big being. Well, you'd have to be to change the world the way that John did.' She made it sound as if John was some kind of guru or a political zealot.

John confessed to another interviewer that his love of flying was partly related to his fascination with fear. 'What you resist you become, you know. I don't think I'll ever admit when I'm frightened, just to make it not happen to me. It's nothing to do with aviation; it would be more on a personal family level. But you can't put too much energy into something negative because, like you said, you could make it happen.'

In December 2003, John was told by the space agency NASA that he could qualify for a trip into space thanks to his skills as an airline pilot. John seriously considered the offer and even joked with reporters, 'I'm thinking that, if I can take five months off from movies to do the training, maybe I will go.'

Up at his biggest home – the £10 million twenty-bedroomed chateau in Penobscot, Maine – John continued to work out manically at least twice a week in his state-of-the-art gym between gargantuan meals. More than a dozen servants attended to King John and his beautiful queen and their two young children. As one former staff member later explained, 'Everything revolves around King John and what makes him happy. Food and family are his two great joys.'

Jett's suite of rooms in one wing of the house included a fantasy playroom with a mini race car, a bedroom built into the shell of a real aeroplane and a life-size ice-cream parlour. The former staff member added, 'John insists on being called "Mr Travolta" or simply "Sir". Kelly is addressed as "Ma'am" and Jett is "Young Master". Every morning John took a long shower and towels were warmed and ready for him when he got out. Another staff member laid out his clothes on the bed for him to step into. Whatever Sir wants, Sir gets.'

Often John – still a bit of a night owl – preferred to stay in bed until midday and then feast on a traditional full English breakfast before going out to play with his toys, including those numerous aeroplanes. Every Christmas, he spent hundreds of thousands of dollars flying at least fifty family members and friends to his Florida estate and lavishing them with expensive gifts, including gold Rolex watches and hand-made leather luggage.

In the autumn of 2003, John flew daily from his home in Florida to the city of Tampa throughout the shooting of *The Punisher*, an action movie based on the antics of a Marvel comic-book hero. Thanks to his special aeroplane-friendly home he could walk out of his front door, under a canopied-walkway and into the cockpit of his 707, open the long mechanised gate taxi on to the runway and be airborne in minutes.

In December 2003, John found himself sitting next to US President George W. Bush during celebrations to mark the centenary of the first flight by the Wright brothers at the very same spot on the Outer Banks of North Carolina. One attempt to recreate the flight of the Wright Flyer had to be postponed because of torrential rain. A later attempt failed because of a lack of headwind but, in his speech, Bush pointed out that Orville and Wilbur Wright had faced similar problems.

In January 2004, John proved once again just how in touch with his feminine side he was by hosting an English tea party for men in drag. During filming, his *Ladder 49* movie co-stars turned up in John's trailer wearing pantyhose and dresses after actor Balthazar Getty challenged John to throw the tea party with scones, clotted cream and jam and little cucumber sandwiches. Getty later explained, 'Next thing you know, we're putting on dresses, handbags and hats – the whole nine yards.'

By early 2004, *Pulp Fiction* director Quentin Tarantino was growing increasingly frustrated with John for not giving him a decision about playing *Pulp Fiction* hitman Vincent Vega in a prequel to the 1994 hit. The new movie was provisionally titled *The Vega Brothers* but, to date, John has not even read the script.

John was told by Kelly to expect a quiet, relaxing weekend to celebrate his fiftieth birthday on 18 February 2004, when the couple travelled down to the Mexican resort of Los Cabos for some complimentary hotels rooms. Instead, 300 of his Hollywood friends had secretly gathered there for a surprise party. There were performances by Tony Bennett and Carly Simon, a cake presented by Tom Cruise and a rendition of Happy Birthday by Barbra Streisand in the Marilyn Monroe-to-JFK style. Singers Roberta Flack and Natalie Cole also took to the microphone.

Ironically, John later admitted, he'd mistaken celebrity guests Oprah Winfrey and Streisand for fans when he spotted them before the party began. He explained, 'I said to Kelly, "See, there are no free rides. All these people are employees and they want autographs and photographs and this is what we're going to get for a free room." I told her, "We'll have to work the whole weekend for it." Then I look again and see Barbra Streisand and Oprah and I think, Oh, this is a surprise party but I was missing the surprise.'John added, 'It was amazing. I thought I had died and this was the afterlife.'

Other celebrity guests assembled for John's fiftieth bash had kept themselves busy; Sylvester Stallone played golf while Meg Ryan and Laura Dern sunbathed. John's only present to himself had been a classic 1972 Mercedes 190SL sports car that he'd bought a few months earlier for use at his home in Brentwood, LA.

There were also video greetings from Tom Hanks, Olivia Newton-John, Steven Spielberg and Bill Clinton. The amazing turnout was an indication of John's true popularity in Hollywood. As John said in an interview shortly after the party, 'Flying or acting – which do I prefer? I couldn't live without either. Flying was my dream, but I found out I was a natural performer, an actor. That enabled me to have the things I have. The joy of creating as an actor is euphoria. The relief I get from airplanes is also immeasurable. One is an expression of my inner self that has to come out. But flying always bales me out. In any state of mind, a photograph of an aircraft can cheer me up, a possibility of a trip can cheer me up. One is my heartbeat, showbusiness and acting. The other is my respite, my relief from stress. It's a lovely balance, and I'm very lucky to have it.'

In August 2004, John began working alongside hot young teenage actress Scarlett Johansson in an indie movie called *A Love Song for Bobby Long*. Sexy Scarlett – who's penchant for older men had been well publicised over the previous year – told friends that John had trimmed down specially for the part. 'Have you seen him in the past couple of months? I won't spoil the surprise, but wait until you see what he's done physically to play this part. It's unbelievable.' The actress also insisted the pair got along famously while making the film. 'We made each other feel like it was a big party,' she added.

In September 2004, John piloted his Qantas Airlines 707 to Venice. 'It was too big to fly to the airfield here on Venice Lido,' he explained after his arrival. 'So I had to park it at the international airport on the other side of the lagoon.' John was in Venice to show his movie *A Love Song for Bobby Long*.

A few days later, John took a pot shot at the big Hollywood studios by accusing them of ruining good scripts 'by committee'. He even said that, if a big studio had made *Pulp Fiction*, his hitman character Vincent Vega might have turned out very differently. John said they would even have questioned why his hair was so long and how his character shuffled.

John said the vast majority of scripts were unworthy of the big screen. 'Only one out of ten is really good, and one out of twenty is really excellent.' He then attacked the studios for rewriting bad scripts too much. 'It's a disaster. When you do a small independent film, you say you will agree to this but, if they change a word, you won't do it. With the studios you can do it to a degree, but there's not a guarantee that there won't be a committee input, removing a scene, adding a scene, manipulating it.'

One of John's few real regrets was turning down a starring role in the Oscar-winning musical *Chicago*. He confessed to one German magazine, 'I'm still angry with myself that I turned down the role of the lawyer that Richard Gere then got.' He conceded that Gere had done a great job with the dance numbers but then added, 'I would have loved to have shown them all what I can do one more time.'

In December 2004, John treated himself to a $5.7 million Zeppelin airship for Christmas. This latest addition to his aircraft collection was bought from a department-store catalogue and John told friends he intended to keep the huge airship at his airport home in Florida.

There seemed no end to his supply of money and many were wondering why he even needed to keep working. But John's work ethic bordered on that of a workaholic. He needed the adrenaline rush and the activity otherwise he might sink into a comfy chair, grab a bucket of cookies and turn into a couch potato. The quest to stay at the top continues and there seems little or no chance that he's even vaguely ready to give up his crown.

FILMOGRAPHY

The Punisher (2004)
Ladder 49 (2004)
Basic (2003)
Austin Powers in Goldmember (2002)
Domestic Disturbance (2001)
Swordfish (2001)
Lucky Numbers (2000)
Battlefield Earth (2000)
Standing Room Only (2000)
The General's Daughter (1999)
Primary Colors (1998)
A Civil Action (1998)
The Thin Red Line (1998)
Welcome to Hollywood (1998)
Mad City (1997)
Face/Off (1997)
You're Still Not Fooling Anybody (97)
Happy Birthday Elizabeth (1997) [TV]
She's So Lovely (1997)
Michael (1996)

Phenomenon (1996)
Broken Arrow (1996)
White Man's Burden (1996)
Get Shorty (1995)
Pulp Fiction (1994)
Look Who's Talking Now (1993)
Shout (1991)
Chains of Gold (1991)
Look Who's Talking Too (1990)
Look Who's Talking (1989)
The Experts (1989)
The Tender (1988)
Perfect (1985)
Two Of A Kind (1983)
Staying Alive (1983)
Blow Out (1981)
Urban Cowboy (1980)
Moment by Moment (1979)
Grease (1978)
Saturday Night Fever (1977)
Carrie (1976)
The Devil's Rain (1975)